Geoff.

The Life of Geoffrey M. Shaw

A biography by Ron Ferguson

Famedram Publishers Gartocharn

Dedicated to the Gorbals Group

The Spirit of the Lord is upon me,
Because he has anointed me
To preach the Gospel to the poor.
He has sent me to heal the broken hearted,
To preach deliverance to the captives,
And recovering of sight to the blind,
To set at liberty those that are oppressed,
And to proclaim a year when men may find acceptance with the Lord.

(Luke 4.18, 19 in the form used in the weekly Communion service of East
Harlem Protestant Parish and the Gorbals Group.)

The royalties from the sale of this book will go to the Six Circle Group.

Photoset in Quadritek Garamond and printed and published
in Scotland by Famedram Publishers Limited, Gartocharn.
© Copyright 1979 Famedram Publishers and Ron Ferguson.

ISBN 0 905489 00 4 Paper covered
0 905489 01 2 Hard covered

Contents

Preface

The gap left since the man died a year ago seems to become bigger by the day.

Geoff Shaw is missed.

The process of researching this book was illuminating. Politicians, churchmen, powerful people and very weak people remarked on how much it had meant to them that Geoff had simply been there—much more than they had realised at the time. Even his opponents. Conversations about Geoff soon turned into reflections about theology, politics, the future of Scotland, delinquency and hosts of other subjects. All who were compelled to think seriously about Geoff Shaw found themselves, at the same time, assessing their own lives.

He was a substantial man. Not a perfect man, or a saint. He must, at all costs, be kept out of the stained glass windows. His life should be celebrated where it belongs—in the world. He was a frontiersman, one of a new breed of Christian who explored uncharted territories that most of us would prefer to leave alone. His journey was more lonely and more costly than most of us recognised at the time. But precisely because he lived at the margins he has the power to address us about central things.

The genius of Geoff Shaw lay not so much in his ideas as in the manner in which he incarnated them. He tenaciously refused to separate speaking from doing, praying from acting, spirit from body, peace from politics. And he knew the difference between being relevant and being fashionable.

Most people who read this book will have encountered its subject primarily as a politician. His political contribution, particuarly in terms of mood, direction, agenda and style was considerable. Yet perhaps his greatest and most disturbing gift to us is the haunting symbol of a battered, ever-open door at 74, Cleland Street, Gorbals.

He represents one alternative model of contemporary Christian discipleship. He reminds us of long-forgotten radical strands in the Scottish Reformed tradition. He stands for imagination and risk-taking, over against ecclesiastical bagpipes, kailyard theology and 'survival without error,' to borrow Iain Crichton Smith's evocative phrase from another context. That is not to say that Geoff's way was **the** way, or that everything he said or did was right. He would have been the very last to support that idea.

Indeed, Geoff would have laughed at any suggestion of his life being a fruitful contemporary sign. One can almost hear him roar with laughter from his present vantage point. (Surely the Lord has too much of a sense of justice—and of humour—to prescribe a spell in purgatory for a man who served his time on earth in **both** the Church of Scotland and the Labour Party....) Yet even in his worst moments—and no one was more aware of these than Geoff himself—his life niggles and points and challenges and questions.

It was felt fitting that this book should be published at the first anniversary of Geoff Shaw's death. This means that it cannot be a definitive work: it is immediate history, with all the limitations that that implies. The time scale also meant that the manuscript was written at strange times of day and night during the course of a busy year.

The book could not have been produced without the willing help of so many of Geoff's friends—and adversaries (who were usually friends too). They are far too numerous to mention, though my debt to some will be obvious from the text. I should like to express special thanks to Geoff's widow, Sarah, and to the Shaw family, for their unfailing courtesy and kindness.

All of those close to Geoff insisted that it be a truthful book. Although many people made helpful suggestions both before and after reading the drafts, I had complete freedom in how I handled the material. So responsibility for all matters of interpretation rests entirely with myself.

Colin Morris was more than an able research assistant: he proved to be a stimulating thinker and a good friend. And how appropriate that the book should be published by Liz and Bill Williams of Famedram, who have kept many causes alive, the *Gorbals View* amongst them. My thanks for help with the manuscript go to Helen Gibson, Helen McCormack, Willie Quail and Alex Martin. On a more personal note, a word of appreciation must go to Alex Smith, an elder of Cairns Church, Cowdenbeath, who opened up for me the world of modern literature. Above all, my thanks go to my wife Cristine, who endured the book and its manic author with amazing forbearance.

The quoted material comes from several main sources. The Gorbals Group quotations come from unpublished minutes, reports and other documents as well as from the *Gorbals View*. Background statistical information also came from the City of Glasgow District Council Planning Department and from the Christian Action Housing Report, 1966. Geoff's political speeches are on public record, and acknowledgement is made to the library departments of the *Glasgow Herald, Daily Record* and *Evening Times* for their assistance. Thanks are also due to Strathclyde Regional Council for granting access to minutes and speeches which had not been published in full. Acknowledgement is made to SCM Press Limited for permission to quote passages from Dietrich Bonhoeffer's *Letters and Papers from Prison*, and to the BBC for permission to quote from broadcast material.

The royalties from the sale of this book will go to the Six Circle Group, a charity nominated by Sarah Shaw. The Six Circle Group organises camps for young people from borstals, mentally and physically handicapped children and adults, youngsters from intermediate treatment centres, and individuals and families under the care of social work departments. In the course of the camps individuals find, often for the first time, that they have gifts to share with others who need what they have to offer. Delinquent youngsters discover that they can assist handicapped children who, in turn, can help to heal adults caught up in emotional problems. Just how appropriate such a recipient is, will become clear during the reading of this book.

R.F., 1979.

Convener Shaw speaking in the rain, watched by wife Sarah.

Introduction

IT WAS, one has to say, an impressive funeral service, though not without ironies.

Glasgow Cathedral, standing room only. Ex-Moderators, an Archbishop, peers of the realm, the Secretary of State for Scotland, Members of Parliament, representatives of the armed forces and the legal profession, councillors, Government officials, housewives, ex-prisoners, alcoholics, down-and-outs, and ordinary, ordinary people.

The soaring voices of the choir singing with moving simplicity *All Things Bright and Beautiful;* the poetic eloquence of Lord MacLeod's tribute, putting the deceased into the same exalted company as St. Mungo, St. Ninian, St. Francis and John Knox: the dignity of the family mourners.

Then out into the brightness. A former prisoner, shouting with anguish: 'I should be there with him' in the direction of the hearse. The streets beside the cathedral lined with silent people, some openly weeping. The cortege moving slowly, slowly behind a pipe band playing a haunting lament, till the hearse disappears down High Street, and out towards the dead man's beloved Gorbals...

It was an altogether unique occasion, almost a State occasion, bringing together a remarkable cross-section of Scottish life. And all this for as man who several years earlier had writen a letter marked 'To be opened in the event of my death'—saying he did not have much money and requesting the simplest possible funeral.

And the multiple ironies! Ecclesiastical dignitaries saying farewell to a cleric whose ministry had been largely ignored by the Church. Military representatives paying their tributes to a passionate campaigner against nuclear weapons. The wealthy doing obeisance to someone who spent most of his adult life in a slum, fighting for the poor and questioning the way in which wealth was distributed. Conservative leaders acknowledging a dedicated socialist. Public officials paying tribute to a man who raised his voice against establishments. Law-and-order campaigners eulogising a former lawyer-to-be who broke the law in the name of what he conceived to be a higher obedience. Peers acknowledging a man who refused a knighthood. Ordinary people standing in silence for a very public figure who was at the same time an intensely private man. The Glasgow poor weeping for a reserved, almost academic person from the top drawer of Edinburgh life. Radical political activists honouring the dux of one of Scotland's best known fee-paying schools. The powerless mourning a man widely tipped to become the first Scottish prime minister in a Scottish Assembly, and who was described by the premier as 'one of Scotland's foremost sons'.

At this funeral, this extraordinary funeral, the contradictions and questions abounded, just as they did in the life and death of Geoffrey Mackintosh Shaw.

Part I: The Sure Foundation
Chapter I
Son of the Father

'Tis happy for him that his father was before him—
Jonathan Swift

The Mackintosh came from his father, and Geoffrey was his father's son. By all accounts, Colonel John James McIntosh Shaw, M.C., M.A., M.D., F.R.C.S. Ed., F.R.S.E. was a formidable man.

He had been brought up in Edinburgh. His father had died in his early fifties, and young Mack had gone to live with his aged grandfather.

Mack Shaw was obviously academically gifted. He matriculated at Edinburgh University in 1902, and studied for the degree of Master of Arts.

He joined the Officer Training Corps at University. As sergeant of the battery, he was chosen one of the members of the artillery team from Britain sent to Canada in 1907. But one of his companions fell ill, and Shaw remained to look after him in Eastern Canada. On his friend's recovery, he struck off on his own, and worked his passage west on a cattle train, watering and tending the animals for his fare. He eventually arrived back at Waverley Station, Edinburgh, with exactly one shilling in his pocket.

He returned to Edinburgh University to study medicine, having considered and rejected law and the church as possible careers. A fit, large-framed man, he was a tennis blue and good athlete. In 1909, he was elected president of the University Athletic Club. The same year he was elected president of the union by students of all years and all faculties. He was greeted by their magazine, *The Student,* as—

> A combination and a form indeed
> Where every god doth seem to set his seal
> To give the world assurance of a man.

Shaw had always won the affectionate admiration of his contemporaries, they added, and described him as "our trusty and well beloved J. J. M. Shaw, gentleman." The

Edinburgh Medical Journal put it thus: "From his schoolboy and student days he was a natural leader of men. His handsome presence and charming personality contributed to this, and with it went that power to command that is given to some wherein they, without personal effort or selfish motive, come to be elected leader by their fellows."

On graduation, he was appointed by Professor Sir Thomas Fraser as resident physician, in charge of his wards in the Royal Infirmary of Edinburgh. He graduated Doctor of Medicine of Edinburgh University in 1913. Having in the meantime gone to London, initially as a G.P., he was appointed resident house surgeon at the East London Hospital for Children, an appointment followed by two years' work in pathological research in neurology.

In London he joined the Special Reserve, and when war broke out in 1914, he was mobilised as a surgeon of the Reserve crossing to France in the original expeditionary force in August 1914. He served there until after the Armistice. In 1916 he was appointed surgeon specialist to No. 44 Casualty Clearing Station, a post he held until February 1919. There was virtually not a single engagement from the Battle of the Aisne and the first battle of Ypres right down to 1918 in which he was not doing major surgery, and for the manner in which this was carried out, Major Shaw, who was twice mentioned in despatches, was awarded the Military Cross and the Croix de Guerre with Star of the French Army. In addition to his military duties, he helped take care of the population of the surrounding countryside.

On his return to Britain, he was appointed to the surgical staff of the Edinburgh War Hospital in Bangour, specialising in the plastic repair of severe war injuries to the face and jaws.

It was not, however, all work and no play. Looking for a game of tennis at Kyles of Bute Hydro, he met Mina Draper. Miss Draper, who was 13 years his junior, lived with her mother and stepfather at Torphichen, near Linlithgow. She had gone south in 1917 to work with the Ministry of Munitions at Woolwich. The following year there was a flu epidemic, to which Mina fell victim. When Armistice was declared, she went home, severely ill and nearly died. She had gone with her parents for a holiday to recover at Skelmorlie and it was from there she found herself at the Kyles of Bute Hydro.

Miss Draper was playing with a schoolboy, when she was suddenly aware of a giant of a man standing beside her, holding a tennis racket with several strings missing. He asked for a game and soon proved that he was no mean player. That evening they danced. Two months later they were engaged. Six months after that they were married—in January 1920, just after the bride's 21st birthday.

Mr Shaw was appointed at Queen's Hospital for Injuries to the Face and Jaws at Sidcup. He served in this hospital for several years and, in the words of the *Edinburgh Medical Journal,* "ultimately came to be looked upon as one of the two foremost surgeons in plastic surgery in the British Empire."

On January 13 , 1921 the Shaws' first child, Vaughan was born. Mr. Shaw was appointed to the Ministry of Pensions Hospital in Edinburgh, and the year following his return he was appointed assistant surgeon to Leith Hospital. Subsequently he was also appointed assistant surgeon to the Royal Infirmary in Edinburgh. In April of the same year, the Shaws' second son David was born.

Mr. Shaw's experience as a pioneering plastic surgeon was sought by the Edinburgh Medical School, and in the lecture room, students and post graduates alike stayed behind for his regular 'after meeting', when problems, many of them personal, were put to him. He was known as a gentle giant with skilful hands, whose generosity of mind ensured that all sides of any question were looked at.

The Shaws lived in Inverleith Place, an aesthetically pleasing and dignified district on the north side of Edinburgh. Contemporaries remember the Shaw home as a place where Christianity, duty and service were simply assumed, without fuss. It was a solid, secure, disciplined Edinburgh household, with two maids living in.

It was into such a home that Geoffrey was born on April 9, 1927.

Chapter II
Floreat Academia

The roll-book is closed in the room,
The clacken is gone with the slate,
We, who were seventy-two,
Are now only seven or eight.
Robert Louis Stevenson, Edinburgh Academy 1861-63

As a child, Geoff was sunny and outgoing. He was obviously secure in what was a happy and close family.

Holidays are still fondly remembered. Well-off without being wealthy, the Shaws regularly took a summer month's holiday in a house in Arran, or at the coast, or in the Ochil hills. The car would be packed excitedly, with the fishing rods tied along the running boards. The family would get in and they'd be off for four weeks of relaxed enjoyment. For Geoff, it was the beginning of a life-long love affair with the outdoors. He loved hills, and rivers: he was often to say later that Neil Gunn's 'Highland River', was one of his favourite books, and that was 'what it was all about'.

When Geoff was five, the family moved house to Kinnear Road in the Inverleith district of Edinburgh. It was a substantial square three-storied building, standing in its own grounds. There was a sense of space and freedom. Father made a little pond in the back garden for the 'wee ones', by now joined by Evelyn who was born in January 1930.

Mr Shaw was by this time deeply interested in the affairs of the University Union, the Athletic Club, the University Settlement, and the Graduates Association.

As plastic surgery became more to do with changing the shape of noses, Mr. Shaw turned his attention to the problem of cancer. The Medical Journal put it thus: 'As an operating surgeon Shaw was a man of outstanding brilliance, and some of the cases he dealt with in the plastic replair of facial and maxillary defects were marvels of heroic surgery followed by brilliant results. As a general surgeon, his judgement was ever sound and his touch sure. At the same time his inclinations were even more towards the administrative side

13

of medicine. Thus it came about that the problem of cancer made a peculiarly strong appeal to him, and he carried through a campaign in this connection that was skilfully conducted and well thought out.'

In 1934 he set up the Cancer Control Organisation for Edinburgh and South-East Scotland.

When Geoff was six, there was no real doubt as to which school he would attend. Vaughan and David were both at Edinburgh Academy, which was recognised as the best fee-paying day school in the city.

The Academy was founded as a school of classical learning in 1824. (The famous High School had no longer satisfied the merchants and professional men of the prosperous New Town. They did not wish their sons to have to go to school through the somewhat squalid and dangerous streets of the old town). The opening speech was made by Sir Walter Scott, one of the Academy directors and from then on the school had a large number of distinguished pupils, as Magnus Magnusson's history of the school, 'The Clacken and the Slate' shows. Future 'old boys' included Archbishop Tait, James Clerk Maxwell, Robert Louis Stevenson and the man who was the prototype for Sherlock Holmes. The school provided many statesmen, judges, scientists, professors, soldiers, headmasters, churchmen, and writers. Its dux medallists were expected to do well. (The weight of such demands proved too much for one such dux, who feigned drowning in the Danube. He re-appeared two years later, saying he had felt himself unable to live up to expectations).

The Academy, then, was a school with a rich tradition, the obvious choice for the Shaw family. In May, 1933, Geoff started in Class IB of the Academy prep school. He soon distinguished himself, winning first prize in his class at the end of the first year. The school records show that the following year, Geoff again won first prize, and in 1937 he was dux of the prep school as his two brothers had been before him.

Miss H.F. McTavish, the prep school headmistress, remembers Geoffrey as a friendly and happy boy who laughed a great deal.

In the upper school, Geoff continued to distinguish himself.   In 1939, he won the Lyon reading prize.   He had developed a love for music, and had become particularly fond of Gilbert and Sullivan. The following year, he was awarded one of the Balfour prizes for singing - for his part as a bridesmaid in 'Trial by Jury'. The other bridesmaid (and prizewinner) was Magnus Magnusson. (To have an idea of Geoff's speaking voice. one only needs to listen to Magnus Magnusson. The enunciation, tone, and modulation are very similar. From the time he won the Lyon prize at the Academy, coached by his mother, Geoff was always a clear, distinct, but somewhat unflamboyant reader.)

The war brought changes. Some of the staff were called up, and evacuation schools for those boys whose parents wished them to be moved were set up. The prep school had to close because the shelter accommodation was not deemed suitable and the number of boys in the upper school was only 260—just over half the usual size. (So bad was the crisis that the possiblity of admitting **girls** to the prep school was considered—and rejected!) Teaching went on with half empty classrooms and the boys carrying gas masks as the air raid sirens sounded.

The advent of war had been particularly dreaded by Geoff's father, who knew too well the suffering of its casualties. In 1939 he had been appointed Rector's Assessor in the university court of Edinburgh University and in January 1940 he was elected full Surgeon-in-Ordinary to the Royal Infirmary.

When it had become apparent that war was inevitable, he took a major part in the preparation of ARP schemes and the education of the medical profession for this work. In the spring of 1940, when Edinburgh was requested to nominate a consulting surgeon to the army in the field he was asked to go. So in the early summer Mr Shaw packed his gear, said farewell to his wife and children and left for Cairo.

The first news that came home was that Mr Shaw (by now Colonel Shaw) had settled down, was happy and was looking forward to good work ahead with his colleagues. Soon after, a warning note was received from his opposite number, the consultant physician, to the effect that Shaw was gravely ill. On September 10, 1940 he died of acute bacillary dysentery.

He was only 54 years old.

The *Edinburgh Medical Journal* stated:

"Thus at the age of fifty four years, and at what was considered the threshold of a great career as a surgeon and administrator, Shaw has died, and the Edinburgh Medical School has lost one who gave every promise of being a leader in academic life, and a surgeon whose brilliant work would attract men from all over the world to his native city. In the death of J.J.M. Shaw, the University of Edinburgh and the Edinburgh Medical School have lost not only a brilliant surgeon, a great clinician and a first class administrator, but also a man whose personality was an outstanding influence for good in every circle in which he moved."

This was the father who died when Geoffrey Shaw was 13 years old.

Chapter III
Noble Tasks for Noble Men

The thing is to understand what I am cut out for, to see what the Divinity wants me *to do. It is a question of finding a truth which is true for me, of finding the idea for which I can live and die.—*
Soren Kirkegaard.

The family circumstances were immediately changed. The well-loved house in Kinnear Road, with so many happy associations, was sold and a modest bungalow in Southfield Terrace, in the Barnton district of the city, was purchased. The maids were reluctantly dispensed with and Mrs Shaw settled down to bring up the three children who were still at home—Vaughan was by this time in the Army—in the manner their father would have liked.

This was not to say that Mrs Shaw did not have a mind of her own. On the contrary, her strength and resilience were now most evident. With the death of her husband she took on a more dominant role. She devoted herself to her family and watched over them with anxious and loving care.

At school Geoff continued to do well. He was popular without being prominent. He preferred the non-combative sports: he is remembered as a bit timid on the rugby field, although he gained his rugby colours in 1943. He never really enjoyed cricket, but as a member of one of the junior cricket teams, he recorded a score of 51 in an Academy victory over Boroughmuir. He began to do very well at tennis and athletics.

By 1943 he was captain of the Academy tennis team (struggling under the handicap of not being able to purchase new or reconditioned tennis balls) and was a member of the athletic team. He became a sergeant in the Junior Training Corps. Life was good.

But the same year Geoff was beset by a further tragedy. On February 22, 1943 his best friend at the Academy, Gordon Philip, was accidentally injured during rugger practice. He went home complaining of headaches and that evening died in the operating theatre.

At the funeral service the Rev. Dr Black spoke again the words of Bunyan which Gordon had read recently to his class.

> "My sword, I give to him that shall succeed me in my Pilgrimage and my Courage and Skill, to him that can get it. My Marks and Scars I carry with me... So he passed over and all the Trumpets sounded for him on the other side."

Geoff was deeply moved.

Gordon's father, Sir James Randall Philip, Sheriff of Renfrew and Argyll and Procurator of the General Assembly of the Church of Scotland, had a book about Gordon published privately. In that book Geoff wrote:

> "This year, a great disaster has befallen the Academy, a disaster which nothing can ever repay. For by the death of Gordon Philip the school has lost one of her dearest children who in later years would have added yet more glory to the glory already won by the long line of noble men whom she has sent forth into the world... He can ill be spared, for next year at school he would most certainly have been one of the leaders of the school, and in later years he would have played a most valuable part in the affairs of the world.
>
> Few boys have been brought up in such a close and loving family as was Gordon, and amid such happiness and joy. Perhaps he is fortunate in having been spared many of the uglinesses of life by being taken so young; for all he ever knew in life was Truth and Love and Happiness, and, as his life on earth was filled with beauty, so will his life in death be no less beautiful."

Although Geoff remained thereafter an amusing companion and a popular schoolboy with ready laughter on his lips, an inward seriousness had entered his soul, never to leave him.

Geoff spent a lot of time at the Philip family home in Great King Street. He was very sensitive to Gordon's parents' loss and what is remarkable is that he became a pastor to them. He **supported** them in their loss.

Lady Philip remembers how much he seemed to grow up at

that time. She remembers him as essentially a very happy boy, who was good fun to have around. After Gordon's death he spent several holidays with the family.

Sir Randall Philip, who was 'Uncle Randall' to Geoff, had a great influence on the boy. A fine, gentle man, he took him to concerts and parks and was generous with time and money.

One need not be a psychiatrist to understand the impact of such an eminent man on a boy who had so recently lost his father. Soon Geoff gave up his original intention of becoming a surgeon and declared that he would become a lawyer.

An illuminating glimpse of Geoff in that crucial year comes from a contemporary, Robin Matthews, now a professor at Clare College, Cambridge. He described the beginning of a 'spiritual awakening.'

"When I first got to know him, that is to say until he was about 15, Geoffrey conformed to his family background. He was a good all-rounder; near the top of his class in work, but not quite at the top; respected and liked, but not a leading personality; not in any sense a teacher's pet, but not prone to question customary standards of behaviour (adolescents were, of course, far more conformist than they are now). He was on good terms with everyone without, so far as I remember, having any particularly close friends or belonging to any clique.

During the war the number of boys staying on into VIIth class was less than normal. There were only about half-a-dozen of us in the VIIth Classical, including those in their first, second or third years in the class, and we all got to know each other pretty well. The change that I remember in Geoffrey in that year 1942/43 was that he became more thoughtful and questioning, particularly about fundamental moral questions. I don't mean to imply that he was an earnest or solemn boy, but he did become more serious-minded, and in a way more worried.

I don't think it is just a reflection of adolescent egocentricity that leads me to say that I was to some extent a catalyst in that process of change in Geoffrey's attitudes, so I can't avoid saying something about myself and my relations with him then. I was at that time a Christian pacifist, a position which incurred the displeasure of the school authorities and some of the boys; at the same time I had a certain standing as the top boy academically in our year.

Although we were not really all that close personally, Geoffrey became extremely interested in my position and we had long discussions about it. These discussions, as far as I remember, were more about pacifism and the position of the pacifist in war-time than about Christianity or religion. A central issue was that of adopting principles and standing by them. I dare say in retrospect that our discussions were dreadfully naive but they were extremely serious, indeed fraught, not just an academic debate.

I left school two terms before he did and there my story ends abruptly — a snapshot of one brief phase in his life."

By this time Geoff was doing very well in the classical stream of the Academy. In his final year, 1944, it was no surprise that he won the gold medal for dux of the Academy, the Academical Club prize for the best in classics and the Clyde and Millar Greek prizes.

At the prize-giving exhibition on July 28, 1944 Sir Andrew Jameson McCulloch, K.B.E., C.B., D.S.O., D.C.M., congratulated him on the high distinction he had won.

Sir Andrew told the assembled boys: "The future before you is difficult. Europe is in a chaotic state, with eighty million people homeless. You have a noble heritage in your country, your city and your school. Noble tasks await you; see that you pay to posterity the debt that you owe to the past."

With the school song, *Floreat Academia,* the National Anthem and the traditional cheers ringing in his ears, Geoffrey Mackintosh Shaw, dux gold medallist, set out on the search for the noble task.

20

Chapter IV
Cramond

The supreme wonder of the history of the Christian Church is that always in the moments when it has seemed most dead, out of its own body there has sprung up new life.—

William Temple

The parish kirk of Cramond stands on the remains of a Roman fort. There has been a place of worship on the site since the sixth century A.D. and the church, outwardly much the same as it was in 1656, stands in a lovely little village of restored 18th century houses set at the mouth of the River Almond. It was in this church that Geoff Shaw learned to express, and to test, his Christian faith.

Cramond itself was not just a lovely old village—it was the place to which the up-and-coming young professionals were beginning to gravitate. By the 1940s it was one of the most desirable residential areas within easy reach of the capital. So it combined the attractions of a sense of history, a loveliness of outlook and the dynamism of a young, growing professional community. This vitality enlivened the kirk. The congregation itself was of a fairly mixed social background, taking in people from a wide catchment area. The Rev. Dr. Leonard Small, the minister of Cramond when Geoff was a teenager, was a noted preacher and extra folding chairs had to be brought in on a Sunday morning after the 800 pews had been filled up. Communicants classes for those wishing to join the church often attracted over 100 people.

The kirk was the social hub of the community. Its organisational life was strong and the welter of activities ensured that there was something for everyone. The presence of a large number of young people contributed to the atmosphere of openness and liveliness. There was no sense of musty traditionalism. It was a professional, suburban church running at peak performance.

Geoff loved Cramond Kirk. The worship meant a lot to him, and he was greatly influenced by Leonard Small. Dr Small, who had studied under the great Swiss theologian

Emil Brunner at Zurich, constantly stressed personal religion, personal commitment and personal service in his sermons. His preaching was very direct, clearly spelt out and well illustrated. Several young people in the congregation studied for the ministry as a result of his influence.

Geoff often helped Dr Small in the manse garden. Amid the bushes, the flowers, and the weeds, a living, very personal theology took shape in the conversations between the preacher (and former amateur international goalkeeper) and the impressionable lad. His experience seemed to confirm the words of his favourite hymn—Christ is made the sure foundation.

Geoff felt at home in the church. He joined the Young People's Fellowship. Here, with other young people, he learned to socialise, stretch his wings, test ideas, flirt, learn to speak in public and find room to grow emotionally and intellectually. Not surprisingly, some of the girls had their interest aroused by the quiet spoken, handsome young man. "Geoff always came to the YPF looking well dressed and dishy, but somehow seeming remote and untouchable, perhaps because of his breeding and accent."

Scouting absorbed a lot of his time and energy. He loved camps. Hiking and hill walking gave him great pleasure and he was remembered as an athletic, clean-cut boy who engaged in activities with great gusto and who was good company. Impressions people have of him at that time are of someone who laughed a lot, who was popular and who fitted in with his background.

He rose through the Scout ranks and became assistant scoutmaster of the Cramond troop.

The boys were not always easy to control. Geoff would stand, looking serious, waiting patiently for order to be restored. He regularly took boys hiking and camping and Alan Small, one of Dr Small's sons, remembers the kind of hero-worship which developed. Geoff, an attractive, likeable person with considerable charm, was looked up to by his charges. They remembered his sense of fun. At one of the many Scout camps at Peebles some of the boys made a raft. Alan Small's pole stuck in the mud of the river bed, while the raft went on. 'Let's do it again for the camera,' said

Geoff as the boy struggled out of the water.

(Leonard Small recalls an occasion when Geoff had a group of boys from Gorbals at camp in Iona. Dr Small was towing some canoes, with Geoff in one of them. Geoff laughed uproariously as he sank into the Sound of Iona!)

The serious side was there too. There was always a right way of doing things and the finding of Spangle papers under the pillow at camp was an offence punishable by an early rise followed by a run in the fields. The picture of Geoff striding around in his kilt, keeping good discipline, 'improving' the boys' outlook, is that of muscular Christianity in which Godliness, cleanliness, fresh air and exercise are indissolubly linked.

Geoff's concern for others, seen already in his pastoral care for Sir Randall and Lady Philip, was developed in his work with the handicapped youngsters of the nearby Trefoil School. He ran their Scout troop for them.

Playing games such as stone-age football with boys in wheel chairs or wearing calipers was dangerous as well as exhilarating. He took handicapped youngsters away for camps and hikes: it gave him great pleasure to help crippled young people reach the top of a hill and see the marvellous views.

He also organised cricket matches for handicapped children. A crippled lad would be at the crease and would make the strokes with the bat: Geoff would do the running between wickets.

This concern for the handicapped was with him all his days. He was later to extend his concern to those handicapped by environment, unemployment or poor home background. Nothing made him angrier than to hear people condemn those who had had an unfortunate start in life. Dr Small believes that Geoff began to recognise at that time that his was a privileged life. He came to feel acutely aware of the fact that other people had not enjoyed the same privileges.

All this might be too priggish by half if it were not for Geoff's tremendous sense of fun and his ability to laugh at himself. He enjoyed writing and acting in Scout sketches and was prepared to make a fool of himself on stage.

His musical tastes were catholic. The first record he ever

23

bought was Tchaikovsky's Piano Concerto played by Egon Petri. Geoff played the piano himself, without ever being particularly accomplished. He was also an avid listener to the regular Saturday night Jack Jackson record show on radio.

When he was 17 Geoff was given a ticket to a mass rally at the Usher Hall. The speakers were Archbishop Temple of Canterbury and Archbishop Garbett of York. During that evening William Temple talked about squalor.

Geoff was later to say in an interview: "This was perhaps the first time that this kind of concern hit me. I'd never heard of squalor. I came from a rather nice comfortable background. I never knew what squalor was." Describing that incident as 'perhaps the first question mark', Geoff felt later that it was right that the Church should bring to people's attention the extent of poverty-stricken squalor in the world.

He went to Edinburgh University in October 1944 to pursue his studies with a view to becoming a lawyer. By this time he was very much the man of the house at Southfield Terrace. David had left to join the Navy. Geoff took his domestic responsibilities seriously and was sensitive to his mother's needs as well as the needs of others. Young People's Fellowship, Scouts, handicapped youngsters, sport and music also took up a lot of his energies and what was left he devoted to his study of English, Constitutional Law and Civil Law. He might well have become an Edinburgh lawyer with a good living and a social conscience had fate not intervened.

Colonel J.J.M. Shaw, Geoff's father.

Young Geoff, with sister Evelyn and father.

Chapter V
The Street Which is Called Straight

Straight is the gate, and narrow is the way, which leadeth unto life, and few there be that find it.—

St Matthew 7.14

And when they were escaped, then they knew that the island was called Malta. And the barbarous people shewed us no little kindness.—

Acts 28. 1,2

The Lord said unto him, Arise, and go into the street which is called Straight.—

Acts 9.11

The call-up papers came when he was eighteen. There was no question of refusing to go, and in the summer of 1945 he was on his way to **H.M.S. Royal Arthur** at Skegness for basic intake training.

The Scots actor Tom Fleming was there and the two became close friends. Both attended the mission hut for 'O.D.s' (other denominations, i.e. non-Anglican). Tom Fleming was a Baptist and Geoff, of course, Presbyterian. During basic training it was forbidden to leave camp and Geoff and Tom spent a lot of time at the mission, taking part in discussions, social evenings and old-fashioned hymn singing. Tom used to play the organ for services at Butlin's cinema at Skegness. He was able to impress the congregation by producing steam whistle and other effects. It may not have been Cramond, but it was a lot of fun.

The two men parted when Geoff went on to Wetherby for his training as a 'Jack Dusty' — a stores assistant. He was then posted to Malta.

During the next two years in Malta he never left base. His job was a that of clerk in Supply and Secretarial—hardly mindstretching for the dux of Edinburgh Academy. That was a time when more people were getting out of the naval service than were entering it. The choice of categories to serve in was limited and opportunities for promotion were few. He later rose to the dizzy heights of Leading Hand.

For Geoff it was a novel experience. In uniform, coping

with people from all walks of life. Living with 60 ratings in a room full of double-tiered bunks. A few cold taps for washing. Exposure to people with quite different ideas, jokes, language, interests, political views. Glimpses, perhaps, of what 'squalor' was about.

Like a homing bird Geoff made for St Andrew's Kirk in Valetta. There he formed a firm friendship with Andrew Wylie from Glasgow, and together they found themselves embarking on a spiritual pilgrimage. For Geoff it was a question of trying to fit new and wider experience into his framework of thought and belief. There was little privacy in the barracks and walks were greatly valued. He and Andrew talked theology as they explored the island.

Hugh Purves, naval chaplain and minister at St Andrew's, Valetta when Geoff arrived, remembers him as a 'quiet, upper middle class lad', who was over-shadowed by the more outgoing Andrew.

Geoff didn't involve himself much in social life. Attractive though he might have been to the Wrens, his primary interests lay elsewhere. St Andrew's Kirk, mainly. He never missed worship on Sunday morning. He was often called upon to read the scriptures and a fellow serviceman vividly remembers sitting in the pew and taking note as the Edinburgh man with the quietly impressive presence and immaculate appearance moved to the lectern to read the lesson in his well modulated tones. After the service there was a cup of tea at the manse and discussion. In the evening the chaplain was 'at home'—more discussion, singing and socials.

St Andrew's Kirk and the rocky island terrain were the crucial staging places in this part of Geoff's pilgrimage. As he looked out to the Mediterranean he was reminded of St Paul's missionary journeys and his shipwreck near Malta. In the town of Valetta, Straight Street, flanked by bars, brothels and dance halls, seemed to symbolise the kind of choice he was being called to make.

Straight was the way. He would become a minister. Christ of Cramond, Christ of Malta, Christ of the shipwrecked St Paul: the sure foundation.

The significant thing about the decision was this: his previous desires to become a surgeon and a lawyer would appear to have been prompted by other more dominant figures in his life. The decision to enter the ministry was his independent choice.

Hugh Purves remembers that when he spoke to him about his decision he had private doubts as to whether Geoff would last the course. Nevertheless, he lent him some books to help him in his theological quest.

Another person who remembered Geoff at that time was Able Seaman John Lang. A commanding figure with a beard, John was something of a 'sea lawyer' and he would insist on his right to leave ship to attend public worship in the denomination of his choice on a Sunday morning. Sometimes he was the only person on board the small craft which took him ashore. John, who was later to find himself a neighbouring minister of Geoff's in the Gorbals, was a socialist, which let him in for some teasing at the hands of Andrew and Geoff. Able Seaman Lang remembered Geoff at that time as a nice, quiet, cultured, well-educated conservative young man.

Life in Malta was not all contemplation and discussion. Geoff enjoyed tennis, cricket, table tennis and billiards; he was initiated into a new sport in the Navy—boxing. He didn't think much of it. On one occasion he had to box with Andrew Wylie. Andrew remembers vividly realising how much more aggressive he was than Geoff. The picture of Geoff Shaw, future pioneer and peace-maker in Gorbals, and Andrew Wylie, nowadays exercising an imaginative city centre ministry in Edinburgh, engaging distastefully in fisticuffs in a ring in Malta is something to be treasured.

After a year Andrew Wylie returned to Scotland. By this time the Rev. Callum Macleod had arrived to replace Hugh Purves. The new man had more radical political views and Geoff found his horizons further widened. He made new friends, too, some of whom were also to the left in their views of what should happen socially and politically after the war.

The man who occupied the bunk below Geoff was George Lawrence.

"We worked in No. 5 Naval Store dealing with most types of stores and equipment required for ships' operation and maintenance. The work was not particularly demanding and, by and large, we had a relatively easy time.

Geoff spent a great deal of his free time ashore. We had relatively few night duties and consequently he took the opportunity of retaining a permanent room at the British Sailors Society hotel.

With his educational achievements, his obvious capability and his social background I was surprised that he had not attempted to obtain a commission. When I asked him why, he replied that he preferred to be just an ordinary rating. I gained the impression at the time that he welcomed the opportunity to live and work with people from a broader social spectrum than those with whom he had previously associated at school.

Very often, as was common at that period, our discussions turned to politics, and I remember registering surprise, particularly in view of his social background, that Geoff had definite leanings towards socialism. He did not, however, give any indication that his interest would flourish and that he would eventually play such an eminent part in local government politics.

Geoff was extremely well adjusted and even in his young manhood had a very equable temperament. Despite the many petty restrictions which became part of our routine, he took things very calmly and rarely, if ever, raised his voice in complaint. The only time I can recall him being put out and at odds with authority was when his request for leave to visit the grave of his father was turned down. He was quite despondent.

The passing years have not diminished in any way the very high regard I held him in and my admiration for him. For me, Geoff Shaw was a quite outstanding human being and a Christian truly worthy of the name."

Mrs Isobel Macleod, widow of Callum Macleod, remembers Geoff as being full of life and ideas and always willing to help. By a strange coincidence, the piano was often played at these church functions by Claude Thomson, who was later to become municipal correspondent of the *Glasgow Herald*. Geoff conducted a choir and arranged a public recital of Scots songs which was so successful that he was asked to repeat it at a concert broadcast from the British Institute in Malta.

Mrs Macleod said: "All of us who knew Geoffrey in those days had the highest regard for the warm and happy personality he had. I seem to see him always smiling. We all knew he would have a great future, though no one guessed what path he would choose."

Later, when Geoff was in Gorbals, he received a request to speak to apprentices on **H.M.S. Caledonia** at Rosyth. The request came from Rev. Callum Macleod and Geoff responded immediately. Later again, when Rev. John Lang was Moderator of Glasgow Presbytery of the Church of Scotland and Geoffrey Shaw, the man who used to tease him about his socialism, was leader of the Labour administration in Glasgow, Geoff used to say to John with a grin: "What would Padre Macleod think about this?"

By the middle of 1947 the peacetime routine of the Navy with its petty restrictions, was beginning to pall. Geoff was anxious to take up his studies for the ministry. He eventually secured an early release.

The time in Malta had been an important phase in his life. Although daily letters from his mother had kept him in touch with what was happening back home, away from the secure Edinburgh life for the first time he had found the space to think through some of the issues of his life. He had never gone through an adolescent rebellion either in terms of his faith or his life style, but the Malta experience had allowed new questions to be raised and new experiences to be integrated.

His Christian faith had not been seriously challenged, but had been stretched to accommodate a wider view of life. Serious political questions had been raised, although it was not till later in his life that they were really thought through in any comprehensive way.

At any rate, as he sailed for home towards the end of 1947, Geoffrey Shaw was alive and well and looking forward to the future as his own man.

Chapter VI
Queen of the Sciences

He unobserved
Home to his mother's house private returned.—

Milton

Merely to talk about man in a loud voice is not to talk about God.—
Karl Barth

In January 1948 Geoff resumed his studies at Edinburgh University and picked up his life in Barnton and Cramond where he had left off. He changed courses at university, choosing philosophy and psychology, subjects more suited to his new intentions. John Macmurray was professor of moral philosophy and Geoff was greatly excited by his work.

Geoff persuaded Andrew Wylie to come through from Glasgow University to join him at one of his lectures. He had tremendous enthusiasm for Macmurray's thinking and saw it as a message for the future.

In his early days Macmurray was a political radical and was for a spell a member of the Communist Party. He was an enthusiastic expounder of the ideas of Martin Buber, the great Jewish philosopher whose central 'I/Thou' concept had a big impact on metaphysical and theological thinking. Macmurray's intellectual pilgrimage eventually led him to embrace Christianity. In his teaching he stressed the total man in the whole community and in later years Geoff frequently referred to his debt to Macmurray.

In 1948-49 Geoff studied moral philosophy and he did well enough to be exempted from examinations at the end of the session. Even so, it is interesting that Geoff did not feature on the prize list, and showed no inclination to become an academic. Despite a capacity for understanding complicated ideas and expounding them with clarity, he did not care for learning for learning's sake. Most of his leisure time was spent at Cramond, or on scouting, or working with the youngsters of Trefoil School.

Mrs Shaw, Geoff and Evelyn were regularly in their pews at Cramond, and Geoff occasionally played the organ. Both he and Evelyn had good singing voices, and on several occasions Geoff sang bass solo at morning worship.

He was very much looked up to by the young people of the church. Neighbours would sometimes complain about him standing on the pavement, talking for hours with young people from the church. He was at his best with small groups and the conversations outside the church are still remembered fondly.

So Geoff's style of ministry was evolving. A good listener, who would take in what people were saying. Skilled at helping people to see solutions to their own problems. Accepting. Popular without being pushing. Affirming what was best in people. Reconciling, avoiding extremes. Clear-headed. Charismatic, with a definite 'presence', yet in a quiet way. Serving the needs of others without fuss. Under the lamp lights of post-war Cramond, Geoff was learning to become a pastor.

There was still an unresolved question, however. Theologically, it was 'Who is my neighbour?' and how did this relate to squalor? The question was put again in 1948, when James Monaghan became assistant minister at Cramond and the two became good friends. James, a Boys Brigade man, was still an officer in the 54th Company in Dalry, a mixed housing area in Edinburgh. He invited Geoff along, and thereafter he went every week, enjoying working with boys of a quite different background. He established after-school clubs for the pupils; the activities included sport, music and drama. He did not spare himself and made considerable demands on his staff.

Geoff helped with the Ainslie Park clubs. He found the work fulfilling. He was greatly influenced by Mr Murchison, whose all-out dedication and vision appealed to the younger man. The headmaster in his turn was very impressed by Geoff's ability.

Meanwhile, Geoff remained a student: one who enjoyed music, tennis, golf and outdoor life. Time spent in the library was limited and at the end of session 1949-50, during which he did junior honours mental philosophy, he elected not to go on for a further year's study. At that time students who had had at least a year's war service could opt for an unclassed honours degree rather than study for a further year and gain, perhaps, a first or second class honours degree. To be given an unclassed (war privilege) honours M.A., the professor had to issue a certificate stating that the student would be expected to gain at least second class honours if he were to pursue his studies for a further year. Geoff wanted to hurry on to New College. He graduated MA Hons. (Unclassed) on July 7, 1950.

The time at New College studying for the ministry of the Church of Scotland was particularly happy. From the moment he walked through the portals of the former Free Church College at the top of the Mound in Edinburgh, past the outstretched arm of John Knox, the 23-year-old intending divine felt at home. New College brought together so many things he enjoyed—study, discussion, theology, music, practical work, all in the setting of the Edinburgh he loved.

It was an exciting time to study theology. Men back from the war wanted more than some vague liberal sentiments about the inherent goodness of man: they wanted a theology that took the full nature of man seriously, that took judgement seriously and yet spoke a triumphant word. The revival in Biblical theology seemed providential: many believed that theology had been restored to her rightful place as the Queen of the Sciences, even though her crown might be askew. The theologian with the message for the hour was Karl Barth.

Barth, who was born in Switzerland in 1886, had been taught by liberal theologians. In 1911 he became a pastor in a Swiss village, preaching the message that the Kingdom of God could be built by the efforts of man. Then came the First World War. All the optimistic creeds were shattered, and Barth ransacked the scriptures for help. In 1918 he published a commentary on the Epistle to the Romans, and with this book a theological revolution was under way. Barth emphasised that God was sovereign, independent of man. Man was a sinner, alienated from God and from his own true being, and could only know God because God had graciously made himself known in Jesus Christ.

Barth's commentary caused a furore. The theologian likened himself to a man who was falling in the dark and reached out for support. To his surprise he found that he had caught a bell rope and had wakened up the whole town.

As a professor in Bonn, Barth began to elaborate his theology. His thinking was radically Christocentric: that is to say his continual starting point was Jesus Christ. Christ revealed God to man, and man to himself. Christ, the Word made flesh, true God and true Man, was the key to all understanding. It was no good, said Barth, trying to come to understand God through all sorts of other concepts. Christ alone revealed God and turned all man's understandings upside down. For instance, man's natural understanding of God as omnipotent would lead him to think of God as a lordly potentate. Christ, however, revealed that God's omnipotence was expressed in lowly service. Man was utterly dependent on God's grace.

Barth was also critical of 'religion', which he understood as man's attempts to get up to God. He stressed instead faith in Christ as the Word Incarnate and opposed 'religion' as idolatry.

It should not be imagined that Barth was some kind of quietist, who stressed the inward life of the spirit at the expense of political action. On the contrary, he publicly opposed the rise of Adolph Hitler precisely because Hitler was setting himself up in place of God. Barth helped to frame the Barmen Declaration which said clearly that the Church's only *fuhrer* was God. As a founder of the Confessing Church which opposed Hitler, Barth was compelled to flee to Switzerland in 1935, after refusing to take the oath of loyalty to Hitler.

Barth also insisted that the place where the Christian served God was in the **world.** He must be involved in the social and political life of the State as a part of his obedience to Christ. On most occasions the Christian would serve the State, but there might come times when he would have to oppose the State.

Karl Barth, then, later to be compared by a Pope with St Thomas Aquinas and his *Church Dogmatics* with the *Summa Theologica*, was a substantial theologian and his star was in the ascendant when Geoff Shaw first went to New College. G.T. Thomson, Professor of Dogmatics, was engaged in translating *Church Dogmatics* into English and a new lecturer who attracted students was Professor Thomas F. Torrance of Ecclesiastical History. Torrance, who succeeded to the chair of Christian Dogmatics the following year, was a convinced Barthian.

Geoff was excited by Barth: the influence of Barth—and of Professor Torrance—on his thinking was often to be acknowledged. Yet Geoff was never a man to adopt whole systems of thought undigested and people always found him difficult to label. Not that Barth had it all his own way at New College in any case. For instance, Principal John Baillie, Professor of Divinity, and a distinguished theologian, stood in the idealist tradition—and he also introduced students to the work of the German martyr-theologian, Dietrich Bonhoeffer. In a book on the Sermon on the Mount, Bonhoeffer attacked what he called the 'cheap grace' offered by the churches ('Confess your sins and you'll be OK') and talked instead about 'costly grace'—radical obedience to Jesus Christ.

A fellow student remembers Geoff going round with a copy of Bonhoeffer's *Letters and Papers from Prison* under his arm. Bonhoeffer did make some impression on him at that time, but it was not until he was deeply involved in Gorbals that Geoff came to regard Bonhoeffer as the theologian most helpful to him in his pilgrimage.

Other important influences were Martin Buber and Emil Brunner. Brunner, although close to Barth in many ways, had a public dispute with Barth over the nature of theology. This dispute was part of the regular diet of all would-be theologians in the 1950s.

This continental brew was heady stuff. Geoff drank deeply from it—and yet he was too much of an Edinburgh Scoutmaster to regard it as the be-all-and-end-all. Barthian theology probably didn't cut much ice at Ainslie Park Club. Nevertheless, Christocentric radicalism, while hardly a slogan to set Dalry alight, gave Geoff a clarifying interpretative basis for thought and action.

The New College student common room was a place of

much laughter, particularly when Geoff and his musically gifted friend Jim Ross sang, with Jack Henderson on the piano, in imitation of the Inkspots singing group. Geoff was renowned for his sense of humour and he loved taking part in students' concerts. The choir of which he was a member would go out entertaining pensioners and women's guilds. They put on sketches in which Geoff would take part with great relish.

His involvement at Cramond continued. In his second year at college he was student assistant to Leonard Small. This involved taking part in worship on Sundays, Youth Fellowship, Bible Class and two nights a week of youth work—all of which brought in the sum of £120 a year.

One of the boys, Alexander Wedderburn, recalls Geoff taking the senior boys' Sunday School: "There were about six of us, including one recalcitrant whom Geoff took great trouble over. He wasn't bad, but was a bit glum-silent and Geoff used to work away patiently and solemnly trying to get him to say what he thought.

"In the YPF he was much more at home, because he clearly took God seriously. I don't remember much of his teaching, except once when he was in a discussion group on sex with us and we all giggled, and he was asking us solemnly to try to explain why we giggled. It was really afterwards, when he would walk with us up to the chippie, or a couple of miles back down the road, listening and talking about all manner of things, that he really rubbed off. He was prepared to listen and talk about anything and he was much better at it than in the more formal setting.

"He was one of the major influences in my life. I haven't done much—I'm a reluctant elder and a keen Community Council secretary. But I would be a different person if I hadn't had the luck to brush against the humble and saintly and cheerful life of Geoff Shaw."

One of Geoff's friends at New College, Bob Henderson, ran a Bible Class for over 50 boys at Sighthill, another corporation housing area in Edinburgh. Geoff went over to help a lot and would often bring guests with him.

The Sighthill connection was strengthened in his final year at college when he became student assistant minister at St

Nicholas' Church. A revealing glimpse of Geoff at that time comes from Mrs Betty McGlashan, then a young member of the Sighthill congregation.

"He had a tremendous influence on the young people and he left an unending mark on all our lives. He cared, he was interested, he gave, he shared and he loved in a very Christian way and there are many of us who, 25 years later, are still influenced in the lives we lead today.

"Perhaps one of the greatest things he did was to introduce a group of us to the children of Trefoil School. These children were physically handicapped and were resident there. Needless to say, they loved him.

"Not only was Geoff loved by the young people, but by all ages and there was a lot of contact with old people of the parish whom we adopted in pairs or singly and visited regularly. They loved him too. Every Sunday morning we all cycled very early into town and helped with the breakfast at the People's Palace and also did some Saturday evening concerts. The worlds that he opened up to us were endless.

"There was a lot of fun in knowing him. The Boys Club concerts in the church hall were hilarious. Enter Geoff as a fairy, all dressed in a tu-tu complete with blonde plaited wig."

But the serious, dedicated note was there too. Mrs McGlashan recalled: "Many and long were the discussions we had in those days of youthful eagerness and Geoff always had so much to offer each and every one. I always remember one rather sad discussion on marriage and of how he felt so strongly that he could never marry because he could not devote his time to the work he knew he would do and be fair to a wife and family. At that time I remember arguing with him on how difficult it would be for him to understand family set-ups and problems if he did not have a family of his own. How wrong I was proved to be."

Another of Geoff's friends at New College was Mary Lusk, a very able student whose application to be ordained later became a *cause célèbre* in the Church of Scotland. Mary and Geoff and Jim Ross went to Paris to attend a conference of Russian and British members of the Student Christian Movement. Geoff was much impressed by the Orthodox

Worship. (A favourite record of his for the rest of his life was a sung version in Russian of the Apostles Creed).

Another friend at that time, George Lugton—Geoff was later to be best man at his wedding—remembers him as a natural leader of the group, middle-of-the- road in his views.

It was no surprise to anyone when Geoff was elected president of the Divinity Student Council, the representative body of the New College students. Student life was not so political then as it later became and Geoff's appointment was a measure of his personal popularity with students of all shades of opinion. At that time he expressed no strong political opinions.

David Torrance, another good friend at College, organised a petition protesting against a proposed visit by the Kirk's Moderator to South Africa. Geoff was in sympathy with the petition and signed it, but he took very little active part in the campaign.

He had no strong views on the parish ministry either. Students at that time tended either to go into the parish ministry or, if they were very bright, into academic work. Geoff, who had chosen to specialise in New Testament, was clever, but not interested enough in an academic career to spend much time on it. He ended up sixth in the order of merit, winning a Cunningham Fellowship and the Mackenzie prize in elocution.

Thus on June 16, 1953 he graduated Bachelor of Divinity of Edinburgh University. Geoffrey Shaw, Edinburgh Academy dux, establishment man, personable and charming, middle-of-the-road preacher with a social conscience, was expected to go far.

He was offered a fellowship to Union Seminary, New York. (The more academically oriented students chose the Continent). This was followed by the offer of a Commonwealth Fellowship—the premier fellowship to be won, being open to all faculties in all universities. It would still allow him to go to New York and also provided a grant for travel. He accepted it.

The summer was spent as full-time assistant at Cramond Kirk. Then he set out on the journey that was to change his life.

Part II: Nothing Lower than the Cross
Chapter I
The American Nightmare and the American Dream

Give me your tired, your poor,
Your huddled masses yearning to breathe free
The wretched refuse of your teeming shore.
Send these, the homeless, tempest-tost to me
I lift my lamp beside the golden door.

Inscription on Statue of Liberty

The traditional forms of the churches we knew as children and young men in middle class America have little power or relevance in a community like East Harlem.—

G.W. Webber

It was in the crucible of East Harlem that Geoff Shaw became a twice-born man.

There had, of course, been influences in his background which helped lay a foundation for what he was to do: the emphasis on Christian service at home and at school, the work with the handicapped, the Dalry Boys Brigade, Ainslie Park Youth Club, Sighthill Church, his spell on the lower decks and his theological preparation. There were strong elements of continuity.

Nevertheless, the East Harlem experience constituted a revelation for Geoff. It was not simply an **addition** to his experience: it transformed and revolutionised his way of looking at the world. What he saw in the slums of New York ate into his soul: the experiment in which he participated crystallised for him life's purpose and pointed the direction of his future destiny.

When he first went to New York he was reluctant to become involved in Harlem. The person who persuaded him was Walter Fyfe. Walter had first met Geoff two years previously at the Student Christian Movement Conference in Paris—and hadn't really taken to him. It was perhaps not surprising. Walter, from a working-class background in Glasgow, was a theological and

39

political radical. During his studies for the ministry at Trinity College, Glasgow he had decided that the parish ministry was not for him. Possessed of an acute mind and a love for the dialectics of political and religious thought, Walter felt that the Church had largely sold out on the working classes. He had been influenced at a distance both by the East Harlem Protestant Parish experiment and the French worker-priest movement. At Trinity Walter made up his mind that his future ministry would be conducted as a labourer in industry. These ideas were shared by a student friend, John Jardine and the two men determined that some time in the future they would attempt a new form of ministry that would try to make sense both of theology and of work.

Little wonder, really, that on the few occasions Geoff and Walter had met there was not a great deal of rapport between them.

Geoff, however, was always generous with people who disagreed with him. Walter and Elizabeth, his wife, were in Edinburgh when they saw a kilted figure running across the street to greet them.

I hear you're going to New York, Geoff had said. I'm going too and I'll see you there.

When the Fyfes arrived in New York they found a note stuck in the door of their quarters in the Union Seminary residence. It was from Geoff, giving them a welcome and offering to show them round New York the next day. (Geoff had been there all of five days). It was the beginning of a rich and close friendship that was to last through good times and bad.

Geoff initially resisted Walter's suggestion that he should become involved in East Harlem and it was only after the failure of two attempts to fix up other, more orthodox appointments that he found himself in the huge slum ghetto, which was literally over the wall from Union Seminary.

By the 1940s East Harlem was probably the worst slum in America. Built towards the end of last century as cheap housing for the immigrants flooding into America it had declined ever since. Into not much more than one square mile were crammed over 200,000 people (roughly 40% American negro, 50% Puerto Rican and the rest from other immigrant groups). East Harlem was the kind of place people yearned to get out of. Those who had come in pursuit of the American dream soon found instead a nightmare of unemployment, violence, discrimination, crime, over-crowding, juvenile delinquency, rats and drugs.

What of the church in this situation? It had largely abandoned East Harlem to its fate. The Roman Catholic Church made only token efforts. Not one of the major Protestant denominations was represented in the area. The only strong Christian commitment came from the sects, whose storefront churches at least offered a warm welcome and the promise of a better life in the future after the hell of this one.

In 1948 three graduates of Union Seminary, Don Benedict, Bill Webber and Archie Hargreaves decided something must be done. They made a survey of the area, cataloguing some of its worst horrors. In his book *God's Colony in Man's World* Bill Webber tells of a survey of church-going which showed that only 30 out of 2000 in one block went to church on one warm Sunday morning.

The two men put forward a plan for a new type of church life in the area and four major Protestant denominations backed the infant East Harlem Protestant parish experi-ment. The ministers were allowed freedom to develop new patterns. They decided from the beginning that they would form a group ministry in the area rather than operate separately; they and their wives and families would live in East Harlem; they would rent stores for worship rather than build new buildings; they would try to be responsive to the real needs of the community.

When they moved into East Harlem they met with a lot of suspicion. Who were these white middle class people? Why were ministers, who normally steered well clear of the place, coming to live there? Were they from the CIA? Or spies? Or police?

Many barriers had to be broken down. The three men visited hundreds of people in the tenement blocks, inviting them to the opening service. When the great day arrived one woman turned up.

From such unpromising beginnings the East Harlem

Group Ministry evolved life and disciplines of its own. As more people joined the staff and as the church and community work grew, they agreed to commit themselves to a discipline of daily worship, of pooling their incomes in a common fund and of full participation in the life of the community. This led them into the political arena, fighting on behalf of the poor. How this happened is best illustrated by an incident recounted by Bill Webber.

Don Benedict was standing at a street corner in East Harlem when an old man was knocked down by a truck. Don called an ambulance—then waited for an hour and a half until it came.

How to rectify this? Webber commented: "The only way to fulfil the Biblical injunction would be to get a better ambulance service for East Harlem. The only way to get a better ambulance service is to put pressure on the local political boss and ultimately on city hall. But you have no pressure to exert unless you and those who feel as you do have been actively engaged in the political enterprise."

The ministers concerned had been greatly influenced by Rev. Dr George MacLeod, who had founded the Iona Community in Scotland in 1938. (The East Harlem documents often quote Dr MacLeod, who paid several visits to East Harlem.) They were fond of quoting Dr MacLeod's view that it was not enough to pray for a child dying of TB; it was also necessary to take political action to eliminate the circumstances in which tuberculosis flourished.

By 1953 East Harlem Protestant parish had really got going, with four store-front churches operating and a full programme of youth work, drug addiction help, Bible study and political and community action.

In East Harlem Geoff Shaw saw life as it was never lived in Edinburgh. A black child coming home from school stole an apple from a shop and was shot in the hip by a policeman. Not quite your friendly Barnton bobby. When the child went to Sunday school that weekend he asked his teacher where he could get crutches. The vicar of the church said: "These negro children cause a lot of problems in our community. Don't do anything to lessen the authority of the police."

Geoff was horrified by the level of drug addiction. Twelve-

42

year old black kids were hooked on heroin. Prospectless teenagers literally died on their feet. There were frequent gang fights and crime was rampant. Geoff sat up night after night listening to youngsters crazed with drugs.

And the unemployment! Men with no prospects of a job became totally lethargic. The pathology of such a community, with its hopelessness and its sense of being written off, appalled him. How could this be allowed to happen in the midst of such affluence? Why had the churches retreated to minister to the successful? Were they not indeed dispensing cheap grace?

Edinburgh suddenly seemed very far away. There was not much in his experience which could help him to cope with this kind of situation. He realised that the Cramond Kirk which he loved, Scottish Prebyterianism at its best, was a million light years away from the horror of East Harlem. What was happening in New York could not be resolved by the personal service of some well-disposed Christians from a secure base in suburbia. In East Harlem Geoff Shaw lost his theological and political innocence and became a full-blooded Christian.

Where did he find the resources to cope with the situation and to make of it something constructive? The answer lay in the East Harlem Group Ministry, in the strengths of the local people, and in his friendship with Walter and Elizabeth Fyfe.

The life of the group ministry made sense to Geoff. The ministry of identification with the people, backed by disciplines of money, time, worship and social action, gave flesh to the idea of Christocentric radicalism.

The group ministry's weekly Communion service meant a great deal to him. The words from Jesus' sermon at the synagogue in Nazareth spoke deeply to him as they were recited each time:

> The Spirit of the Lord is upon me,
> Because he has anointed me
> To preach the Gospel to the poor.
> He has sent me to heal the broken hearted,
> To preach deliverance to the captives,
> And recovering of sight to the blind,
> To set at liberty those that are oppressed,

43

And to proclaim a year when men may find
acceptance with the Lord.

This passage had been spiritualised and anaesthetised by
the Church. But in the context of the misery of East Harlem
the ancient words were charged with new power. Signs of the
coming of the kingdom of Jesus were very physical: healing
and deliverance and liberation from oppression! In the
hearing Geoff understood personally what recovering of
sight to the blind was all about.

He was amazed at the way some of the people of East
Harlem coped with their problems. He was put in charge of a
group of youngsters in East 102nd Street and he enjoyed
their vitality and honesty and cheerfulness. He got very close
to a number of youngsters and their families. One Puerto
Rican teenager, Angel Camacho, virtually became a
community worker with him.

Angel has a vivid and unforgettable memory of the time
Geoff showed the boys how to pack their bags for camp. One
of the teenagers was picked up by the police on his way
home. Geoff and Angel went to the precinct at about 10 pm.

"We found a knife in his bag," said the officer.

"I know," said Geoff. "I put it there." It was clear to him
that George had been beaten by the arresting officers. His
smile faded, and his face turned red. He asked George about
the bruise on his face.

"They beat me up. They wanted me to confess about some
fruit that was stolen." Geoff confronted the officer with the
question.

"We didn't touch him. He was like that when we found
him."

"He wasn't like that when he left my house," Geoff
replied.

"These people give us a hard time. You don't know what
we are up against when we have to do our job. I bet you this
guy is a junkie."

Geoff's eyes were on the police officer, trying to meet his
eyes. The officer went on: "You must be from the church?"

"Yes sir, I'm one of the do-gooders from the Church of
Our Redeemer. Well, officer, are we going to be beaten up,
or are we all under arrest?"

44

"You haven't committed any crime," said the officer.

"Neither has he," replied Geoff.

On their way home, Angel recounts, they didn't dare look at Geoff's face.

The lessons Geoff learned while doing youth work in East Harlem formed the style of his later work with youngsters in Gorbals. The basis was the small club, in which the leader could really get to know the youngsters. It would be reinforced by outdoor work and the widening of young people's horizons through camps and trips.

Geoff's compassion for those who had started off in life with a handicap found new expression. He had endless patience for the outsiders who were in trouble.

A year later, referring back to his youth work in America, he said it would not do to write off all those who would not fit into the Church's pattern of youth work. There were no young people who were ever outside the Church's sphere of concern.

Writing of the dope addicts, he said:

"The real problem is how to help those who can't do without it; the mainliners who inject heroin into their veins. They live in a world of dreams of greatness, and so they escape from their surroundings the easy way. Their work has become useless; they are unreliable; they cannot take even the group activities of a club; they are listless and without purpose. About the only thing that can be done is to spend evening after evening with them, perhaps just sitting in a candy store playing records and talking. Eventually it may be possible to persuade them to take the hospital treatment by which alone they may be cured; it lasts about three months, and at the end of it, when they come back to East Harlem there is the almost more difficult job of trying to keep them from drifting back into the habit again. It is a long job, and one which requires great patience; it is a job, above all, in which it is terribly necessary to remember that for the Church even the worst of young people, even the most unlikely are of supreme importance.

"Plainly not all the dope addicts, not all the delinquents, not all the straightforward young people of East Harlem

45

are covered by the churches' work. But here, at least, is an attempt to meet young people of every sort, where they are and as they are: with no condemnation because they are not as they ought to be, but with a deep concern to point them to what under God they may become."

Ever more conscious of his own privileged upbringing, Geoff often observed how remarkable it was that people managed to remain cheerful and make something positive of their lives in such difficult circumstances. He genuinely regarded such people as his betters and tutors. He had a particular admiration for one warm-hearted black woman, Mrs Leroy Harris, who had had a very difficult life. It was her idea that: "In East Harlem you bring up each child for fourteen years, wondering all the time whether you will win them or the street will win them, but knowing that almost certainly the street will win them."

These words made a deep impression on Geoff, and he was often to quote them in Gorbals.

All this time he was attending Union Seminary. He made his mark in different ways. More than once a college audience was in stitches when he sat at the piano and he and Walter Fyfe sang a duet *Seven Drunken Nights*.

He and Walter attended the same classes, and as they were both involved in East Harlem they had a lot to share. The dominant figure at Union was Professor Paul Tillich, a magisterial thinker steeped in European philosophy and theology. Deeply interested in culture, art and psycho-analysis, Dr Tillich provided a wide-ranging contemporary theology which posited God as the somewhat impersonal Ground of Being rather than as personal God-up-there. His theological system was worked out in a Germanic prose which ranged between the totally illuminating and the totally incomprehensible.

Geoff and Walter and Elizabeth found Tillich very stimulating, even though they rarely agreed with him. In discussions over coffee they argued through Tillich's theses.

In a term paper, for which he gained an 'A' grade from Dr Tillich, Geoff took the professor on. Arguing for a more classical orthodox understanding of the Christian faith and belief in the bodily resurrection of Christ, he wrote: "I find myself closest to what Dr Tillich described as a supra-naturalistic position, as distinct from naturalistic or existentialist. That is, I would hold that reality is most meaningfully described by talking in terms of God as being God in himself over against the world, or any world created by him; of God who remains love, truth and power even where, hypothetically there is not, or has not been, any other reality; of God as most adequately to be addressed in personalist terms rather than to be talked of in ontological terms." So there.

Reinhold Niebuhr was also teaching at Union, though he was at this time much less active because of illness. Niebuhr's theology took seriously the sociological and political realities of life, and he opposed the prevalent American optimism.

The Scottish students enjoyed the class on 'Church and Community' conducted by Bill Webber. America at this time was in the grip of the McCarthy witchhunt. At one class, civil rights leader Patrick Murphy Mullin said he would support the dismissal of a Government building janitor whose sister had married a Communist. Geoff was very angry. He leapt to his feet to complain about the unfairness of what the speaker had said. The confrontation between the two big men looked almost as if it might have come to blows. Geoff was infuriated because he had seen the civil rights of the poor ignored. He knew from his own experience that those who were at the bottom of the heap and had no power were ignored or manipulated. And he determined that from then on his ministry would be with these losers of this world.

Out of the discussions over coffee with Walter and Elizabeth came the determination to try an experiment in Scotland which would be effective both at the neighbour-hood and the industrial level. Walter wrote to John Jardine—who was by this time assistant minister at Govan Old Parish Church—telling him of their views and arranging to meet when they got back.

Geoff wrote to his mother explaining his future plans. Using a naval analogy he said that an escort ship's job was to guard the convoy, but sometimes one of their number had to go off to help another crippled ship. This was what the

47

Church should be doing—helping those who were most in need.

So the time in New York drew to a close. Despite excellent term marks Geoff decided not to take a degree; Walter, who gained an 'A' from the rigorous Professor Tillich for a thesis on William Blake, graduated STM.

It was a wrench to leave East Harlem and all his friends. He was moved to tears when some of the Puerto Rican and black youngsters in his care presented him with a Burl Ives LP.

Angel Camacho recalls his final night at the youth club. Some of the teenagers cursed him for going away after such a short time.

"Geoff said nothing. He raised his hands as if he were trying to touch us all at the same time. One said: 'Big man, do you know how to pray?'

"At a signal we bowed our heads. Geoff whispered 'Oh God' louder and louder, and then the silence came. We heard the gentle steps fading up the stairs and we knew that Geoff, the man, was gone. I thought I heard somebody crying."

Geoff stayed on in the States to attend, as an observer, the Second Assembly of the World Council of Churches held in Evanston, Illinois in August 1954.

He was impressed by Evanston. The main message of the Assembly was that the churches should work much more closely together: they must join in the struggle for social justice everywhere: and the role of   the laity must be seen to be crucial. There was a new-found optimism and determination in the air at Evanston, not unrelated to the fact that the post-war austerities had begun to be relaxed and the future looked brighter.

After the Assembly he linked up with Mary Lusk and another friend, George Buchanan-Smith, and toured New England in an old jalopy. He showed his two Scottish friends round East Harlem with great enthusiasm.

Then, buoyed and chastened, sobered and enthusiastic, Geoff left the New World for Edinburgh. He still had a lot of questions to sort out. But although he did not know exactly where he was going, he was now sure of the general direction.

Chapter II
To Dwell Amongst People

I simply argue that the Cross be raised again at the centre of the market place as well as on the steeple of the church. I am recovering the claim that Jesus was not crucified in a cathedral between two candles, but on a cross between two thieves; on the town garbage heap; at a crossroad so cosmopolitan that they had to write his title in Hebrew and in Latin and in Greek (or shall we say in English, in Bantu and in Afrikaans?); at the kind of place where cynics talk smut, and thieves curse and soldiers gamble. Because that is where He died. And that is what He died about. And that is where churchmen should be and what churchmanship should be about.—

George F. MacLeod

Geoff may have been shaken, but Cramond stood firm. Not long after his return to Edinburgh, he was invited to preach at the morning service. He graphically described the poverty and deprivation in East Harlem and challenged the congregation to new endeavour for social justice. After the service the verdict was unanimous: he was wonderful.

He was soon spending a lot of time in Glasgow, in conversation with Walter and Elizabeth Fyfe and John Jardine. Fired with enthusiasm, they started to outline proposals for a new style of ministry in Glasgow, inspired by the East Harlem pattern.

They walked round different areas of Glasgow: Anderston, Bridgeton, Cowcaddens, Dalmarnock, Govan, Townhead and Laurieston. The housing conditions appalled them and they noted that the ministers of the churches in these areas seldom lived in the communities they served. Indeed, they were expected not to.

The group wanted to live and work in an area which was deprived, but in which there was a possibility of helping to build a sense of community. Anderston was felt to be too far gone: the dereliction was such that only ambulance work could be done. Laurieston Gorbals was the place they decided on.

The name of Gorbals was, of course, associated in the public mind with squalor and violence. It had not always

49

been so. In 1750 Glasgow was still confined almost entirely to the north of the Clyde. The small village of Gorbals, set in open country, had grown up on the south side of the river. With the settlement of weavers in Gorbals at this time the village began to expand and by 1790 the population was around 500.

During the Industrial Revolution and the consequent population explosion Gorbals developed as a residential suburb for the new merchants. It had handsome buildings made of cream sandstone and wide elegant streets. Gorbals was a very desirable residential area. But as Glasgow expanded, the rich merchants moved further out. Gorbals became more of a transitional residential area for the middle classes. They too left as the city grew. Working class housing was built in what became known as Gorbals-Hutcheson-town. It consisted mainly of single ends, or rooms and kitchens. Laurieston was always regarded as being the 'toffy' part of Gorbals.

The pogroms of Eastern Europe at the turn of the twentieth century meant an influx of Jewish immigrants, and Hutchesontown was the favourite settling area. Irish immigrants moved in too. By the 1920s and 1930s the social and religious differences, backed by debilitating unemploy-ment and misery, helped to establish the notoriety that was later to be romanticised in the novel *No Mean City*.

The post-war housing shortage saw homeless and desperate families moving into Gorbals in big numbers. The once magnificent houses had by this time been sub-divided and hundreds of families were crammed into single rooms, for which they paid exorbitant rents.

As the group walked round the streets of Gorbals they were confronted with decaying tenements, broken windows and rat-infested back courts. A local authority survey ten years later was to quantify the misery: of the 5,500 houses in Laurieston Gorbals (population 18,500) 99 per cent fell within the three lowest categories of structural condition and in terms of sanitary condition 62 per cent were regarded as either unacceptable or incapable of improve-ment. Thirty per cent of the houses had shared lavatories and only 11 per cent had baths and hot water. Many families had a communal kitchen on the stair landing and in cold weather housewives used to huddle round the open stove to get a heat.

In 1955 overcrowded, decaying Gorbals was acknowledged to be one of the worst slums in Europe, although it was not uniformly desperate. A considerable number of families lived with dignity and never came in contact with either the welfare service or the police. There were streets and closes with a tradition of stable family life. But for too many, especially the battered and defeated, life in Gorbals was a matter of survival. It had to do with unemployment benefits, bail, trouble and keeping body and soul together.

Walter, Geoff and John did their own survey of church-going in one area of Gorbals. Their report revealed that, at most, 9.6% of the population were active members of the Church of Scotland ('active' meaning attending church at least once a month). Of the adult population 46.8% claimed Roman Catholic affiliation. Of young people 3.6% claimed active affiliation to the Church of Scotland. They also noted that a high proportion of those attending church were people who had actually moved away from Gorbals.

Out of the analysis, surveys and excited talk emerged some firm proposals. A plan would be put forward to the Presbytery of Glasgow (the Church of Scotland's governing body for the area). Walter and Elizabeth, Geoff and John would move into a small area of Laurieston Gorbals. Their intention would be to work as a team with the people resident there, in the hope of building up some kind of Christian community. It would be regarded as an experiment in evangelism, supervised by the Iona Community Board and under the general responsibility of the Presbytery.

The documents prepared at that time reveal a number of influences—most obviously East Harlem Protestant Parish, the worker-priest movement, the Iona Community, the Evanston philosophy and the general ferment in Scottish church life at that time.

The French worker-priest movement had a very limited impact in Scotland, but the thinking behind it was undoubtedly an influential part of the Gorbals philosophy. In a paper Geoff explained the movement:

"The priest workers in France were men who moved into the secular world of industry to labour with their hands, not for the aggrandisement of the Church, nor as a bulwark against Communism, but in order in the first place to be there simply because Christ is already there; to bring, if need be, their own insights into the problems of industry; to meet working men on terms of equality rather than from a position of priestly status; to share in the struggles of industrial tension and the search for justice and for dignity; and to declare, where possible, God's judgement and God's promise in the place where they worked."

The Iona Community had been founded in 1938 by the Rev. Dr George MacLeod. A very successful parish minister in Govan, Dr MacLeod had been dissatisfied with the Church's attempts to say something relevant to men at a time of high unemployment. He felt church life had become separate from the world; that theology inhabited its own private world, while the rest of the world went to hell. God was not just a God for Sundays, but for every day of the week, at the factory bench or the dockyard or the dole queue.

A brilliant preacher and a dedicated socialist, MacLeod had the vision of rebuilding the ruined abbey on the holy island of Iona—a project to be shared by ministers and craftsmen. In the sharing of work and worship, spirituality and the common life, lessons might be learned not just about rebuilding an abbey, but about rebuilding the world at large. Thus the Iona Community was born.

After an initial period of training on Iona, members were sent to work in industrial or urban parishes. They shared a common discipline of daily prayer, planning for each day, economic sharing and a commitment to work for social justice. The founding of the Iona Community was not appreciated by everyone. Its sacramental worship was regarded by some as half way towards Rome and its politics half way towards Moscow. The aristocratic, charismatic MacLeod, with his Celtic mysticism, his romantic socialism and his willingness to stand on ecclesiastical toes, was not loved by all.

The Iona movement was followed by wider stirrings in

Scotland. The new Barth-inspired Biblical theology allowed broad coalitions to appear and the rise in ecumenical interest and the rediscovery of the laity helped bring about the Tell Scotland movement. The movement was born of discussions between representatives of the Church of Scotland Home Board and the BBC in 1952. It became a nation-wide evangelistic movement with the following principles—evangelism is the job of the whole church; evangelism is a constant and not an occasional activity; the Church itself, as the Body of Christ, is the agent of His Mission; the Church is both universal and local; the role of the laity is crucial.

Geoff wrote a basic policy document early in 1955. He began what was a markedly church-based paper as follows: "It is not a new thing in Scotland to express concern about a situation in which great numbers of men and women and young people are outside the life of the church; are strangers to the new life in Christ; have seldom heard and never responded to the word of God preached vitally and relevantly. We are concerned, as ministers of the Church of Scotland, to undertake a ministry to such people which, we believe, will be for us the only way in which we can act realistically in terms of the situation. We believe that we must try some new ways to bring a knowledge, so far as we can understand and interpret it, of Christ's person and of his will for individuals and for a community in a predominantly pagan district."

In the course of the closely argued paper Geoff said that existing parishes were too large. Ministers were having to spend most of their time with church members. The Gorbals experiment would attempt to move in other directions.

"In our consciences we have chosen the other way and have committed ourselves to a ministry to those who are far outside the Church and to whom the Church has become entirely a side issue."

What was needed was a team ministry, working in a small area of Gorbals. "This small group must become the outward-looking nucleus of a Christian congregation—a congregation centred on the sacraments, on preaching and on worship, a congregation committed to carry the Gospel to the whole life of the community."

The group would live in Gorbals and would rent, but not buy or build property for their use. They chose to do this for "many practical reasons, the most important being that we must be familiar to the people and available at any and every time.

"But there is more. The Church must cease to be an occasional visitor and must really learn to dwell among people—this we believe to be true of every parish and congregation. But especially, in our most pagan areas, we believe that this must start with ministers who will be prepared to leave behind the traditional building and the traditional privileges—perhaps even reputation—and dwell in the midst of their people, because Christ first dwells there."

Geoff said that two out of the three ministers would seek secular employment. They would visit the community and would work with the families of local youngsters. He stressed: "We do not claim to have discovered some new solution which will revolutionise the Church of Scotland and make it adequate to its responsibilities in such a situation. We claim nothing. We ask only that we be allowed to approach this problem in one way which seems to us to be a realistic step towards meeting the situation."

He insisted that there was no wish to do something separate from the Church of Scotland. They did not wish to start a new sect; the scheme would serve to complement the parish system. He concluded: "We may be accused of trying some new stunt, or trying to concern ourselves only with the so-called romantic situations of crime, etc. Here again, we refer back to our time in East Harlem. From the outside it is characterised by some as a stunt. For those engaged in working there, there is nothing of a stunt, nothing romantic about it.

"There are only people—people in sometimes very distressing situations, people who desperately need to be told of, and to experience for themselves, the new life of Christ."

While all these discussions were going on John Jardine was still assistant minister at Govan Old Parish Church, Walter Fyfe was labouring in the shipyards and Geoff Shaw was working as a full-time field secretary for the Scottish Churches Ecumenical Association, a job he took up at the beginning of November 1954.

The Association, which promoted ecumenical activity in Scotland, wanted to capitalise on the post-Evanston mood. A huge 'Evanston to Scotland' rally had been held in the Usher Hall, Edinburgh at the end of October, 1954 and was attended by 1600 delegates from 550 congregations from all over Scotland.

Local conferences and committees began to spring up and Geoff was appointed for a short term to help co-ordinate activities. This involved him travelling all over Scotland promoting the Evanston message of unity and mission. At that time the Rev. Campbell Maclean, a minister in Campbeltown, wrote to Church of Scotland headquarters asking for a speaker on Evanston. He was disappointed to learn that he was being offered a student, Geoffrey Shaw.

"But from the time I met him at the airport I realised that this man was someone different," he recalled. "He was a real winner. He spoke at the meeting without notes, in an apparently casual manner, but with great assurance. He was very impressive."

In the course of their discussions Geoff told Campbell Maclean that there was a vacancy at Cramond, a place that he had not even heard of (Leonard Small had moved to St Cuthbert's Church in Edinburgh). Six months later, when Campbell Maclean was elected minister of Cramond, he received a postcard of congratulations from Geoff Shaw.

Geoff gave up working for the ecumenical association at the end of January to concentrate on the Gorbals project. In April 1955 the die was cast. The proposal to set up the Gorbals Group experiment was sent to the Presbytery of Glasgow.

Chapter III
Bridgeton

Show me the whisky stains on the floor
Show me the drunkard as he stumbles out the door
And I'll show you a young man
With so many reasons why,
There, but for fortune, go you and I.—

Folk Song

I am come that they might have life, and that they might have it more abundantly.—
John 10.10

The Presbytery said a firm 'No.' Their minute stated: "The Presbytery is unable to give its approval to the proposed experiment for the following reasons: (a) manpower; (b) the setting up of a separate organisation within the parish; (c) the unsatisfactory nature of the accommodation and the living conditions, the house proposed having four rooms and kitchen, with inside lavatory and bathroom. That is three bed-sitting rooms, kitchen as dining and sitting room and one large room free for any public activities; (d) the uncertainty of the financial arrangements.

"The Presbytery is further of the opinion that an experiment such as that proposed could be done better by providing extra assistance to the parish minister and the Kirk session in co-operation with the lay witness of the congregation."

The three young ministers were left high and dry. After their initial disappointment they agreed not to commit themselves to any long term work in order to have one more go. The more they thought about it, the more they saw it was unlikely the Presbytery would allow a radical experiment to be conducted by three relatively unknown people. They resolved to work within the bounds of the Prebytery in order to establish their credentials. Thus Walter Fyfe became minister of Hall Memorial Church in Dalmarnock and John Jardine took up an appointment as youth secretary of the Iona Community.

In September 1955, after a short spell on the staff of

57

Ainslie Park School and after leading a summer youth camp on Iona, Geoff turned down the offer of a post as a lecturer at New College. He took up instead the position of full-time boys leader in Church House, Bridgeton.

The story of Church House in Glasgow is one of the best examples of Christian service and commitment in Glasgow. Established in 1942 by the Rev. Arthur Gray, following on pioneering work by the Rev. Sidney Warnes, it has provided since then a place to go for young people in the Bridgeton area of the city. The number of boys and girls who have the club to thank for keeping them out of trouble must be legion.

(Church House has gone through numerous developments. It still serves the youth of Bridgeton, under the guidance of the Rev. Bill Shackleton who was assistant at St Francis-in-the-East when Geoff was appointed and who has been in Bridgeton ever since. At the time of writing this book the club is under the leadership of Alex Mair.)

During the period of Geoff's £300 a year appointment the House was run the by the kirk session of St Francis-in-the-East church, through a management committee of which the minister, the Rev. John Sim, was chairman. The building used was that of the former congregation with which St Francis-in-the-East had united. The programme was aimed largely at young people who would not normally fit into church organisations.

Geoff was immediately at home in Church House. He loved it. It was a bit like picking up where he had left off in East Harlem. Bridgeton had similar problems to Gorbals, with its bad housing, high unemployment and gang sub-culture.

He threw himself into the work unsparingly. He quickly established himself as a good leader and the characteristics of his style of youth work were soon apparent. He offered the youngsters himself, on unlimited call. His special concern was for the delinquents and outsiders. He had a personal firmness, yet he refused to throw people out or to bring charges against them.

His style was an unusual mixture of authoritarianism and permissiveness. He ran the club like the scoutmaster he always was—doors open at 7.30 pm and closed at 10.00 pm,

no matter who wanted in. No sandshoes, no gym.
Youngsters weren't allowed to do what they wanted in the
club.

Geoff had a presence which cooled situations, yet it was a
totally unflamboyant presence. He never used violence
towards any youngster and club helpers cannot remember
him shouting or losing his temper. He refused to call the
police—he felt that was an evasion of the issue and he was
not impressed by some police methods. If police arrived at
the scene of a fracas he would decline to press charges. He
preferred to deal with problems in his own way.

This meant some battles of will. If someone refused to
leave the premises Geoff would sit with him till 3.00 am if
necessary, till the boy cracked.

He was admired for his judgement. Monica Morris (now
Monica Campbell), the girls' leader, recalls a dance at which
one of the club's violent car-stealers smashed a bottle and
faced up to a six foot two Korean war veteran who was
helping. Monica ran from the canteen and separated them,
taking the drunk boy off to the kitchen. Geoff in the
meantime stood on the balcony, watching.

"I really think he felt I could cope. I had got there first—so he
just let me handle it my way. If he had interfered the
balance would have changed."

Geoff remarked to Monica afterwards that Mary Slessor in
darkest Africa never had to face anything like that.

He set himself high standards and he demanded a great
deal of the club leaders. He usually got it.

Not all of his helpers handled things in the same gentle
way, however. At a party in the club a boy started tearing
things off the Christmas tree. One of the leaders, Tom
Milroy, shouted at him to stop. There was a deathly hush in
the club as the two walked towards each other. When they
met the boy punched Tom in the face. Geoff came over and
said quietly to the youth: "Go up to my office," then he
turned to Tom: "You go and interview him."

The two went upstairs into Geoff's office. Tom closed the
door behind him. He went over to the youth and punched
him on the mouth. One game each. No words needed. Issue
resolved.

When they went downstairs Geoff said: "You've settled it all, then?" Little did he know.

Tom Milroy, remembering Geoff when he first came to the club, said: "At first I didn't like this upper class do-gooder, but I came to have a great respect for him."

The club evenings used to finish with an epilogue. Geoff was skilled at taking ordinary incidents and making a good theological point. The youngsters of course did not sit there with folded arms lapping up the Gospel stories. The speaker often shouted through a barrage of flying chips. The boys also excelled at reciting the Lord's Prayer backwards!

Activities were not restricted to club nights. Geoff took boys for football on Glasgow Green each week and he led many camps. Iona and Mull were favourite places. For many of them it was their first time away from Glasgow.

Stewart McGregor, now chaplain to Edinburgh Royal Infirmary, found himself stranded in Oban, having missed the last ferry to Mull. He knew that Geoff and some Bridgeton boys were camping near Kilmore at the head of Loch Feochan, so he hitched a lift to the roadend.

"Eventually I got there and found Geoff and his lads camped in bell tents beside a burn, having a whale of a time", he said. "They cooked me a supper of potatoes and beans and made me more than welcome. The next morning, I wanted to get back to Oban to catch the King George for Iona at 9 a.m. Geoff had to go into Oban too and he drove me there in a dormobile.

"It was a glorious morning, the herons were standing at the edge of the loch feeding in the early morning light and Geoff and I revelled in what we saw around us. I remember he looked very tired and he told me he was exhausted ferrying lads from Glasgow up to Argyllshire and back and getting very little sleep because of the late nights and early mornings in the camp."

Geoff exhibited endless patience for the delinquent and the outsider. When he was at Church House, the balance of the club changed in the direction of the 'tough guys' and he found himself criticised for the time he spent with delinquents. He would reply, "You can't get lower than the cross."

60

In response to his experience, Geoff's theology was developing two polarities—the cross of Christ and the idea of the abundant life. Jesus, God's son, was crucified on a rubbish dump between two thieves. He was despised and rejected and spat upon. Therefore the Christian disciple who believed in costly grace had no right to look down upon any human being. There was nothing lower than the cross and there was no human being who was outside the scope of redemption. Geoff believed this with a passion that never left him.

He also meditated on the idea of the abundant life which Jesus spoke of. What was there in life for youngsters from broken homes, brought up in slums, dealt with harshly by the police, institutionalised, robbed of prospects? He felt that such crippled young people needed the compensation of extra care and time and the opportunities of widened horizons.

One night Geoff sat in the corner of the club, playing with matches with a boy for two hours. George Buchanan-Smith, who was helping, said to Geoff, "I hope your university degrees helped you tonight!" Geoff replied that for that boy, matches were his way into the Kingdom.

A prayer which meant a great deal to him was appropriately, the Prayer of St Francis. It summed up for him the essence of what he was striving after and he was often to use it in services.

Lord, make me an instrument of Thy peace.
Where there is hatred, let me sow love.
Where there is injury, pardon;
Where there is doubt, faith;
Where there is despair, hope;
Where there is sadness, joy;
Where there is darkness, light.
O Divine Master,
Grant that I may not so much seek
to be consoled, as to console;
to be understood, as to understand;
to be loved, as to love.
for it is in giving that we receive;
It is in pardoning that we are pardoned;

It is in dying that we are born to eternal life.

Geoff lived in a very spartan single end in London Road. Boys and helpers would go round during the day or after the club for a cup of coffee and a chat. He would never let anyone go, no matter how often he was let down. The door was always open. He would listen to problems patiently and help the youngster to analyse his own life situation.

There would be evenings of great hilarity and singing. Often they'd talk till two and three in the morning. The address of 983 London Road became known as a haven of acceptance, coffee and fun and listening—even if the house was freezing!

Geoff dealt with things through personal relationships rather than rules. This was time-consuming and costly. At times he got depressed and moody: boys who let him down badly would be dealt with coldly—to such an extent that some would have preferred a quick punch on the mouth. Nevertheless, they were never rejected.

Although Geoff's time at Bridgeton was happy and fulfilling, he also knew days of black despair. Dealing with people's problems could be a lonely business and sometimes he felt overwhelmed by the enormity of the social and economic network in which so many seemed trapped. What depressed him, too, was the slowness with which his own vision of what life could be came to pass. His sense of duty and his desire to see immediate changes made him impatient with others who didn't see things in the same way.

George Buchanan-Smith's lasting vision of Geoff at that time is of him looking determined, leading a group of ragged 13yearolds hurriedly towards the promised land....

Geoff had in those days the relentless air of a man driven by a Calvinist duty ethic, perhaps working out a guilt complex related to his deeply felt sense of privilege. There were those who thought there was an element of romanticism in his defence of boys habitually in trouble. 'All Geoff's geese were swans. There were no rogues in Bridgeton when Geoff was there.' (Geoff was aware of the criticism and knew the boys concerned were rogues. But he defended them as no worse than a lot of people in more fortunate circumstances who got away with it.)

Attractive girls from the east braved the culture shock of Bridgeton in order to have tea with Geoff at London Road. Some may have been disappointed to encounter a determined man with a mission. Here was this tall, athletic, handsome, hazel-eyed hero labouring among the poor. They found him aglow with East Harlem and the priesthood of all believers.

He preached ouside Bridgeton now and again, but his message did not please everyone. His good friend George Buchanan-Smith was assistant minister of Glasgow Cathedral and he arranged for Geoff to preach one Sunday morning. At the end of the service, the clergy processed out, led by the beadle, who turned to Geoff and said in a voice which reverberated throughout the Cathedral,"Yon wisnae a sermon!" Far from being offended, Geoff roared with laughter. Over 20 years later, the same cathedral was crowded with the high and the lowly paying tribute to the same preacher whose best sermon had been his life.

One old friend who came to see Geoff in Bridgeton was Tom Fleming, by this time an actor with an established reputation. After his spell in the navy, Tom had decided to study for the Baptist ministry. At his interview, he was asked why—he said because he was interested in people. He was told, "You must be interested in souls" and was asked if he was applying for the ministry because his theatrical career was a failure! Exit potential ordinand.

Tom was interested in different types of ministry and he was part of a group in Edinburgh which met for discussion and prayer every Monday morning before work. Geoff was interested in this.

The two men agreed that churches generally seemed to convey an impression of certainty and aloofness at a time when people were struggling with their doubts and uncertainties. Much more humility and flexibility were needed.

Tom remembers one particular conversation with Geoff in1955. He had been asked to portray Jesus of Nazareth on television—the first time this had ever been attempted. Up till then in religious films, one saw the whisk of Christ's robe or his footsteps in the sand. He wondered if he should take the role on. It was a difficult decision because television was beginning to make its presence felt in a big way: and the programme was to be screened live.

Geoff's advice was that he should do it, but that he should make sure Jesus came over as a young man, and not as a toff, or someone very holy.

The programme was a great success. Geoff and the Bridgeton youngsters watched it with approval. Robin Hood was on the other channel, but young Jesus of Nazareth, with his sleeves rolled up, beat him out the park.

At this time Geoff's political philosophy took a further radical turn. 1956 was the year of Suez, an issue which divided friends and families.

Anthony Eden's decision to send troops to Egypt caused impassioned debate up and down the country.

Geoff was angered and dismayed by the British Government's conduct. He took part in a public debate at Bridgeton Cross. His New College friend, Bob Henderson, who was by this time in Drumchapel, remembers Geoff coming to him in great distress about Suez.

Geoff's further shift leftwards was not made easily and he thought long and carefully before voting Labour at the subsequent election. He was to write later, "As a boy, I lived in a world in which it was unthinkable that anyone other than the Tories could make a fitting Government for Great Britain. And I remember clearly feeling the election of 1945, bringing a Labour government to power, was an unmitigated disaster.

"I was, of course, wrong, and the dramatic legacy of the 1945 government was the Welfare State, with a whole new structure which even the following Tory Government of thirteen years did not, or could not, dismantle."

Geoff, Walter Fyfe and John Jardine had met from time to time to discuss future plans. Geoff had become so immersed in Church House that he would have been more than happy to stay on in Bridgeton. Nevertheless, they had committed themselves to another attempt at setting up the Gorbals experiment.

The date for discussion in Glasgow Presbytery was fixed for Tuesday October 1, 1957.

Chapter IV
The New Family

And they continued steadfastly in the apostles' doctrine and fellowship and in breaking of bread, and in prayers. And fear came upon every soul: and many signs and wonders were done by the apostles. And all that believed were together and had all things in common; And sold their possessions and goods and parted them to all men, as every man had need.—

Acts 2 42-45.

Our training in discipleship is our training in ordinary life—in the daily choices and decisions of common life, in all the questions that life brings.— **T. Ralph Morton**

On the afternoon of the Presbytery debate Walter, John and Geoff felt very tense. They decided that climbing a mountain would make them feel better.

Geoff rode pillion on Walter's motor bike and with John on his scooter they sped towards Ben Ledi. Climbing the mountain did make them feel better. But they needn't have worried. The 'Gorbals Evangelistic Experiment' was passed by the Presbytery by a healthy majority.

Since the last time there had been changes in personnel, a getting-used to the idea, closer aquaintance with the men concerned and a feeling that there was no real harm in giving the three idealists their heads.

As was pointed out in the debate in the Presbytery, if a scientist was approached by younger men who wanted to try an experiment, he put them to the outer edge of the establishment so that if things went wrong, the only people blown up would be themselves.

Thus the Gorbals experiment began, if not with the Presbytery's active blessing, at least with its cautious acknowledgement.

According to memorandum approved by the Presbytery, "the aim of the experiment would be to provide each small natural community (street, part street or block) with a centre of worship and to break down the large and anonymous area into smaller and more personal groups. In these groups we would get to know the entire population by visiting their

65

homes, meeting them in cafes and chip shops and in the streets. As time went on, we would hope that the centre of worship would become real in the lives of many people and that a congregation would serve this small area, meeting perhaps in the homes, perhaps in a disused shop or warehouse, which would not only be a centre of worship, but a family centre for all in the area."

The words were Geoffrey Shaw's.

Geoff was appointed assistant minister of Gorbals John Knox Church—a legal fiction to enable him to work in a section of the parish and receive a salary from the Church of Scotland's Home Board. The agreed memorandum proposed: "That he be free to devote his whole time to working in cooperation with his two ordained colleagues in an experimental, evangelistic outreach to those in the parish outside the fellowship of the Church.

"That this group be free to conduct worship in their own home or in any buildings which they might subsequently use; that they might be free, further, to administer the sacraments in accordance with the order of the Church of Scotland, only with the consent of the parish minister and Kirk Session.

"That they be free to admit persons to full membership of the Church of Scotland, the names of such people being first submitted to the Kirk Session and subsequently added to the membership roll of the local parish church.

"That they be free to engage, as they are able, in such activities as seem to them to fulfil most nearly the total mission of the Church to those round about.

"That the group and the Kirk Session be committed to the experiment for a minimum period of three years."

The die was cast. Some of Geoff's friends were horrified that the 30-year old minister with a promising career should settle for obscurity, or worse. Rev. Dr Ronald Selby Wright, well-known minister of the Canongate in Edinburgh, recalls: "When he decided to 'bury himself' (as it was thought) in the Gorbals, it was regarded by many, including most of his friends, as a great mistake. The Church, it was argued, needed men like Geoff and he seemed to be leaving the main stream of life in the Church, while little knowing how much he was really entering it. The fear was that this active, so popular and so promising young minister would be wasting his talents and indeed burying them, while little realising how great was the work he was doing and continuing to do in a way that only he could do it. He who had been brought up in comfort and security and what might be called 'privilege', was now prepared to live and work in a quite different environment and with considerable sacrifice; and though many admired him they equally thought it was a pity that he had not followed the more orthodox line of the other not so gifted ministers of his time!

"Of course the many were wrong and he was right and the lack of encouragement he must have had must sometimes have been rather hard to bear. Here was almost a parable of the Rich Young Ruler in reverse—a young man with great possessions who had knelt at the feet of Jesus whom, having given up all, he followed."

It was indeed painful for him. Some people felt threatened by his move: it seemed to be putting a big question mark against their own lives and values. In a sense it was. Yet Geoff never believed that his way was the only way, nor did he write off what others were doing. Nevertheless, his was a lonely journey and he had to make it without the support of some of his friends.

It was with great excitement that Walter and Elizabeth, John and his new bride Beryl and Geoff made plans to move into Gorbals. They rented a house at No. 33 Abbotsford Lane—five big rooms and kitchen, up a stair, over a shop, for £38 per annum.

The first official meeting of the Gorbals Group was held in Community House, Clyde Street on October 7, 1957 and Geoff moved into Abbotsford Lane on October 29. Before Christmas he was joined first by the Fyfes and then the Jardines. On December 22 the Gorbals Group ministry was formally inaugurated at a communion service conducted in the house by the Rev. Tom Crombie, the sympathetic convener of the Presbytery's Home Mission Committee.

There was so much to do! Decisions to be made about the domestic arrangements, worship, group life, economics and strategy, never mind responding to the day-to-day crises of Gorbals life.

Walter gave up his church job at Dalmarnock and started work as labourer at Dixon's Blazes. Geoff got a part-time job—working between 4 and 7 pm each day in a newsagents shop in Rutherglen Road owned by the Rev. Jack McLennan. A dux of Edinburgh Academy dishing out *Daily Records* and five Capstan! He loved it. John still had eight months to do in his Iona Community job, but it was agreed that he should go into teaching in Gorbals after that. The Church of Scotland worker priests were in business.

Geoff was soon busy meeting headmasters, doctors, social workers and council officials, trying to establish the needs of the area. Demands were quickly made on the group— matters of rent, broken windows, lads out of Borstal, and so on. By the time of their Christmas Eve service in the house— the first of many—the Gorbals Group was well and truly off the ground.

The Group had long discussions on the shape of their common life, and what their strategy was to be. The discussions were not all sweetness and light—tempers were lost and insults sometimes traded. Let no one portray the Gorbals Group as a saintly bunch of retiring wallflowers. It was one of their rules that discussions should be open and frank. They said what was on their minds.

On one occasion Geoff was taken to task about the visits of so many club boys from Bridgeton to Abbotsford Lane. He would never let friendships go; if people needed him, he was available. End of discussion. At the group meeting Geoff said he felt that the new family should welcome friends coming to visit one member.

The minutes drew a discreet veil over the details of the discussion, but concluded: "All the members having fallen into a somewhat tense silence, the meeting ended."

One of the most important decisions of the Group was to pool all their money and share it out according to need. Each member declared his or her assets at the beginning (GMS: £90, plus furniture). Household bills were paid from the common fund and each person received an agreed allowance for food and personal money. What was left went into a common fund to help finance Gorbals Group projects.

Walter and Geoff had noted that in East Harlem members

went out to speak at suburban church meetings. In return they were given donations for their work. The trouble, Walter and Geoff felt, was that in the speaking the East Harlem situation tended to be glamourised and trivialised. It was too high a price to pay.

They thought it was better not to have activities dependent on outside bodies which might withdraw financial support when the going got rough.

There were other reasons for the economic discipline. The Group felt, following the Book of Acts, that the sharing of money was a symbol of commitment to one another within the Christian fellowship. Costly grace meant putting their money where their mouth was. The pooling of money was also a personal form of social security whereby it was possible to maintain continuing standards during time of unemployment or sickness. Geoff was put in charge of the common purse. He insisted that while the Group should be generous in its attitude and actions towards others, it should be 'meany-minded' in its spending on itself. The phrase stuck and was frequently quoted in discussions on the economic discipline.

Worship was important to the Group. Household prayers were held at 10.00 pm each evening and Holy Communion was celebrated on Sunday evenings. The liturgy which developed was a mixture of Church of Scotland, Iona Community, East Harlem Protestant Parish and Govan Old Parish.

The early discussions, held each Thursday evening, centred around Group policy. It was agreed that there should be no publicity—they were afraid of distortion by the media. Instead of speaking at meetings they invited organisations who wrote requesting a speaker to send two delegates to an open day in Gorbals held each year. They agreed not to take on individual outside commitments without the consent of the whole Group. All decisions about finance and holidays were to be made by the Group.

What was being hammered out here was the principle of **accountability**. The Group felt strongly that current ideas of Christian fellowship were too wishy-washy. Both support and critical challenge were needed.

Sometimes all this could become too serious for words. Later, for instance, the Group spent time solemnly debating whether one member should be given extra money for shoe leather because of the extra walking she did. Margarine or butter was a major debate. The spending of money on a rug became a time-consuming crisis.

At times the Gorbals Group were in danger of taking themselves too seriously, by talking as if the coming Kingdom of God depended on their next decision. The intensity might have been unbearable were it not also for the humour and the compassionate commitment both to each other and to Gorbals. The 'tense silences' in the midst of debates about matters of economics and politics which the Church at large tended to ignore altogether—were usually punctuated by outbursts of hilarity.

There was continuing debate about the role of the Group. Was it to work to evangelise or to fight against the miseries which people faced?

Walter Fyfe, the most radical of the Group, asked: What does ministry to the people round about mean? In a later paper he expressed his view: "I believe that Christ spent his life, intentionally, among ordinary people—more in the pubs than in the synagogues. This was the new thing that came into the world—God among ordinary people, living an ordinary life, without any official purpose, backing or status... our efforts should be towards doing the things that Christ commands—being disciples, not towards creating disciples (other people). Mission, evangelism, must grow out of obedience, which is primary."

John Jardine, the gentlest of the Group and the most church-oriented, argued as time went on: "I think one important failure in our purpose as a Group is our failure to share our group life with other people in the area. We have been quite static in this. I wonder if it is because we are not all sure that we really believe in the Church."

Geoff agreed with Walter that the primary purpose of the Group was obedience, "but this is in order to fit us to share the gift of knowledge that Christ is Lord. The preaching of the Church is communication of this knowledge and its implications—namely making sense of the life of the individual, the family and society."

As regards the role of the Group Geoff added: "I am agreed that we are moving towards something and should not be hurried. The basic essential is that of waiting to see how God uses the Group, rather than determining the limits or activities.

"I still feel we might do more to receive—the whole Church is wrong to divide people into contemplatives and doers. The Group must be both and while the Group receives by conversation among ourselves and with other people, I still feel there is room for waiting on the Lord."

Despite the recurrence of the internal debates, it must not be imagined that the Group spent most of its time looking at its own life. Many of the meetings consisted of a series of brisk, business-like decisions.

As they wrestled with the problems and tried to cope with the unattractive environment and the pressures of Gorbals life it was not surprising that domestic tensions surfaced. With all of them living together in one house, Beryl Jardine being pregnant and delinquent boys from Bridgeton always dropping in, it was a recipe for strained relationships. The move of the whole group into one house had always been intended as a temporary measure, but Geoff was disappointed when John and Beryl moved into the nearby 10 Abbotsford Place. Geoff was a bit oblivious to the problems. He enjoyed being part of one big family and also felt that the communal family was an expression of true Christian community. He always argued at Group meetings that Christian community was more than a matter of simple friendship, it was a matter of vocation. "In Christ" meant more than being pals together.

The Group was now faced with the problem of operating from two bases. It was agreed that all would meet together for the Sunday Communion and the Thursday business meeting which would be preceded by a common meal. Evening prayers would be held in each household and would follow a common liturgy.

The life of Gorbals was beginning to suggest the Group's agenda. Housing was the major issue, of course, and individual Group members argued cases with factors and helped speak for people at rent tribunals. The three men visited the neighbourhood to ask for help in establishing a junk playground for the local youngsters. A playroom was established at No. 33 Abbotsford Lane and Flossie Borgmann, a dynamic American girl who had served in East Harlem Protestant Parish and who had come over to work with Geoff at Church House, took over the running of it.

The state of Gorbals raised political questions, as had the state of East Harlem. Was it enough to provide facilities for youngsters? Was there not a need for social and political change? The three men joined the local Ward Labour Party (average attendance at the fortnightly meetings, five to seven people). On December 18, 1958 Walter was elected chairman, John a member of the executive committee and Geoff, secretary.

Referring to the need for political change, Geoff often used to say: "It's not enough to feed the goldfish, you also have to change the water in the bowl from time to time."

Thus the Group began to dig in. One obvious area which had to be tackled fairly quickly was that of youth work. In his walks round the streets and contacts with different groups Geoff had got to know quite a number of youngsters, most of them involved in crime or drifting dangerously near it. The priority matter on the agenda was to find a meeting place.

Chapter V
Gold Things from Aimless Floss

"One of the Bridgeton flymen was over at Gorbals Cross only half an hour since. He just shouted 'Tell your mob we'll be ready on Sunday night.' An they say he was away again. That wis aw."—

No Mean City

The Kingdom Hall at No.2, Abbotsford Lane had a roof through which the sky could be seen. It was a long, ramshackle hall built over two shops.

And the person pointing it out to Geoff Shaw and Walter Fyfe was Lilias Graham.

Lilias, an Episcopal church worker, had been attached to St. Margaret's and St. Mungo's church in Gorbals since 1954. When she was appointed she told the bishop she wanted to live in Gorbals. To protect her the bishop had said, no, you can't. But Lilias moved into a house in the close at 10, Abbotsford Place in 1955. So she was in a position to observe the setting up of the Gorbals Group from close at hand.

Lilias, one of that rare breed of people of aristocratic background who can work in slum areas and be immediately and warmly accepted, was a one-woman Gorbals experiment. With no fuss, and no struggle with governing bodies, she simply went ahead.

St. "Maggie-Mungo's" had 60 names on the roll and 25 regulars on Sunday. So Miss Graham started to develop things on her own. Children came over to her house to play. Harrassed mothers dropped in for a cup of tea and a chat. And as relationships with young people developed, she, too, was looking for premises.

She searched Laurieston Gorbals and came to th. conclusion that the old Kingdom Hall was the only place. She knew that the Gorbals Group wanted premises, so Lilias, who had known Geoff through his work with the Scottish Churches Ecumenical Association, arranged to meet him and Walter on site.

The old Jehovah's Witness Hall looked somewhat derelict, and the rickety wooden stairs did not seem too safe, but it had possibilities. It was agreed to rent the hall (£30 p.a.), which the Gorbals Group and Lilias would share jointly. Geoff managed to get a grant from the Bellahouston Trust to put a new roof on, and he soon had a squad of boys working to get it in shape. Geoff saw that the hall could be easily sub-divided into three open sections—a place to sit around, a section for indoor games, and a work area.

By this time he was so busy that he had to give up work in the newsagent's shop. He had been reluctant to do so, but the Group made the decision for him. Over the summer of 1958 the work on the roof was completed. Geoff took the boys away camping and for runs in the old Fordson van the Group had bought for £75. He also ran football teams and during one Group policy discussion, he insisted that the poor players as well as the good should get a regular game and that the teams should be chosen on a non-sectarian basis.

Geoff's ecumenical bent was not shared by everyone else. One of the local Roman Catholic priests went round the homes of boys who were helping to clear up the hall warning them not to go back. Three never returned to the club: the rest continued to come. This, of course was a thousand years before Vatican II.

In February 1959, the club opened. Soon it was in use almost every night of the week, with activities for different age groups. Sunday night was family night. The old Orange Hall at 73, Bedford Street became available and the Group rented it as a gym and training centre, for £28 per year. The whirring sound which could be heard at the time was presumably the sound of Orangemen and Jehovah's Witnesses turning in their graves at the thought of such a welter of ecumenical activity going on in their premises.

The demand was considerable and was a threat to Geoff's policy of working small. Leaders from outside were recruited. They were volunteer helpers who had contact with the Gorbals Group.

All age groups were represented at the clubs. The era of television and pop culture had well and truly dawned and Tommy Steele and Elvis Presley records blared forth. Rock 'n Roll, skiffle, drainpipe trousers, bootlace ties: Geoff was there, though definitely not in mod gear. The creaking timbers shivered as the jiving classes began.

Geoff's policy was the same as that in the Church House. Personal contact and unlimited availability were the keys. No one would be thrown out permanently. The police would not be called. Violence would not be met with violence. And he would stand for ages under the lamps at the street corners of Gorbals talking and listening just as he had done at Cramond. The talk was much cruder than at Cramond, but the principle was the same. This was twenty years ago, long before there was any vogue for detached youth work.

The boys from the early days of the club remember Geoff's style well. Now grown men of course, they recall him with affection and gratitude. They recognise how he listened patiently and helped them to see the solutions to their own problems. Some of the boys used to become infuriated because he refused to reject them at the point that they had expected to be rejected.

He only talked about religion when asked. He would say often how important it was that Christ died for one person. The important thing was that Geoff Shaw affirmed these Gorbals youngsters. Many of them had never known a kind word from an adult. He paid them the supreme compliment of listening to what they had to say and discussing issues with them, without ever being patronising. What they said and were mattered to him, deeply, no matter their background. You can't get lower than the cross.

One of Geoff's great gifts as a youth leader was his ability to see the potential in youngsters. His football teams would at first be beaten soundly, but the boys would gain confidence because they kept their place in the team. Then they would start winning. It was a parable. He transmitted a kind of sparkle, a 'something' which communicated itself to the youngsters. He loved them and they knew it.

The widening of horizons was important. In Geoff's presence they were able to put forward serious ideas without being laughed at. In the discussion group he developed at the youth club, they could talk about issues without having to be ready at all times to defend the Pope or King Billy. Some of them became, in the words of one young man 'Geoff Shaw kind of Christians'—that is, people who cared about

75

others, no matter their religion or state. Geoff Shaw was their conscience.

It was important to him that the Gorbals youngsters should get the chance to see places they had never seen before. So a friendly town scheme was developed. Each summer, Gorbals children went off to stay for two weeks with families in parishes in Dumfries, Castle Douglas and elsewhere. It didn't always work out well. On one occasion the Gorbals Group received a letter asking that the children should be de-loused next time. But, generally speaking, it was a good experience for the children and their host families.

The Easter and summer camps were much enjoyed. The gear would be piled into the old van and off it would roar full of singing youngsters. Programmes of sport and adventure activities would be arranged for the daytime and in the evening round the camp fire Geoff got out his guitar and led the singing.

It wasn't fun all the time. Some of the tearaways would sneak out of camp at night and cause trouble. The sight of the van being driven round the field did not amuse Geoff. On one occasion the shopkeepers of Oban knew the Gorbals boys had been when they counted their stock. Geoff demanded that the missing goods be returned and said that the camp would not continue until they were. It was more than once that sheepish boys made their way back to Woolworths with their haul. Shoplifting was one form of redistribution of wealth that he did not approve of.

When a boy kicked over the traces Geoff would go cold. He wasn't good at giving short sharp lessons and getting it over with. But once the lad apologised things got back to normal.

Robin Buchanan-Smith, George's brother, who was minister of Christ's Church, Oban at the time used to keep the boys' gear in his outhouse when camps were held on Mull. He remembers: "The back wall of my manse would be climbed and the confusion of the camping gear extricated from an outhouse. On a Monday everything happened in reverse, but Geoff was usually in such a hurry that tents and pots and pans would come in a jumble over the wall for me to tidy everything up in the evening and pack it away. Far from feeling imposed upon and taken advantage of, as one might feel with many people, I simply regarded myself as making a very small contribution. No words, no particular communication over the transaction and it seemed so right and proper.

"Geoff was an enthusiastic supporter of my 9 a.m., 20-minute service, on a Sunday morning: where he came from or what his destination was, didn't seem relevant. He would be there, surrounded by 10 or 12 boys: 'Hey, mister, we'll put the numbers up on the board for you.' Quite immaterial if the numbers went on upside down; they bellowed out the old favourite hymns. So much together, worshipping in God's house—and at the end of it they would disperse as quietly and inconspicuously as they had gathered."

But what happened when the young people went back home to the Gorbals ? Geoff worried about this and agonised over whether it was fair to take children away and then bring them back to the same conditions. At the end of the day he felt the advantages outweighed the disadvantages.

He was much influenced by a passage in Neil Gunn's "Highland River" in which the boy, Kenn, reflects on an experience of wrestling with and killing a huge salmon.

"It is a moment of sheer unconditional delight that may not be described or explained and nothing can ever explain away. Delight is here not so much too strong as too uniform a word. For the moment may be troubling in the old panic sense; it may be ecstatic; or it may, by a lure of memory, evasive as a forgotten scent, draw one towards it as towards a source."

Geoff believed in the importance of these moments of "sheer unconditional delight". He wanted the Gorbals youngsters to experience them. And many of them did. Geoff was never happier in his whole life than when he was out on the hillside with a group of lads from Gorbals.

The Gorbals sub-culture into which the youngsters returned was one in which it was easy—and normal—to drift into crime. The gang system was like the old feudal clan structure. It was difficult not to belong. The territorial gang was the Cumbie (originally from Cumberland Street). It had different branches, although there was no central control.

They were the Young Cumbie, Young Young Cumbie (17-18 years), Tiny Cumbie (15-17 aggressive, carrying weapons, stealing cars, house breaking), Toddler Cumbie (13-16 Years, centred on particular street corners), Mini Cumbie (highly delinquent, drinking young), Baby Cumbie (11-14, street group beginning delinquency), Rebel Tiny Cumbie (new group in Hutchesontown).

The structure was not unlike the Cramond Sunday School and youth organisations, but there the similarity ended.

Most boys and girls living in Gorbals felt themselves as belonging to Cumbie, however remotely. On going into another gang's territory in Geoff's van, they would be obliged to shout "Cumbie" at youths out of the window and pray that they didn't break down. One group member recalls a particular panic when he was chauffeuring a football team through Bridgeton. After a loud cry of "Cumbie", the traffic lights promptly turned red.

The youngsters would even cry "Cumbie" in the Gorbals streets. It was a kind of talisman, a protection, in case they were suspected of having affiliations with some other gang and therefore be attacked or even chibbed (cut with a razor or knife).

The system gave boys and girls a territory and a common enemy. Toon Tongs controlled the area north of the Gorbals. Enter at your own risk. (In later years, some boys offered to help Geoff with canvassing, but withdrew when they discovered it was in Calton).

The club gave the youngsters a place to meet and a chance to stay out of trouble for a bit. The first gang to use No.2 was not Cumbie, but a small group of youngsters whom Geoff had got to know in the street. They were not yet tough or criminal. Their name was "The Clarty Dozen" (clarty = dirty). The club was not exclusive to them, but they formed the basis of the original membership.

Sometimes there was trouble at the club itself, when gang or personal feuds exploded into violence. Now and again the premises were raided or vandalised. But considering the potential for trouble among teenagers with little money and a lot of time on their hands, No.2 deserves a special place in

Pictured not long after his father's death.

Leading Hand Shaw.

the annals of influences for good in Glasgow.

Geoff's views on crime and punishment were developed in this situation. Time and again he spoke out against the calls for the reintroduction of the birch or for more repressive measures.

In an article in *The British Weekly,* he argued that the delinquent was never simply the 'ned' of the popular newspaper nor the 'thug' of popular fear and fantasy. Nor on the other hand, was he, in most instances the pitiable character to be protected by the charitable. Both those attitudes denied his personality and treated him not as a person but as an object, as a specimen of a separate and inferior class. Within the Christian perspective this was never permissible.

Why was the individual delinquent?"The only true answer to this question," he wrote "can be that in each instance different contributing factors are at work. More disturbing for the Christian," he continued, "is the recognition, which no amount of scorn or anger against the delinquent can hide, that somehow we are all involved, that in each delinquent, society is itself on trial...It goes deeper than the recognition that the society which has segregated itself into little fragments according to wealth and background must not be surprised if sometimes there is a kick-back; that the society which idolises affluence will increase offences against property; that the society which, in national affairs, tolerates an ever-increasing scale of violence will increase the scale of violence at home.

"It goes indeed to a corporate awareness of Christian understanding that in human nature there is a basic contradiction of the will to do well and continual failure; that the delinquent is, as it were, the pimple on the skin that too clearly betrays the poisoned bloodstream. For this reason, society can achieve greatness only when it follows through the costly and difficult problem of reforming and restoring. Neither anxious repression nor muddle-headed molly-coddling are adequate substitutes."

The practical steps Geoff advocated included more effective family service to problem families in high delinquency areas; better family/school relationships won

79

through a hard process of mutual respect; detached youth work on the streets; more money and time spent on the potential delinquent—"remembering always that prevention is for the sake of the person, not for the sake of society at large."

Here lay the key to Geoff's social and political philosophy—the individual is what matters. There is nothing lower than the cross. Nothing is more important than the fact that Christ died for an individual person.

He concluded the article: "This emphasis on the individual, on his family, on his group, on his local community, must apply also in action which society may take towards the delinquent who has been convicted. It is necessary that experiments should be made with attendance centres in the cities, where the convicted delinquent would be required to attend nightly; still resident in his own home, still working at a normal job, occupying his time to some purpose and in crimes of violence, working to compensate the victim.

"But underlying all these practical steps must be a renewed sense of the utter tragedy of lives so stunted, so lacking in purpose and aim, so unimaginably undeveloped as to result in what we call delinquent behaviour.

"Our delinquents are people, created under God to live gloriously. Whatever in society makes this impossible must be attacked; whatever in the individual may make it possible must be nurtured and strengthened."

The last paragraph hints at the political implications of his personalist philosophy.

Given that such youngsters filled Geoff's youth club, how was he to strike the balance between authoritarianism and permissiveness? In an article in *Contact,* the journal of the Scottish Pastoral Association, of which he was a member, he wrestled with the problem. He wrote: "The most understanding of parents, teachers, youth leaders from time to time find their anger boils over, feel that they should have laid down the law long ago, discover that the flog-them-all brigade may have something after all and worry in case they have left their young people with no adequate supports. In any event they feel guilty, realising the patience of the saint

80

or the analyst is not theirs and that they are continually halting between two opinions.

"The truth is that the adolescent group will demand from the adult an astonishing variety of things. It will demand that the adult fulfill an astonishing variety of roles, from the figure of authority through the big brother to the teddy bear who eventually gets kicked around, discarded, only to be taken up again in a new relationship."

A poem about a teacher expressed for Geoff the heart of it all. Here is a part of J.P. Fletcher's "Unprofitable Journey" in *Tally 300* (**Hand and Flower Press**), which describes his child-to-man life in the Leicestershire pits.

> I brought my empty soul
> Eroded, bruised,
> And old, resentful will,
> A mouth hard-closed,
> The unimaginable
> Mind of a child ill-used.
>
> Not sweetened and bright and clean
> Like a new house
> For you to settle in
> Eager assiduous
> Tenantry to spin
> Gold things from aimless floss.
>
> Lonely, unloved, a stark
> Rebellious oaf
> You kindled with your spark,
> In that poor stuff
> Setting at last to work
> The miracle of love.

The 'miracle of love' was what it was all about and the sparks were kindled in lonely, unloved lives at the club, on the Gorbals streets, under the lamplights and on the hillsides of Mull.

Geoff helped to set these miracles to work not just because his technique and his philosophy were right, but because he cared. As one former charge of his put it: "Geoff? He was brilliant. Magic."

Chapter VI
Blankets and Lady Bountiful

*The Pharisees knew how to take care of the poor in such a way that the
poor were always with them.—*   **Fr. Thomas Merton.**

*What warkis are reputit gude befoir God....to save the lives of
innocents, to repress tyrannie, to defend the oppressed....*

The Scots Confession, 1560

The real goal is not to convert the proletariat but to abolish it—

Abbé Godin.

Meanwhile, back at the group. The demands were increasing
all the time and it was difficult to keep pace with what was
happening.

What certainly wasn't happening was packed worship
services. In fact, hardly anyone came to Sunday communion
at all. In August, 1959, it was decided to depart from the
Sunday celebration and to have Communion once a month
as part of the common meal at the Group meeting on
Thursday evenings. The order of events was: meal,
Communion, dishwashing, discussion, prayers of intercession, benediction. No member of the Group was allowed
to miss the Thursday night meeting without good reason.
Each member of the Group took a turn at leading. In May
1960, it was agreed that Communion should be celebrated
every week, on Thursday evenings.

By this time, membership of the Group had changed. In
October, 1958, Kirstie Wedderburn from Cramond, who
had worked with Geoff at Church House, applied to join.

She sat quaking on the stairs outside as the members
deliberated. Answer, Yes. Kirstie taught at a primary school
in Garthamlock and was a gifted worker with children. She
helped in the playroom. She moved into a flat rented by the
Group at 3a, Abbotsford Place. One month later, Ray Soper,
a physiotherapist, also joined the group and moved in with
Kirstie. Flossie Borgmann had to return to America in
January, 1959.

The childrens work flourished under Kirstie and Ray.
Progress was gradually made with the junk play-

ground. Walter and Geoff were engaged in seemingly endless negotiations over its site in Nicholson Street,but eventually the plans were finalised. Walter managed to get various pieces of equipment from his work, and on May 21,1959, the minutes recorded triumphantly: "Walter reported on the establishment of the junk playground last Saturday. The work had been a real community effort. Local men had rejoiced in the idea and taken pride in the work. Many children had helped with the construction. Over the weekend, some 2-300 children had played on it." Summer games, crafts and outings were organised for the children who didn't go away for holidays.

John who was now teaching at Adelphi Terrace School, Gorbals and Walter and Geoff got more and more involved in the Labour Party. The property rented by the Group was used for Labour Party activities and the three men helped with duplicating and canvassing. At the beginning of 1959, the Campaign for Nuclear Disarmament was starting to get under way and Geoff and Walter became increasingly active. There were not enough hours in the day.

Theological discussions within the Group continued. What was the role of the Group? Was it fulfilling its remit? Was it evangelistic enough? Was too much time being spent on politics? Or too little?

From time to time there were visits by representatives from the Presbytery. There was something faintly amusing about the scene. Decent, honourable men in black suits and clerical collars wending their way through the rubbish and shouts of abuse in Abbotsford Lane and up the dank stair into the house. Onward, Christian Soldiers. Sharing bread and wine, slightly distastefully, from common household implements. Anxious, honest, men of good will trying to fit this bewildering experiment into their categories. And the questions! All about ecclesiastical matters in the midst of this ghastly mess. How many members have joined,asked one minister as he pulled the visitation form from his pocket. (There must be some way we can get this down on the Presbyterian form) None. None? Well....there's a girl from downstairs who sometimes comes to Communion...Good. We'll put her down. How Geoff used to roar with laughter when he told that story!

In the course of the discussions with the Home Mission Committee members about worship, the sacraments, and the common life, Geoff would often quote John Knox. He had a great affinity with the Scotish reformer and believed that the Gorbals Group ministry had its roots firmly in the Scottish Reformed tradition. He felt the Church of Scotland had domesticated and trivialised that tradition, enslaving it within a Scottish bourgeois culture. The teeth had been drawn from the Reformers. Geoff's Christocentric radicalism caused him to view with dismay what he regarded as the emasculation of the Scottish Reformation. He argued that the greatest mistake the Church of Scotland had made was to ignore John Knox's Book of Discipline. The Christian community must be bound by discipline and the Gorbals Group was at least making an attempt at it. The Rev. Geoffrey M. Shaw was never a trendy theologian.

Much to some of the visitors' unconcealed amazement the women in the Group participated fully. Elizabeth, Beryl, Kirstie and Ray could more than hold their own in theological and political discussion. They often felt they were being patronised by the clerical visitors.

The hard facts of the matter were that many of the Presbytery didn't understand what life was about in Gorbals: and not a few didn't want to know. For their part the Gorbals Group members were often too weary, or too impatient, to make the necessary efforts to help the Presbytery to understand. And perhaps too arrogant. At any rate the relationship settled down to a mutual live-and-let-live.

The annoying thing was that the visitors from the Presbytery had a point. The proposal approved by the Presbytery in 1957 had been for an 'evangelistic experiment', and Geoff Shaw's documents had envisaged little centres of worship in different streets. It had not happened, and the Presbytery, even if it didn't really grasp the full implications of living in Gorbals, had a right to ask why not.

The point was taken up by Ray Soper, who often acted as the Group's conscience. Leading the discussion at the Group meeting, she raised the issue of the 1957 memorandum.

85

What do we mean now by local centres of worship? We spoke of a congregation serving the area. So far we have no congregation. At the moment we are apart from the people. Will we always be like this? How much time and energy do we have at our disposal? Sometimes our ideas seem too big for our potential.

Ray had raised questions which were to exercise the Group for years. The dilemma can be stated thus: who was the life of the Group **for**? Was the communal life to enable and strengthen Group members in their work in the world? Or was it to be available to the whole community in the shape of a worshipping congregation?

If the Group life was meant to be shared with the whole community there were the two obvious problems of the economic discipline and worship. How many Gorbals people would want to pool their incomes with the Group? And would the rather traditional worship of the Gorbals Group appeal to local people? If they really wanted to share their life with their neighbours, wouldn't the Communion service pose an insurmountable problem to the Roman Catholic members of the community?

On the other hand, if the economic discipline were abandoned and Communion withdrawn, wouldn't the corporate life of the group fall apart, or at least become impoverished? And if it were decided to have two kinds of meetings, one with more popular appeal, wouldn't this create first and second class Christian citizens?

There were obviously two competing views of the Group here. The dilemma was a real one and the Group agonised over it. In the meantime things remained largely as they were. In those early days the Gorbals Group was a tight-knit, close fellowship of dedicated, intellectual Christians, whose committed obedience was strengthened by their somewhat élitist forms of worship and discipline.

The role of the Group socially and politically also caused heart-searching. Extract from minutes, October 22, 1959: "**Blankets and Lady Bountiful.** Long unresolved discussion about means of providing blankets (or any other necessities) for people who need them. There was general agreement that all possible use should be made of the National

Assistance Board, but no common mind as to what should be done when that service proved inadequate to an immediate occasion."

The recurring question was whether the Group should invest its time in ambulance work, or concentrate on longer-term objectives. Should they work for the revolution or major on meeting the immediate day-to-day needs as they arose? The Group attempted to do both. Political change was pursued through the Labour Party and individual crises were responded to immediately. Windows were repaired. Blankets were arranged. Youths were represented in court. Drunks were dried out. Cases were won at the Rent Tribunal. Group members took on the legal guardianship of several delinquent boys. The Group set up regular meetings of Gorbals social workers, doctors, health visitors and probation officers.

Geoff loved the Group. For him it was his family, his strength. Here he could relax and find refreshment. He loved the worship and the discussion. He was notorious for interjecting at the end of every discussion the comment, "Just one wee point..." The Group would laugh, knowing they were about to hear not just one wee point, but probably four or five others in addition.

The Group was the arena in which Geoff was working out his new life style of Christian discipleship. He found challenge, criticism and support. He felt at home there. He could be himself.

Being himself usually meant having fun, laughing, enjoying jokes, praying and discussing serious issues. It could also mean being moody. The black days, which contrasted strongly with the much, much more frequent enjoyable days, were still there. The pressures, the occasional oppressiveness of Gorbals life (the communal sense of inadequacy could sometimes become almost tangible), the exhaustion, the disappointments, the let-downs and the loneliness now and again caught up with him and seemed to take hold of an interior lurking melancholy. He had no wife to shout at or to share things with. The Group got it instead.

It has also to be said that Geoff was like many a passionate democrat—he was an autocrat at heart who got very impatient when his own ideas weren't immediately accepted. The one who could spend hours patiently listening to a delinquent youth could get upset when not all of his peers immediately saw the point of what he was saying. Geoff would occasionally come up with hare-brained schemes for the Group, like opening up a commercial café or setting up a taxi business, only to be shouted down in no uncertain terms. Abbotsford Lane on Thursday nights was not for the faint-hearted.

As time flew by in the hectic round of Gorbals life, 1960 posed its own questions. The Group had been set up for three years—did they want to continue? If they did, what was to be the shape or form?

It became a matter of some urgency in May 1960 when Geoff was sounded out by the vacancy committee of St Francis-in-the-East about succeeding John Sim as minister. He asked the Group members their views about the future. They were unanimous. We stay on here, no matter what the Presbytery decide at the time of review. Geoff turned down the approach from Bridgeton.

In discussions on the Group's report to the Home Mission Committee in November 1960, John Lang, minister of Laurieston Renwick Church (ex-Malta) moved that though the Gorbals Group was a failure as an experiment in evangelism, it should be allowed to continue. Despite large question marks, he recognised the immense amount of good the Group was doing and felt it should go on.

The committee report, recommending that the experiment should continue for a further three years, was approved by the Presbytery. The report made the following comments—

"The Committee is of the opinion that this experiment raises questions of an exceedingly interesting nature which cannot be answered except after a much longer time than three years. The team do seem to be making a one-sided presentation of Christianity, but it may well be that this in itself is a challenge to the Church to ask whether its whole witness may not be too strongly biassed on the other side. The lack of statistical results from the experiment need not be a criticism—the area would appear to require that a climate of thought should first be created from which statistical results might later be obtained. Nor can it be objected that this is work for laymen, since few, if any, members of the Church in full Communion reside in the limited area of the experiment.

The Committee is also of the opinion, however, that the team must learn from the experience of the Church as a whole and that this would provide a valuable corrective to them in certain aspects:—

(a) While the team sincerely profess loyalty to the Church of Scotland, their work does not seem to be interpreted to the traditional pattern of the work of the Church of Scotland.

(b) They do not seem to be witnessing clearly to a definite need for corporate worship.

(c) Their one act of corporate worship, the Holy Communion, gives no opportunities for entering into a fellowship of worship to children or to those who do not feel prepared to join in Communion.

(d) The team's emphasis on the importance of economic sharing leads to the view that only those prepared to join in the economic sharing can become full members of the community. Such a stringent condition was already departed from by the Church in New Testament times.

(e) While the emphasis on witnessing by sharing in life and not merely by preaching is to be welcomed, the witness of the word—and especially by definite preaching as opposed to witness in conversation—seems to have been undervalued."

So, an extension was granted, cautiously. But stormy days lay immediately ahead.

The group had agreed to invite people who were in sympathy with their purpose to come on Thursday evenings. Several local people started coming, as well as Lilias Graham, and Richard Holloway, a young Episcopal priest from Pollokshields. Ray Soper had left to get married and a young teacher and his wife, Robin and Mary Cameron, had joined the Group.

The changes posed the inevitable questions. What was to be the pattern of Thursday evenings? What about Holy Communion? Was the present financial pattern appropriate? Should they split up into smaller groupings?

John and Beryl Jardine, in consultation with Lilias Graham, came up with the suggestion that there should be two groups: a monthly plenary; and common Sunday worship at 10.30 am. Each group should decide on its own format. Walter, by this time a full-time trade union official, felt deeply that such moves would weaken the Group and that the disciplines would go.

John felt equally strongly that not to make changes would leave the newcomers on the perimeter.

The discussions were inconclusive. John and Beryl indicated their intention to leave at the end of 1961. Kirstie Wedderburn announced that she was leaving to get married. A chapter in the life of the Gorbals Group was at an end.

Chapter VII
Seventy Four Cleland Street

When Jesus Christ calls a man, he bids him come and die.—
Dietrich Bonhoeffer

I am for everything that helps anyone through the night, whether it is prayer, a sleeping pill, or a bottle of whisky.—
Frank Sinatra

Then Peter came to him, and said, Lord, how oft shall my brother sin against me and I forgive him? Till seven times? Jesus saith unto him, I say not unto thee, Until seven times: but, Until seventy times seven.—
Matthew 18. 21,22

A new phase was under way for Geoff as well. In January 1960 he had moved out to a house on his own, rented by the Group. Seventy-four Cleland Street was a few streets north of Abbotsford Place, at the junction of Cleland Street and Gorbals Street.

The tenement was not one of Gorbals' more distinguished properties. Built originally as working class accommodation, it had deteriorated over the years. ("Started off bad and fell away," as the Gorbals wags would say.) Geoff's flat was two up, built over shops. To get to it one had to climb worn-down stairs, up a dark close which could, at any one time, reek of a mixture of stale urine, dampness, beer and fish suppers. The battered main door opened into a two room and kitchen flat. There was a biggish living room with a kitchen recess, a smaller bedroom and an inside toilet. There was no bathroom: a tin bath hung in the lavatory. Seventy-four Cleland Street was unlikely ever to be featured in *Homes and Gardens*. Geoff loved it. There was never a house he cared about more than that battered building in Cleland Street, Gorbals.

In many ways Geoff Shaw was a secular Gorbals monk. Poverty, chastity, obedience. They were all there. And 74 Cleland Street was his own cell. The only difference was that instead of being a place of quiet and contemplation, it was one of the busiest addresses in the West of Scotland.

Geoff was fashioning for himself an ascetic freedom. He had turned his back on wealth, or a career in the Church. He had sacrificed personal security and comfort. He had given up the leisured life, with lots of time to read books and listen to good music. He had little privacy.

He had also renounced marriage for the time being. He told several friends that he would never marry while he was in Gorbals and he stuck to that vow. He knew that the kind of life he was leading and his philosophy of total availability to those in need would not have been possible had he married.

His relationship with women deserves some comment. A man of immense natural charm, he was very attractive to women, though there were those who found him a bit untouchable. Many attractive women came and went, hoping to catch his eye, but to no avail. He did have some social dates and there was one girl he seriously considered marrying, but he felt it would be unfair to expect someone to share his kind of life. He was therefore somewhat vulnerable. He would sometimes try to cope with the situation by being a bit remote. One or two women in Gorbals said they were a bit frightened of him at first until they got to know him. But he had good relationships with the wives of his friends in the Group because he knew he was safe with them!

One rather amusing Valentine he received, titled "To a Reluctant Valentino," put things rather well—

O, thy luve's like a red, red, rag
Tae every unwed Scot.
O thy luve's like the tentless airt
—Embracing a' the lot.

As fair art thou, wir bonnie Geoff
Yet far beyond wir ken
But do we luve thee still, my dear
Thou cannyiest o' men.

Till a' our tears gang dry, my dear
And your heart melts in our sun!
Yet we will luve thee still, my dear
Tho' though choose from us but one.

92

And fare thee weel frae one, my luve
My ee'n are fu' o' tear
For choose thy maun e'er Ne'er day comes
Afore the passing year.

For if thee dinna choose, my chiel
Some lass wi' bear thee gree
For Leap Year is aboot us
And you'll na lang gang free.

Then let us pray that come it may
(As come it will for a' that)
Better tae marry than tae burn
As Burns well kenn't for a' that!

Geoff's concepts of ministry and discipleship pointed him
in the direction of sharing the privations and life style of
those he was working with. As East Harlem Protestant Parish
staff had gradually done, he rejected the concept of
'identification' in favour of that of 'participation.'

He knew himself that he was not the same as other people
in Gorbals. He had had a good education. He had a different
accent. He had a job. He could get out when he wanted. He
had other options open to him. But this did not mean that he
could not honestly participate in the life of the comunity. He
could expose himself to the same health hazards, the same
housing frustrations, the same vandalism, the same violence.
He never believed in the kind of phoney identification which
tries to pretend that everyone is the same. He did not
develop a pseudo Glasgow accent, or pretend to like beer or
bingo. He was just himself, sharing the life of those round
about him, and making himself available in a self-effacing
kind of way. He genuinely admired the people of Gorbals,
and was amazed at how many struggled successfully with the
sort of difficulties he had never had to cope with.

When he moved into Cleland Street, people who didn't
know him wondered what his racket was.

"What's his game?" was one of the regular questions. Who
was this rather shabby minister, who never wore a dog collar?

93

Why did he not live in a manse? Why did he not have a church? Where did he preach? Was he a secret agent? Or a police informer? Or an experimenting social worker? Maybe he had been thrown out of the ministry, and was involved in crime. Or was he bent?

In a fairly short time he was accepted for who he was and the stairs in the close became even more worn as a constant procession of people beat a steady, or unsteady, path to his door. It was a door they knew would always be open for them. Getting into the house, mind you, could be quite a feat. Papers would be piled on the living room table and on the floor. The room could be full of people and Geoff might be conducting different conversations with different people at the same time. A drunken youth might be sobering up in the corner, two delinquent boys in another, while a CND committee member discussed plans with Geoff. Snotty-nosed children would be lying on the floor reading comics.

Then the phone, the interminable phone, would go. Geoff would say "South-oh-one-two-nine" and settle down again for yet another hard luck story. The door bell again. Another visitor would be waved in and pointed to the coffee jar and the old tin with the chocolate-covered digestive biscuits. Tea was the favourite drink in Gorbals, but Geoff's coffee became famous. James Donachy, one of Geoff's club boys, dubbed Geoff "the man who introduced coffee to the Gorbals."

All this would be happening during the day, when many people in Gorbals had time on their hands. Geoff would often ignore what was happening in the room and sit typing or working on his papers. Then, a quick tin of soup in the evening and out to the club. Three hours of noise, patient listening, disputes, laughter. More conversation at the street corners. Back to Cleland Street with some of the club boys for more coffee and discussion, or songs with the guitar.

After ten when the pubs closed, staggering feet coming up the stair. More problems. More coffee. Someone being sick on the living room floor. The phone ringing. South 0129. Yes, I'll come over to the station right away. How much is the bail? And so on. Night after weary night. Bed, 3.00 a.m. after typing letters.

There was nothing romantic about the life-style of total availability. It was costly and exhausting. Sitting listening to a drunk teenager till 2.00 a.m. endlessly going over the same stories, could be stupefyingly boring.

The pastoral counselling continued out into the street. When one Gorbals man thinks of Geoff Shaw, he sees him standing outside 74, Cleland Street in the early hours of the morning, dressed in pyjama jacket and a pair of trousers, dealing with a hopelessly inebriated teenager. (Tell me, Mr Shaw, how many of your young people have become church members?)

For Geoff, the commitment was total. He would often say that the one thing you should never do to another human being was to turn him away. People who were written off by everyone else would turn up at 74, Cleland Street. At one point Geoff was near to physical and mental breakdown because of one alcoholic who made enormous demands on his time.

The house became a favourite place for young people to sleep off their drunkenness at the weekends. There could be as many as seven or eight people sleeping on the living room floor at the same time. One club boy stayed at number 74 every weekend for one year. He says Geoff was rarely in bed before 6.00 a.m. and sometimes never got to bed at all. If he wasn't sobering people up or sorting out problems, he was over at the police station. Lads from approved schools whose parents refused to have them back would stay at number 74 for weeks and sometimes months. One boy's first recollection of Geoff was of turning round to see who was dipping his head in the sink to get him sobered up. He was all of 11 years old at the time. He stayed, off and on, for six years.

There were boys who were allowed out of borstal on condition they could stay at Cleland Street. Some lads stayed for days, until they got alternative accommodation, others for longer. One of the boys from a very troubled family background was more or less adopted by Geoff. He lived at Cleland Street for years and Geoff worried over him as he would have his own son. Geoff often talked of him as his son and one of his most treasured moments was the first

95

time the boy referred to No. 74 as "home." When the lad married, one of his sons was called after Geoff and the children called him "Grandpa."

Geoff would never allow women to stay overnight for fear of what the neighbours might think. In this respect he was rather naive about boys. One policeman, who didn't like his helping local toughs, said to him that he would get him for being a "queer", because he had so many boys staying in his house. Geoff was angry, but typically he listened patiently. The suggestion was absurd and entirely without foundation but he was obviously vulnerable to this sort of accusation.

Some policemen, although not all, felt Geoff was undermining what they were doing. Many a youth, hauled into Gorbals police station for loitering, or worse at 2.00 a.m., would be told, "I suppose that swine Shaw will be over to bail you out." They were generally right. "That swine Shaw," if he knew, would be over.

Geoff in his turn was shocked by some of the police attitudes and methods. From his Barnton background, he had regarded the police as, in a way, servants of the public. What he saw in Gorbals opened his eyes. The rules didn't always apply if you were poor, or unemployed, or had a criminal record. It was not unknown for youths to be beaten up in police custody, or to be picked up just because they were near the scene of a crime. Geoff complained about police brutality and often spoke for the boys in court. Who else would speak for them?

A few policemen harassed him and suspected him of being a "fence," a receiver of stolen property. They thought he was a kind of Glasgow Fagin, sending boys out to steal! It was more than once that he was stopped at 2.00 a.m. and asked to open up his parcel—containing shirts, or football strips, nicely ironed by Elizabeth Fyfe!

On one occasion, two policemen thought they had got him. There had been a break-in at a cash and carry and sweets had been stolen. The police arrived at Cleland Street. He welcomed them in. On the floor were boxes of sweets. At last! Not really. Geoff had bought them that day for the summer camps and had the receipts to prove it.

How ironic that "that swine Shaw" should later become

Master of Arts.

Group outside East Harlem church.

Scout camp, 1957.

Nicholson Street, Gorbals. On the right, behind tenements, is the 'wee' club.

head of the police authority in Strathclyde!

It would be fair to point out that some of the Gorbals police admired him enormously and one or two came to speak at the club discussion group. He was always concerned to defend the police before the boys, to defend the boys before the police and to plead for understanding.

Seventy-four Cleland Street was broken into several times and Geoff usually knew who had "screwed" the house. Sometimes it was boys staying with him. He refused to bring charges against them and normally dealt with the matter himself. He would confront the person and hope that the relationship which had developed would be enough to bring the thieving to a stop. Sometimes it didn't, but more often than not it did—to the amazement of more cynical observers. Hardened criminals were often astonished to find themselves washing and drying dishes in Geoff's flat!

He would never let a boy go, would never turn his back on him. He used to say, 'they have to know there is someone who'll never reject them.' When boys he knew got into trouble, he would visit them in prison and keep in close touch with their families, some of whom had given them up.

Jimmy Boyle once of Gorbals, now serving a life sentence in the Special Unit at Barlinnie Prison, remembers how Geoff kept in touch with him and other prisoners in Peterhead.

"Never have I heard of people let down by Geoff Shaw," he said. "No matter what time of the night you went to Cleland Street, you were welcome. People who'd been kicked out of the house would get a bed there. Trouble usually happened at night, but he never made you feel you were wrong to go there. You were always welcome. Even though you had woke him up.

"When Geoff moved into Gorbals, he was looked on as a bit of a nutcase. He had a lot of barriers to break down. Gorbals didn't like outsiders, not even working class outsiders. People used to run away from the probation officer. And here was Geoff Shaw—a middle class Protestant minister. Any connections we had with people of his class were people in authority—police, the means test people who ruled our lives. He came from the outside. He was a symbol of all these people should have been. He treated you as equal.

"Geoff had a magic about him. He always made you feel, you're important to me. He always left you feeling good. He challenged everything you thought you knew about churchmen. We were all conditioned to accepting the Protestant/Catholic thing, but he challenged all that. He made you think.

"Hardened prisoners aren't good at expressing emotion. They would say, 'Geoff Shaw, he's no bad cunt.' That spoke volumes. He represented tenderness and love and all the things we were repressing. All the prisoners I knew really respected him."

Drunken, desperate youths and men and women cried their eyes out in Geoff's flat. They always got help. No one will ever know the extent of the generosity of the man who only had one shiny suit and didn't have a cheque book.

Never let go, that was his motto. Setting down on paper a number of options for a youth who was living at his house, he scribbled: 'Have proceeded on the basis of refusal to reject, no matter how foul.' Foul could be really foul. Vomit over the chairs. Theft. Madness.

Case histories are not being used in this book. But there could be many. Instead there is this sad story.

"Andy" was a Gorbals boy who had been in a lot of trouble. Geoff, who had known him in the boys' clubs and in camps and had worked with his family, saw a lot of possibilities in him: he could write well and had a lot of good ideas. Geoff encouraged him to try drama college, but he failed to get in.

He started taking drugs and mixing them with drink. Sometimes he would come to 74 Cleland Street literally frothing at the mouth. He felt from time to time that Geoff was rejecting him and this worried Geoff.

After a bout of drink and drugs, Andy's body was found in the Clyde. It wasn't absolutely clear whether he had jumped in or fallen in. Geoff was absolutely distraught with a mixture of grief and guilt—he felt he had let the boy down.

That Sunday, Geoff had to conduct the baptism of the son of dear friends of his in Laurieston Renwick church. During the words of the first hymn, "All that hath life and breath, come now with praises before Him," he couldn't get Andy out of his mind. The whole service he was near to tears, and when it came to the sermon, he broke down completely in the pulpit.

On the morning of the funeral, a boy staying in the house saw Geoff standing in the bedroom, tears rolling down his cheeks. It was raining outside, very still, with no wind and it seemed to Geoff as if the whole Gorbals was weeping. He was deeply upset about the apparent waste of young life. Like Gordon Philip of Edinburgh Academy Andy had been taken young, but he had not been spared the uglinesses of life.

In order to avoid breaking down at the funeral parlour, Geoff did something he had never done before. He wrote down the service, word for word. This was his prayer—

> In proud thanksgiving we remember the times of Andy's life.
> The times of his childhood, and the times of his youth.
> The times of his weakness and the times of his strength.
> The times of his failure in temptation, and the times of his triumph over temptation.
> The times of his sorrow, and the times of his gladness.
> The times of his loneliness and the times of his happy companionship.
> The times of his despair, and the times of his high, high hopes.
> And because for him all torment is over,   all danger is past and all sorrow is ended, with gladness we commit him to Your care, that he may rest in peace.

Chapter VIII
Never Let Go

Give me your poor
your maladjusted
your sick and your beat
your sad
and your busted
give me your has-beens
give me your twisted
your loners
your losers
give me your black-listed.

Dory Previn

O stand, stand at the window
As the tears scald and start;
You shall love your crooked neighbour
With your crooked heart.

W. H. Auden

Not all the people who climbed the stairs at 74, Cleland Street were in desperate need of help. Certainly not people like Mario Borrelli, Danilo Dolci, Adam Faith, Albert Finney or Tom Fleming.

Mario Borrelli was born in the dockland of Naples in 1922. After studying for Roman Catholic priesthood he was ordained in 1946. He was troubled by problems of the *scugnizzi*— the urchins on the streets of Naples who were never out of bother. He decided to set aside his priestly regalia and dress as a *scugnizzo* himself. He was accepted by the urchins and only narrowly avoided being jailed by the police. Eventually he revealed his true identity and set up his famous House of Urchins, where the *scugnizzi* could get a bed, food and help. The story was told to the world in the book *Children of the Sun* by the Australian novelist Morris West.

Father Borrelli first came to Scotland in 1961, when he was interviewed on television by Walter Fyfe. This led to an invitation to the Gorbals, which the priest readily accepted.

As a communicator with the Gorbals boys, he was brilliant. The locals' questions were first of all translated into "English," then put slowly to Borrelli. His replies immediately showed that he was on the same wavelength as the Gorbals kids, who responded to his warmth and honesty.

What astonished the youngsters was that here was a Roman Catholic priest being introduced by a Protestant minister! It didn't make sense; it flew in the face of all they had been taught. It was a breakthrough to a new kind of thinking.

Some of the local priests warned Fr. Borrelli not to go near the Gorbals Group or their clubs. He came back one day in despair, saying 'I used to think there was nobody more conservative than an Italian rural priest. Now I know there is —a Glasgow Irish one!'

He shared the bread and wine on his visits to the Gorbals Group. He was first asked if he would be allowed to. "As a priest, no,"he said,"as Mario Borrelli, yes.'

Fr. Borrelli felt at home at 74, Cleland Street and enjoyed the discussions after the club—and the coffee. One person remembers finding in the room Mario Borrelli, Archie Ianello and Joe Capello—not names normally associated with the Scottish Reformed tradition. (Many of the youngsters attending the Gorbals clubs were Roman Catholics. The activities were run on an ecumenical basis and no bigoted sentiments were allowed. This worried some of the local priests more than others. Mrs Roseanne Irvine remembers a priest taking her to task for allowing her son, Dennis, to attend the Gorbals Group club. She told him, 'What he does out of school is my responsibility.' Dennis continued to attend. The truth is that the Gorbals Group were closer to the ground than either the Roman Catholic Church or the Church of Scotland, and they had established their credentials with the working and non-working, classes in the area in which they operated.)

Geoff and Fr. Borrelli had a great rapport. Geoff took 14 Gorbals boys to Naples to meet the priest on his home ground. They drove from Glasgow to Dover in the old van— Geoff having naps at the side of the road—and took the train from Calais, across to France and Switzerland.

Willie Hannah, one of the boys on the trip, remembers it well. "It was great. We had never been abroad before. We saw Capri and Pompeii and camped outside Naples. It was like Gorbals—there were lots of kids around. Geoff was a bit like Father Borrelli."

Moments of unconditional delight? Not for one boy though. He got himself lost, and Geoff wouldn't speak to him for a day. The boy told him, "I wish you'd just hit me, or bawled me out." Geoff used to tell that story ruefully himself.

(Geoff's idea of a holiday was to take the boys camping or on trips abroad. He took one group to Italy to see Rangers play in Florence. Every second year he took a group of boys down to watch Scotland play England. One return journey he was driving over Shap, when he noticed a wheel rolling past him. It was a wheel off his own van!)

Another visitor to Cleland Street was Danilo Dolci, the Italian social reformer who opposed the Mafia in Sicily. After giving a lecture at the University, he came out with Geoff to the house. Stepping in the door, he looked around the paper strewn room and said immediately, "Now I am at home."

No.74 could be a place of serious discussion. The senior boys from the club took part and their points of view were treated like everyone else's. Politics and peace were favourite topics. An Indian psychiatrist fascinated the boys by uncannily explaining to them how they ticked. Geoff was a regular visitor to the Citizens' Theatre which was just around the corner and Albert Finney and Tom Fleming came round to drink the coffee and take part in the chat. Pop singer Adam Faith came too, but was unfortunate enough to have the tyres of his Rolls Royce slashed.

The club boys loved ghost stories and Geoff told them well. The lights would be put out and Geoff would tell about a train journey he had gone on. He whispered as he told how the lights in the carriage began to go dim....(He was a master of timing; the railway ran past his house and he knew there was a train due)...and the faces in the carriage suddenly turned to skeletons! Loud shrieks from the tough guys as the 10.43 to Glasgow Central thundered past and 74, Cleland Street vibrated!

Geoff got great enjoyment from the Glasow patter and the ready wit. Over coffee the fags would be passed round—

that was how Geoff started smoking—and the stories would be told long into the night. One descriptive phrase by a boy called Tam Moffat, stood out in his mind with luminous clarity—"Gorbals is a dump, but it's a good dump."Geoff was to quote it repeatedly.

He appeared to be enjoying a delayed, vicarious adolescence in Gorbals. Although he always appreciated the more refined Edinburgh, he came to love Glasgow deeply. He enjoyed the noise, the humour, the warmth, the immediacy, the openness and the rough-and-ready frankness of Glasgow. He liked the way the club youngsters said what they felt and he admired the Gorbals women for their cheeriness in the face of continuing adversity.

It was almost as if that was the kind of person Geoff would have liked to have been himself. Not that he lacked warmth. Far from it. But at the end of the day he was a reserved, inward man, a private man, a thinking man, his own man. People felt close to him and he inspired great affection and yet....there was sometimes a distance, a remoteness, a holding back, a mysterious centre not accessible to others. "Never let go" was true of Geoff's philosophy in regard to others; it was also true of himself in regard to his own emotional life.

Generally speaking, he was in control. Sometimes, though,the control went and the dam burst. He was very sentimental, especially where friends were concerned and he hated saying goodbye. Parting would reduce him to tears.

He was very, very fond of children, too and was marvellous with them. They loved him and responded to his uninhibited playfulness. He mystified one visiting child by beckoning his toy car with a finger and it came back to him—the floor at Cleland Street sloped! The boy tried to beckon his ball back from the sea and found that it didn't work. A woman friend was very moved when she saw the tenderness with which Geoff lifted his "grandchildren" from their sleep one night when he had to move them to another house.

Deep down he was a shy man, who didn't like to bare his soul in public and didn't easily expose his true feelings to others. Could it be that the boy of 13, shocked by his father's death and the boy of 15, grief-stricken at the loss of his best friend, had endured such inner hurt at a critical stage in his life, that an inner decision, conscious or unconscious, had been made to stay in control of the uncontrollable? Was there an interior disposition not to trust the world overmuch in personal matters? Was that at least part of the reason for his postponing marriage? Could that be the ultimate explanation for the black days? Was there inside this refined, subtle, controlled, "Edinburgh" man a "Glasgow" boy struggling to get out?

One thing is true: in most of his relationships in Gorbals, Geoff was the strong one, the one on whom others were dependent. He was like a rock. He was the one who was giving, even though he saw himself as receiving. The others were the ones who exposed their inadequacies. The boy who was pastor to the Philips family at the age of 15, who ran the scouts, who helped the handicapped kids up the hills, had become a kind of "father-mother" to some fairly desperate youngsters in Gorbals. Whatever else collapsed round them, they could depend on Geoff Shaw.

If he had to leave Glasgow, he would always try to get back to Gorbals at night. He knew that was when he was most likely to be needed if there was a crisis. He took very little time off. Holidays were nearly always spent in camps with Gorbals youngsters.

Some of Geoff's Edinburgh friends felt he was shutting himself off, and they regretted it. They always had to take the initiative to see him, although he would welcome them to Cleland Street. They would come through to visit him, but in the confusion of kids, door bells and the telephone, it was often difficult to carry on a conversation.

One former Cramond scout recalls going through to see Geoff at Cleland Street. The experience for him was a bit like James Cameron's in going to see Albert Schweitzer. He found Geoff washing football strips in the sink and somewhat preoccupied with current crises. In the conversation, it was almost as if Geoff had frozen this man in the previous relationship of scoutmaster to scout. He sensed a danger that Geoff, in his commitment and his exhaustion, was isolating himself in a little Gorbals world.

Reflecting on his knowledge of Geoff, the visitor described

him as the most Christocentric and egocentric person he had ever met. By egocentric he did not mean selfish: in fact it was the reverse of that—a self abnegation. In using the phrase of Geoff, he was trying to put his finger on that sense of an interior agenda which had its roots, perhaps, in a guilty sense of privilege and a need to compensate. Yet for him, Geoff was totally Christ-centred as well. The two things are by no means incompatible.

There is certainly something slightly masochistic, even a shade messianic, about Geoff's way of life—the lack of holidays, the refusal of time off, the insistence on being back in Gorbals at nights. More time for relaxation would have been good for him and made him more able to cope with the strains. Or perhaps he just wasn't made that way. He certainly looked well on work

If he hadn't have been back at Gorbals one night, the crisis would have happened and people would have survived, as they usually do. But then, yes, that might have been the one night a body was fished out of the Clyde.

Perhaps Geoff needed to be needed. Perhaps he was partly driven by a middle class Protestant guilt complex. But to analyse Geoff Shaw's ministry in Gorbals so one-sidedly would be to trivialise it. If that kind of commitment could be reduced to such simplistic psychological terms, then many Gorbals people would surely want to shout "Hallelujah" for middle class guilt complexes.

Geoff's standard of Christian discipleship frightened some people. Even though he insisted that his was not the only way and that each person must find out what is right for himself or herself, there were those who found his committed life style a stumbling block. His life was a living challenge and some who regarded it as an examination question addressed to themselves were depressed by their own failure. They had to think their way past the secular Gorbals monk in order to be free to find an authentically Christian path for themselves.

It would be absurd to characterise Geoff at 74 Cleland Street as some kind of neurotic. He had none of the intensity of the fanatic. Indeed there always seemed to be a balance about his life. The life he led was, for him, fulfilling. And he did relax now and again. He listened to classical music on his mono record player—sometimes in the midst of the hubbub. He occasionally got the chance to read books and was a great fan of Tolkien long before that was fashionable. He enjoyed the conversations he had with the boys; it wasn't a case of a tolerant man putting up with inferiors' ideas.

He greatly enjoyed the company of friends who dropped in—people like Neil and Kay Carmichael, Norman and Janey Buchan and Giles Havergal, artistic director of the Citizens' Theatre. As usual the discussion would go on long into the night, and Geoff would accompany the visitors downstairs and continue the conversation on the pavement under the lamplight. He also went to the theatre whenever he could, sometimes coming in near the end and standing at the back of the stalls.

Giles Havergal remembers long discussions in Cleland Street. "He genuinely respected the boys as human beings and therefore he got a lot out of them. Because they knew they were respected they would say some very deep things. It required great maturity and patience on Geoff's part."

Despite the fact that he had the Group as his family and his home was always crowded with people, there was a loneliness about his life. When he left the Group meetings the others were conscious that he was going back alone to his own cell. To have people depending on him all the time was draining. Yet in his freely-chosen celibacy and in his genuine detachment from money and possessions Geoff Shaw was free to give himself. He was, in Bonhoeffer's phrase, a 'man for others'.

Behind that battered door in Gorbals there went on a brave and continually caring life amid tears, laughter, vomit, cursings, singing, despair, disappointments, letdowns and oceans of healing coffee.

Seventy-four Cleland Street was a bit like Gorbals itself. It was a dump, but it was a good dump.

Chapter IX
I am Dead

How beautiful upon the mountains are the feet of him that bringeth good tidings, that publisheth peace.— **Isaiah 52.7**

The coward prays: 'Send peace in our time, O Lord.' The brave man prays: 'O Lord, if there must be trouble, let it be in my time and let my children see peace.'— **Jewish saying**

The Campaign for Nuclear Disarmament was the last great political mass movement in Great Britain. At its peak it could mobilise thousands of people for marches and demonstrations throughout the country.

CND started early in 1958, calling for Britain to renounce her nuclear weapons unilaterally as an example to other countries. It became a mass movement very quickly and converted the Labour Party conference to a unilateral policy at Scarborough in 1960 before being rent by a major hierarchical split over tactics. The movement declined in the early sixties under the twin influences of the nuclear test ban treaties and the growth of the international policy of *détente*. The Iona Community, inspired by Dr George MacLeod's pacifism, had long been concerned about peace. The Gorbals Group shared that concern. In 1959 the Group organised a series of meetings and exhibitions, some of which were well attended. In February 1959 Geoff joined the committee of Glasgow CND and within two years he was secretary. Two years later he was chairman.

The Gorbals Group minutes for June 1959 record that during 'Anti-Nuclear Week' in Gorbals 350 people had seen the exhibition with its large map showing the extent of radiation should the American nuclear base in Holy Loch be attacked, a petition had been signed by 112 people, the film 'Children of Hiroshima' had been seen by 50-60 people and 18 men had come to the men's discussion on nuclear warfare.

As secretary of Glasgow CND Geoff helped to organise several demonstrations. He was regarded as a dependable secretary who would get things done without fuss. The letters were often typed at 3.00 am, but they usually got

109

there in time.

Geoff's style was well suited to CND. The movement was a coalition of all kinds of groups and interests whose one point of common concern was the nuclear issue. Geoff, always and essentially a reconciler, would listen carefully to the other person's point of view. He helped to consolidate the movement in Glasgow and the West of Scotland, and despite his non-pushing style he came to be recognised as one of the CND leaders in Scotland. The combination of outstanding ability, quiet but authoritative moral force, reliability and obvious integrity won him wide respect.

CND was a 'nice' movement, full of well-meaning, high-minded people. Committee meetings tended to turn into rambling, friendly and disorganised discussions. It always seemed amazing that any business got done at all.

Ron Clydesdale, who succeeded Geoff as secretary, remembers 'working lunches' at 74, Cleland Street.

"Blokes with problems would come wandering in and kids would read heaps of comics on the floor. Geoff would make lumpy soup, then would have to go out for bread. The last five minutes were the working bit."

If there was a demonstration and Geoff wasn't there it seemed very strange. Howard Horsborough, a former lecturer in philosophy at Glasgow University, now in Canada, said: "His presence made the rest of us feel more assured of the value of our work and the basic wisdom of our views on nuclear armaments. He had the kind of strength which gives perpetual reassurance and support to the weaker brethren— and that includes most of us from time to time.

"He was invariably helpful, friendly and moderate, never dismissive of the wilder suggestions of younger members of the campaign. He was usually able to turn their contributions to some kind of positive account. He was one of the most purely good-willed men I am ever likely to meet."

Geoff was a like a rock, an anchor. If he was there, things were all right. He would try to be reasonable with police at demonstrations—'Couldn't we just move over there, please?' Reply: 'I'll give you ten seconds to shut up or it's a night in the cells.' Geoff also had his name taken for refusing to walk in the gutter with his placard.

At one CND rally a bright-eyed girl bounced up to Geoff, who was wearing his clerical collar. "Are you Mr Wright?" she asked.

"For you, my dear, I could be," he replied.

At its height the anti-nuclear campaign was torn apart by a dispute over tactics. It began with a leadership quarrel between Lord Bertrand Russell and Canon John Collins resulting in the formation of the Committee of 100 in 1961. The new group felt democratic methods of change were too slow and that direct action was needed. Sit-downs were the order of the day. A submarine in the Holy Loch was boarded. The whereabouts of Government fall-out shelters were revealed. Covered by the omni-present television and newspaper cameras, the peace guerillas seemed to be winning the tactical battle.

The Gorbals Group was undecided about the new approach. It was left to the conscience of each individual. The Group decided they would be prepared to pay fines of those prosecuted. Walter Fyfe was fined for his part in a sit-down at Dunoon.

The dilemma was an acute one for Geoff. As one who had originally studied law he had a great respect for the law. He did not approve of the more extreme tactics of the Committee of 100, and much preferred democratic action. And yet, did not the New Testament say that Christians should obey the laws of God rather than the laws of men, and was not the nuclear bomb an offence in God's sight?

It was not an issue that Geoff took lightly. It came to a head in 1962, when he was asked to speak at a Committee of 100 meeting in George Square. It was not permitted to hold political meetings there and the tactic was to get people to talk in small groups. Various people spoke and Geoff was one of those who mounted the rostrum. Plain clothes policemen were present (dressed as workers, wearing Transport and General Workers Union badges), and Geoff had his name taken.

Around this time Geoff spoke at various different meetings in Glasgow—for example, at a meeting organised by the Christadelphians in the Dixon Hall. He was not a

111

histrionic orator: his speeches were calm, reasoned authoritative, cogently argued.

For CND rallies Geoff donned his clerical collar. At one such meeting he was greeted by a friend, Charlie Shields:

' Geoff, I've never seen you before in your workin' claes!'

Meetings, film shows, demonstrations, folk concerts: there was a continual round of activity. The City Hall was taken over for a folk concert. There were movies and poetry readings. One hundred and fifty thousand leaflets were printed for a demonstration at Dunoon. Plans were made for a peace factory. The committee attempted to hire a plane to fly a CND banner over Glasgow. At Aldermaston housewives marched pushing prams and young people sang the new protest songs.

Geoff was not an out-and-out pacifist, but typically sought common ground between pacifist and non-pacifist. In a pamphlet outlining the Christian arguments for unilateral nuclear disarmament he wrote: "We re-affirm our faith in Jesus Christ, the Son of God, as King of Kings and Lord of Lords, and as judge of all the nations. We confess that within the present political situation we share in many of the confusions and uncertainties inherent in all the affairs of nations; for the consequences of political action can never fully be guaranteed nor foreseen. Nevertheless, within this confusion there are certain clear and definite principles and facts which we are compelled to accept and on which we personally must take our stand. On these too we must found the policy which we would advocate should be followed by our Government. This duty of political decision is laid upon us, as on all British people, in virtue of our citizenship within a democracy.

"The church must now say emphatically No," he went on. "For not only are nuclear weapons capable of indiscriminate destruction such as has never before been known, but they even threaten the whole life of future generations."

Replying to a common argument of the time, he continued: "We can conceive of nothing, not even the temporary victory of communism, as more offensive in

God's sight than the annihilation of countless millions of His people in the cause of 'peace'.....The real choice for the Christian in the present nuclear situation is not between death and life under communism—if this were all, a Christian might well choose death. Rather in the last resort, the real choice may be between life under communism and participation in mass murder and genocide."

After rehearsing the standard CND arguments about the ineffectiveness of the deterrent, the possibilities of accidental nuclear war, the waste of money in a hungry world and the need to take a new initiative to break the deadlock, Geoff concluded by calling upon Christians to oppose the Government's defence policy, to speak boldly of their firm belief that the earth and its fullness were God's, and to pray with renewed urgency for peace and the coming of God's kingdom.

Not surprisingly Geoff's theology of peace was rooted in his concern for individuals. He composed a poem about peace called 'I am dead,' and scribbled it down in his notebook. The issue was seen through the eyes of a seven year old child.

> I come and stand at every door,
> But none can hear my silent tread.
> I knock and yet remain unseen,
> For I am dead, for I am dead
>
> I'm only seven although I died
> In Hiroshima long ago.
> I'm seven now, as I was then.
> When children die they do not grow.
>
> My hair was scorched by swirling flame,
> My eyes grew dim, my eyes grew blind.
> Death came and turned my bones to dust
> And that was scattered by the wind.
>
> I need no fruit, I need no rice,
> I need no sweets, nor even bread.
> I ask for nothing for myself
> For I am dead, for I am dead.

113

Along with Rev Douglas Alexander, Geoff organised a group called Ministers' Unilateralist Group, known as MUG. Ministers were circularised and lobbied at the time of the Church of Scotland's General Assembly. George MacLeod normally had a pacifist motion before the Fathers and Brethren at that time. He was usually given an ovation, then the Assembly voted massively against him.

On each Friday before Remembrance Sunday, MUG ran an all-night vigil of readings and prayers in George Square. Geoff was usually on stewarding duty from midnight till 3.00 a.m.

For Geoff, peace, politics and theology were closely linked in an increasingly coherent philosophy. He refused to separate care for individuals from a wider concern for world issues. He saw no difference between spending hours listening patiently to a delinquent and working on a wide front for nuclear disarmament.

His political work in Gorbals consisted mainly in attending meetings, writing letters and canvassing with leaflets. In April, 1961, when Prince Philip was due to come to look at new housing in the Hutchesontown area of Gorbals, Geoff suggested that he also look at the "squalor" of Laurieston Gorbals. He wrote: "We do not wish in any way to detract from the rebuilding already being done, which no doubt is the best which can be done with the resources available. But the problem is that such rebuilding covers only a very small part of the need. Our own area, for example, is outside the particular development scheme which you, Sir, will visit. But the conditions prevailing in it are of appalling squalor; of no adequate playing space for children and young people; of an extensive and disgraceful system of sub-let housing; of decaying buildings badly maintained. Yet this area and many others like it can have no hope of renewal for perhaps another ten or fifteen years.

"We believe that you, Sir, by your interest and concern, could give a renewed sense of urgency to the whole problem of squalor and decay. We earnestly ask that if it is at all possible, your Royal Highness will take this opportunity not only of visiting the new, but also of looking into the conditions of what is old and urgently in need of renewal."

114

The Prince's programme remained unchanged. On a later occasion, Geoff wrote in a similar vein to the then Prime Minister, Harold Wilson, when he was due to visit Glasgow. Marcia Williams, his personal and political secretary, replied that the Prime Minister 'made it a rule not to receive deputations on visits of this kind.'

The Group insisted that despite the immediate and pressing problems of Gorbals, wider issues should not be forgotten. Petitions on Nyasaland were organised. An exhibition about South Africa was held. The housewives in the Group bravely agreed that they should 'ostentatiously refuse to buy South African goods.'

It was through activities such as these that Geoff Shaw's reputation as a Left wing socialist was first developed.

Chapter X
Miracle in the Gorbals?

Qhilk Kirk is catholike, that is, universal, because it conteinis the Elect of all ages of all realms, nations and tongues.—

The Scots Confession, 1560

"Clergymen!" he repeated with bitter irony. "Sure; they're grand when you're deid."—

No Mean City

Woe unto you when all men shall speak well of you.— **Luke 6.26**

The argument over the direction in which the Gorbals Group should move refused to go away: in fact it was intensified by the increasingly active participation of the Episcopalian workers associated with the Group.

Lilias Graham had been attending Group meetings on a fairly regular basis, though not participating in the Communion service. She was joined by Joyce Livingston, a school teacher who was also an Episcopalian. In October 1962 Richard Holloway, who had been doing more and more work in Gorbals, was given permission by his bishop to concentrate all his attentions there and in 1963 he was appointed priest in charge of St. Margaret's and St. Mungo's. He, too, was attracted to the Group and shared a lot of its concerns.

By May 1963, the composition of the Group was—Mrs. Josephine Forbes, a young housewife living at No. 3, Abbotsford Place, who was in charge of the playroom; Walter and Elizabeth Fyfe; Lilias Graham; Richard and Jean Holloway, who had a flat in the same close as Lilias Graham; Joyce Livingston, a teacher in Gorbals Primary School; Violet Shearer, a member of staff at Braehead Nursery School; and Geoff. Five of the Group were Church of Scotland members and the other four were members of the Scottish Episcopal Church.

The issue of intercommunion was at that time a very thorny question. Episcopalians were not permitted to take Communion at the hands of a Church of Scotland minister, whose ordination was not regarded as valid. So the Episcopalian members came to the Gorbals meetings at 8.30 p.m., after the Communion was over.

This was an intolerable situation. The controversial issue it raised directly was that of the nature of the Church.

There was a clear difference of attitude between Episcopal and the Church of Scotland members of the Group. The Episcopalians were deeply rooted in the life and worship of their local congregation; they were members of the Church first and the Gorbals Group second. The Church of Scotland members tended to see the Group as their church and they had a somewhat tenuous relationship with the local congregations. They did not attend the worship of the Gorbals Church of Scotland congregations on Sunday mornings and their relationship with the Presbytery was ambivalent, to say the least. There was a growing gulf between the Gorbals Group and the "official" Church of Scotland, partly because so many of the Presbytery were either too busy, or indifferent, or hostile and partly because the Gorbals Group didn't really take much trouble to interpret what they were doing for the benefit of the doubters.

Geoff's attitude to the Church had changed perceptibly. At the time of the initial plans to set up the Group, he had talked about complementing the parish system, insisting that they were not starting sect. Yet there was little real attempt on either side to establish relationships with the local parish churches and the Group was undoubtedly in danger of becoming a sect, unrelated to the 'whole catholic church'. Geoff was in the process of fundamentalising the Gorbals Group: it was his church.

He did not attend public worship on Sundays. His attitude was that his Sunday worship was on Thursday evenings: there was no reason why worship had to be on Sundays.

John Lang, who was a sympathetic critic of the Group, remembers tackling Geoff about Sunday worship. Geoff rounded on him: 'You're like the others—worried about appearances!' John said no, he was worried about Geoff. Not attending church could easily become a habit. Geoff said it was the first time anyone had put the issue to him like that—out of

118

concern for himself rather than out of a defensiveness about church ordinances. There was of course, one obvious practical difficulty: if he was up till six in the morning dealing with problems, it wasn't easy to be at Sunday worship that same morning. There is no evidence, however, that Geoff would have chosen to be in his pew week by week had things been different.

The man whose faith had been nurtured by regular attendance at worship at Cramond had moved to a more radical position. He had little time for 'official' religion and church hierarchies. Trumpeted pronouncements by church leaders fell on deaf ears as far as Geoff was concerned and indeed amused him. He detested pomp and ceremony. Deference to the clergy as special people was anathema to him. Yet he was no angry rebel either. He loved the Church and recognised his debt to it. He always saw himself as a minister of the Church, standing within an orthodox theological tradition.

Although he was often disilllusioned with the Church of Scotland and felt that it allied itself far too much with the powerful and wealthy in the land, Geoff was not obsessed about his relationship with the Kirk. He did not see himself as an ecclesiastical reformer, battling to change things. He just didn't think it was worth the energy. He simply wanted to get on with the job—in the name of the Church—and let the rest of the Kirk do what it wanted. The worship and the fellowship of the Gorbals Group—all within the Reformed tradition—sustained and strengthened him. He felt no obligation to seek anything else.

Walter Fyfe was impatient with the discussion on ecclesiastical issues. He felt that if the Episcopalian members wanted to 'save souls' they should do it at St Margaret's and St. Mungo's. From his stance of working in industry and his leieisure-time political involvement in Gorbals, he became irritated with suggestions that bringing in only a few church members was a shortcoming of the Group. He argued that they were in a largely Roman Catholic area, that many of his workmates were Sikhs or Muslims and that there was more to be done than worrying about church membership and the relationship of the Group to the churches. He recalled that

119

in East 100th Street in New York there were 4,000 people, of whom 100 were members of the East 100th Street church. The 4,000 'contacts' was the more important figure, since the church was only catering for minority needs. The same was true in Gorbals.

So the argument about the nature of the Church and the role of the Group went on. The Episcopalian members, with their much more catholic understanding of the Church, felt strongly that these issues were important and should not be evaded. They wanted to share the bread and wine with their colleagues, but their loyalty to their own tradition did not allow them to break the rules.

The matter was resolved by Richard Holloway. Both clever and impulsive, he invited the bishop to his home. He had prepared a memo for his superior saying it was a nonsense, and indeed wicked, to attend Gorbals Group meetings week by week and not share in Communion. The bishop was startled when he read the memo, but simply commented, 'I can't say I approve' and wisely began to talk about other things.

For those who understand their ecclesiastical diplomacy, it was an indication that he wouldn't try to stop the Episcopalian members sharing in Communion, but for God's sake don't keep bringing the matter to his attention! Of such nuances are ecclesiastical breakthroughs made.

So the Gorbals Group was now a properly ecumenical community and they became even more so when they were joined by Quakers who were working in the area. An interdenominational baptismal service was held, at which Richard Holloway and Walter Fyfe officiated. More neighbouring families became involved in the Group's worship and study programme. But the impact of the new members was loosening the corporate ties of the Group, as the Fyfes had foreseen.

The Church of Scotland and Episcopalian members operated different systems of economic discipline. The Episcopalians agreed with the principle of financial accountability, but wanted more personal liberty. They agreed to pay as nearly as could be worked out the same as the others, but have more control over the spending of what remained. The Church of Scotland members continued to operate the original pooling system

The change was acknowledged in the Group's report to the Home Board in May 1963, when a further three years extension was granted. It stated: "In the past two years we have deliberately become rather more flexible and in talking of membership of the Group we refer now to a group of people who are more or less consistently sharing in the life and concerns of the Group, though not all sharing in precisely the same way in the economic discipline."

Turning to the ecumenical developments, Geoff wrote: "The life of the Group is a continuing attempt to discover in our particular situation the ways in which a small group of people together may serve the needs of people in accordance with the command of Jesus Christ. We have discovered with great happiness the "given unity" which underlies the separateness of the churches and which means that at grassroots there is no barrier whatever; it is this perhaps that has most made us sensitive to the need of families in which there is a mixed marriage of Protestant and Roman Catholic, over which the ecclesiastics haggle, while the people remain unable to belong fully to either communion. We have found no neat solutions to the problems of the church's ministry to those who for one reason or another belong to no church."

The Group in the meantime had been strengthened by the presence of John and Molly Harvey. Molly, a daughter of the Rev Dr Hugh Douglas, Dundee, had first had contact with the Group when she was placed with Lilias Graham while studying social work at the London School of Economics. John, a former pupil of Fettes College, Edinburgh, had come into touch with the Group while a student at Trinity College, Glasgow. They were married during John's final year at college and moved into 3a, Abbotsford Place. A member of the Iona Community, John was appointed assistant minister of Govan Parish Church in 1963, and the kirk session had agreed to his continuing to live in Gorbals.

Molly, was appointed family case worker, thanks to a generous donation from America. A warm and outgoing person, she made contact with many local families. John was a reconciling influence in the Church of Scotland— Episcopal debate, sharing as he did much of the Episcopalian thinking about the nature of the Church.

When John Harvey's assistantship finished he stayed on in Gorbals. Part of his remit was to help create the centres of worship which Geoff had written about in his initial memorandum. It did not work.

John Harvey reflects: "Thinking about all that now, I suspect that both Geoff and I shared a view of the Church which, had we been Roman Catholics, might have led us into some sort of radical Order—perhaps Jesuits or the Little Brothers of Charles de Foucauld. Not being Roman Catholics, we had to deal with the reality of the church at the corner—what David Rice, one of our Americans who was sent to us from Bossey to do practical work, called 'The church-is-the-church-is-the-church' sort of thing. I 'dealt' with it by accepting Bonhoeffer's dictum that a congregation has not been entrusted to the pastor in order that he should become its accuser before God and men. For Geoff, on the other hand, the church really became irrelevant—although when challenged as to why he bothered about the equally hardened and difficult institution of party politics, I always felt his answer, that it was relevant to the life of man, left a little to be desired in terms of adequacy."

In the early and mid sixties the demands on the Group seemed to be never-ending. Childrens' work, youth work, political work, community work: the days and nights were crammed full of activity. Students from the London School of Economics and Glasgow University School of Social Studies were seconded to the Group for training. The Gorbals Group was recognised as being ahead of its time in youth and community work. And the experiment was becoming internationally known as a project which had lessons to teach.

Late in 1963, the Group took over a disused infant school in Nicholson Street, Gorbals, to meet the demands of the mushrooming youth programme. Two gyms were constructed and the activities were extended to include pottery, canoe making, library, chess, playacting, netball, basketball and badminton. Church members from the suburbs came in to help and to learn. Lydia Barge, a gifted teacher in the Glasgow School of Art, encouraged the Gorbals children's

122

interest in the arts and crafts, especially pottery. Because the school was situated at an important junction, the whole youth programme was named "Crossroads".

Geoff could not find enough hours in the day, so he took them from the night. His availability became further stretched when an extension telephone line was run from 74, Cleland Street to 3a, Abbotsford Place. When he went out, he switched the phone through to the extension and Molly or John Harvey would receive his calls. On returning, he would buzz over and ask if there had been any messages.

Housing continued to be the dominant political issue. Walter Fyfe prepared a paper on housing policy for Glasgow Corporation and had articles published in *The Glasgow Herald*. In one of the articles, he described the problem. "In 3 houses, 59 persons live; the lavatories have not worked for a year and have to be flushed with a bucket. Tenants cook either on their own spirit stoves or on an open fire. The lighting was rigged up by tenants and in one place repaired with a plastic head square. In these houses where the light failed the tenants have to do without it and are expected to pay their rent as usual... It has to be repeated over and over again, however, since so few people are willing to accept this, that the laws affecting tenant and landlord must apply to the "socially undesirable" as much as to anyone else. This principle is denied again and again by all sorts of officials and particularly by lawyers representing the interests of landlords. The problem is worsening all the time. Glasgow Corporation must take the vigorous action taken by all other cities in Britain."

As more and more reports were published, the conditions in Gorbals deteriorated. In one year, over 10,000 rats were killed in Gorbals. Mrs Josephine Collins, who lived in Gorbals, complained that rats were being killed, but their bodies were not being taken away. The result was that they were floating in pools of green scum in the back courts.

"Our children are running about throwing dead rats at each other," she said.

Not surprisingly, the health authorities admitted that dysentery was worse than it had ever been thirty years ago. This was Glasgow 1965, eight years after Mr. Harold

123

Macmillan had told the nation they had never had it so good.

Some of the housing factors exploited the situation to the full. They charged high rents and did no repairs. Some intimidated tenants in order to get them out. They then charged higher rents.

The Gorbals Group made themselves very unpopular with the factors and with the local authorities. They took cases to the Rent Tribunal and stopped big rises. They had factors prosecuted for intimidation. Evictions were halted. One local activist's abiding memory of Geoff is of him standing in a Gorbals street surrounded by furniture. Rent strikes were organised in order to force necessary repairs. The Group wrote letters to the press and the Council officials. They lobbied politicians.

There had been promises of comprehensive action. Gorbals -Hutchesontown had always had the worst housing problems and the worst notoriety and in 1951 the Gorbals—Hutchesontown scheme had been drawn up. The first of the tower flats in Hutchesontown were opened in 1962. At the ceremony, Mr. Michael Noble, Secretary of State for Scotland, said: "People in Glasgow have a picture of Gorbals. It is often a bad one and a wrong one. In putting Glasgow into focus in the world's eye, it was a masterly stroke to begin at this point. Here, ladies and gentlemen, the world is going to see the real miracle in the Gorbals."

This kind of public relations work merely angered the Gorbals Group. In 1964 the first new houses to be built in Gorbals—Laurieston for nearly a century were opened. They were flats for 79 families.

Two years later, on June 19, 1966, a Comprehensive Development Plan for Laurieston Gorbals was approved. The report stated that it was the opinion of the Corporation that comprehensive development was the only method of dealing satisfactorily with the conditions of bad layout and obsolete development and of effecting the necessary co-ordination of major building and road developments proposed for the area.

The whole of Gorbals was to come down.

The proposal was to reduce the population of Laurieston Gorbals from 18,500 to 8,500. They would be housed in blocks of flats. The mass of small businesses and shops would be demolished and modern schools, shops and health facilities would be built. Open spaces would be planned. The number of pubs in Gorbals would be reduced from 132 to12.

That was for the future. In the meantime, the announcement of compulsory purchase orders meant that even fewer repairs were done.

Richard Holloway had the idea of starting a Housing Association. He proposed to take over houses in nearby East Pollokshields, renovate them and let them to Gorbals families who would not have the chance of a house in the foreseeable future.

The idea was debated in the Group. A Christian Action Housing official came up from London to spell out the theory and practice.

The Group declined to back the idea. Walter and Elizabeth argued that such schemes merely let the local authorities off the hook. What was needed was a concentration of effort on a long term housing solution. Geoff agreed.

Richard and Lilias felt that while future plans had to be made, action was needed now to help families in need. It was the classical argument about long term aims and short term needs. Thus the Christian Action Glasgow Housing Association was born.

In 1967, the keys to the first six renovated houses in Pollokshields were handed over at a ceremony in Community House. Although Geoff had initially opposed the scheme, he did later use it to get houses for newly married boys in his club.

Since the beginning of the Gorbals Group, Geoff had been paid an assistant minister's salary. In 1964, his pay was raised to the dizzy heights of the minimum stipend of any parish minister of the Church of Scotland. For seven years while he worked in the Gorbals, he had been paid an apprentice's money. That itself spoke volumes as to how the Gorbals Group was truly regarded, although it was to the credit of members of the Presbytery's Home Mission Committee and the Home Board that, despite criticism, the project continued at all.

Strengthened by the coming of Anne McPherson and Elizabeth Dabbs, a Community Service Volunteer, the Group continued to develop its service to the community. A nursery school was opened in conjunction with the Guild of Aid. Lilias Graham's women's group opened up The Hen House, a shop for selling jumble. The work of the playrooms continued.

In January 1967, Crossroads Youth and Community Association was set up to take responsibility for the youth programme. And in April 1967, the Group published the first edition of Britain's first community newspaper, the *Gorbals View*.

The Group had felt for years the need for a newspaper which would provide a means of communication to the people of Gorbals. The paper would tell them about events in Gorbals, plans for redevelopment, housing rights and family welfare. They also hoped it would be used as a means of communication by and on behalf of the people of Gorbals. Thus, out of the concern of the Gorbals Group and funded through the economic discipline of its members, the father and mother of community newspapers was born.

Its first editor John Harvey wrote:"We care about the Gorbals—mainly because we live in it. For thousands of us, the 'miracle' of Gorbals has not yet happened: we still live in one of the worst slums in Europe; we watch our children grow up in overcrowded and insanitary houses. We grow weary of the endless promises while the years roll our lives along. That's why the *Gorbals View* will focus on housing conditions and on the pressing social needs of a large part of our area—and where necessary we'll not hesitate to get involved in controversy with the powers that be."

It certainly fufilled its promise to get involved in controvery with the powers-that-be. Geoff Shaw, who had a year as editor, wrote the kind of material that might have embarrassed the Convener of Strathclyde Regional Council.

It has to be remembered that Geoff's activities in Gorbals did not make him universally popular. He had, of course, many friends and admirers. But apart from those who felt personally threatened by his all-out commitment, some policemen, several landlords, a handful of officials and a few

126

politicians were no friends to Geoff Shaw and his name was not music in their ears.

The *View* never made a profit. It was heavily subsidised from the Group's Outreach Fund. Publisher Bill Williams kept it going through one particular crisis. Still it ensured that the decaying Gorbals had a voice. And each year it inspired the publication of more and more community newspapers, whose ammunition was generally fired in the direction of local authority politicians.

Internal matters continued to exercise the Gorbals Group. The questions of membership and economics were continually debated and it was eventually agreed that rather than laying down formal conditions of membership of the Group, it was more desirable that a factual statement of the nature of the Group should be provided and full membership of the Group accorded to anyone who wished to join on that basis.

The statement was as follows;

"The Gorbals Group is a community of men and women sharing common purpose and a common way of life.

The Group takes as its reference point the words of Isaiah which Jesus quoted: 'The spirit of the Lord is upon me, because He has anointed me to preach the Gospel to the poor. He has sent me to heal the broken-hearted, to preach deliverance to the captive and recovering of sight to the blind; to set at liberty those that are oppressed and to proclaim a year when men may find acceptance with the Lord.'

In the light of these words, the Group seeks to express its common purpose in practical action of social, political and personal concern within the neighbourhood of Gorbals.

The Group expresses its common life in these ways: by living in the neighbourhood of Gorbals; by meeting together every Thursday evening, this meeting taking priority over all other commitments; by sharing in the Communion meal, which is itself a continuing reminder of the common purpose; by sharing in the discussion of common neighbourhood and Group concerns which are gathered up in prayers of intercession; by sharing of financial concern, which is expressed by contribution to an Outreach Fund; by discussion together of the ways in which each member may share in the common purpose through their own job and through involvement in neighbourhood and Group concern.

Where any member of the Group finds difficulty in sharing some part of the common life, it is agreed that this shall openly be stated to and discussed with other members of the Group."

The old economic discipline was abandoned: it was agreed that each member would be responsible for his or her own income and would make a contribution to the Gorbals Group Outreach Fund. Walter, Elizabeth and Geoff argued against the move, but were in the minority.

With the adoption of such flexible membership and the dismantling of the tight economic discipline, the Gorbals Group was formally completing the move from a tightly-disciplined, structured group to an open, flexible, less-demanding association—a move which had, in fact, been going on over the years.

This did not mean, of course, that all the disciplines had been abandoned or changed. Every application for membership was debated thoroughly and each member had to fulfil the newly agreed conditions.

Nevertheless, the changes posed questions for Walter and Elizabeth Fyfe. Their house was beginning to fall down and they were faced with the prospect of moving. They believed that the Group members should make a commitment to a wider area (Gorbals, Pollokshields and Govanhill). This, they felt, would require an even more binding commitment on the Group. Instead, the disciplines were becoming less stringent. They decided to leave Gorbals—and the Group—at the end of 1967.

When Walter and Elizabeth and their three sons left Abbotsford Lane ten years after the adventure had begun, Geoff Shaw wept. So much had been shared that his feelings could not be expressed in any other way.

Chapter XI
Crossroads

In East Harlem you bring up each child for fourteen years wondering all the time whether you will win them or the street will win them, but knowing that almost certainly the street will win them.—

Mrs Leroy Harris

When, in his teens, Kenn read that Leonardo da Vinci had gone about the streets of Florence buying caged birds for the pleasure of liberating them, the knowledge excited him to that momentary ecstasy where thought is lost in pure light.— **Neil Gunn,** Highland River.

It had seemed just like an ordinary visit. The elderly lady who wanted to see round Gorbals and to find out about the work of the Group was dutifully escorted by Geoff. At the railway station to catch her train home she had thanked him profusely and had given him an envelope containing a donation for the work of the Group.

Geoff forgot about it until he got home. He pulled the envelope out of his pocket, opened it and found a cheque for £15,000.

Suddenly the Gorbals Group, which had been counting each others' pennies to finance community projects, was wealthy.

It was agreed that the money should go towards employing staff to help run the youth programme and towards a permanent outdoor centre. Crossroads Youth and Community Association had grown out of the work of the 'wee club', as it was known, and the Nicholson Street school.

Geoff had a clear understanding of what he was trying to do in the youth programme. He spelt out his philosophy in a memorandum to Glasgow Corporation.

Influences on what they were doing, Geoff wrote, included the current emphasis on learning-through-doing and learning-for-living: the emphasis of much modern psychological thinking on the small group rather than the large organisation as a means of personal discovery and healing; and developments in modern thinking on child care—finding a proper balance between authoritarian attitudes and

129

undirected permissiveness.

Geoff stressed that the policy of Crossroads was geared towards small groups.

"We are providing a place where small groups of young people can meet together and, in the undirected processes of doing things together and talking things over together and with adults, can discover themselves and something of their own aims and purposes and can enjoy just being themselves," he wrote.

He was not interested in 'keeping people off the streets.' He wanted the streets of Gorbals to be full of interesting life. His vision for the Gorbals youngsters was that of a 'university of the streets,' in which young people would learn new skills, excel in sport, become involved in community service, learn to analyse their own situation and solve their own problems and to experience moments of 'unconditional joy.' Geoff wanted to reverse the process of Gorbals youngsters going to Oxford, as in John Buchan's novels. He wanted Oxford to come to Gorbals.

He recruited a wide range of people with skills and the old St John's School in Nicholson Street became a cross between a youth club, a community school, a centre for creative art and a gymnasium. The youth programme ran every evening in the week and many youngsters 'graduated' with a better understanding of themselves and a fuller appreciation of what life had to offer. The helpers, too, discovered that they were learners at the hands of youngsters practised in the art of survival in the tough school of life.

In his memorandum Geoff said that all the activities and non-activities must be geared especially to suit the needs of young people who might be: of lower than average intelligence; of delinquent tendencies and occasionally of deep disturbance; from 'problem' families; disorganised in themselves and irregular in attendance and interest or individualist and anti-authoritarian.

He did not run a tidy club from which the bad boys were banned and the problems pushed elsewhere. His policy was "a fairly intensive and wide-ranging concern with a few young people, as opposed to a more superficial provision of facilities for a large number. We have," he wrote, "especial regard for those young people who would normally be excluded from the larger or more formalised youth activities and for those who perhaps get lost in the anonymity of mass approach: and for a few we see Crossroads as something approaching a therapeutic community."

The constitution of the Crossroads Youth and Community Association, which was approved in January 1967, had care for the delinquents built into it. One of its declared aims and objects was to 'undertake such experiments in youth and community activities as may be thought, in the light of modern knowledge, to meet most effectively the needs of delinquent or potentially delinquent children and young people. "

The large donation enabled John Harvey to be employed as a full time worker and John Anderson to be taken on as project officer, with the particular remit of developing outdoor work.

The youth programme expanded even further. David Lunan, one of the helpers at the Friday night club for youngsters aged 7-9 in Nicholson Street School, recalls a number of nights when older boys burst into the club and terrified the youngsters. The leaders would return to Cleland Street for a coffee and chat with Geoff and on several occasions they appealed to him to help keep out the intruders. He steadfastly refused to do so, saying it was up to the helpers to build up relationships. If he were present the helpers would become superfluous. David comments: "This was obviously not to protect himself (would that he had), but to practise his theory of small groups in youth work. Geoff himself kept his own close contact with all members via their families—he always seemed to know them intimately."

Football was a mania with the boys and Geoff became an expert manager and coach. He took the boys all over Glasgow in the van to play in matches. When John Carrie, one of the leaders, asked what to do when the boys seemed to take football too seriously, Geoff's answer was: "Take it even more seriously than the boys."

All of the club leaders remember Geoff's extraordinary physical presence. In the midst of violence he himself never used violence. Some of the people he was dealing with were really tough and Geoff was threatened with stabbing on more than one occasion. There were hatchet marks on his door at Cleland Street.

There were times when the leaders felt taken for granted and he certainly expected—and got—a lot from them; yet he would often find time to give each person his undivided attention.

Because of his heavy programme Geoff rationed speaking engagements carefully. He made talks at police training seminars and probation officers' conferences a priority. At the end of 1967 he prepared a memorandum on delinquency for the Secretary of State for Scotland.

Arguing against the use of the birch, he wrote: "I believe we cannot swing indefinitely between hard and soft, between authoritarian and permissive. Each of these can, in their own way, be destructive if made into a firm principle. We have to look at the most constructive possibilities, both on the short and long term basis, and recognise that this needs a much greater flexibility of enterprise than hard positions held on permissiveness and authoritarianism can allow."

Dealing with the police issue, Geoff wrote: "There is a complete refusal to recognise the extent of resentment against the police in many areas of the city and to see that this resentment is on the one hand partially justified and on the other hand itself a major contributing factor to juvenile crime.

"It is common knowledge in an area such as Gorbals that there is widespread rough handling of young people and adults by the police. It is generally assumed that verbal cheek or recalcitrance is sufficient provocation to warrant "roughing up" and young people will expect to get a "doing" from the police on arrest. It is recognised that many individual policemen are exceptions to this rule....There is widespread respect for the individual policeman known to be 'fair'; there is a much greater resentment of the police force in general, based on many experiences of injustice and incompetence."

He proposed the abolition of the law of loitering between the hours of 8.00 a.m. and 10.00 p.m.; restriction of powers of arrest of known thieves; and the setting up of trained

132

youth squads—specially chosen policemen who would specialise in juvenile work, get to know the families of young people in trouble and run social and recreational youth programmes in the community such as he had seen in America.

He also argued that the treatment of juvenile offenders in institutions should be used only as a last resort. From experience he knew many boys learned more about crime when they were 'inside' and faced many problems when they came out. He proposed the setting up of compulsory attendance centres in Glasgow—offenders would remain in their own jobs and would attend at specified times—and the formation of counselling groups.

Dealing with community aspects of the problem, Geoff called for a wide variety of experiments. He advocated the appointment of youth and community officers who would work with families and help find jobs for young people. He wanted small youth centres rather than large ones to be set up because the large ones tended to exclude trouble-makers. Detached youth work in cafes would be more effective than the running of huge centres. Advisory counselling services for young people would also help. He also advocated the setting up of a municipal council of youth, which would be elected on ward basis and would meet once a month in the City Chambers in Glasgow.

Geoff asked the Secretary of State for a proper community service programme and the setting up of a youth corps organised on a basis similar to the Territorial Army. There would be no weapons instruction or drill; this would be replaced by an emphasis on community service, majoring on mountain and sea rescue, flood or fire drill, crowd control and first aid.

He wrote: "There is in many young people a desire to be a bit more regimented; to escape, perhaps, from the freedom of choice demanded in a more permissive setting. Many young people respond well to the structured discipline of institutions and are confused by their own inability to make the right decisions when they come out again into a free society. Much of the attraction of crime for young people is the prospect of being together with other young people

133

under duress in a communal living situation of authority. The abolition of conscription for young people meant often the cutting off of the way in which they could naturally leave home as a boy and return as a man."

Geoff's vision for the youth of Gorbals and similar areas was not, of course, restricted to the streets, but embraced the outdoors.

He must have supervised literally hundreds of camps in his lifetime. He took Gorbals boys to Perthshire to camp with handicapped youngsters. Hillwalking excursions were organised at weekends, with Geoff usually hurrying back to attend meetings. Girls' leader Margaret Morris, sister of Monica, remembers having to lead a group alone across a hillside on Lairig Ghru and drive them back to Glasgow in the van; Geoff in the meantime had hurried off and driven Margaret's car back to attend a CND meeting in Glasgow! No doubt to arrive late and breathless, as he inevitably did for meetings.

On one camp on Iona, a group of boys, with their bootlace ties and "winkle picker" shoes, wanted to stay in their tent and play cards. Geoff, in his shorts and climbing boots, surrounded on all sides by some of the most beautiful scenery in Scotland, was rarin' to go. Despite his threats to cancel tea, the boys refused to budge. Nothing but nothing, was more important than cards, not even the call of Columba's sacred isle. It took the lads a while to humour Geoff out of that one.

But mostly they got on well, with moments of real hilarity. It was on Iona that Geoff offered ten cigarettes to the first boy to swim in the Atlantic. One lad stripped off and plunged into the icy waters only to be told by Geoff that he was disqualified because he still had his socks on. On another occasion Geoff roared with laughter when a boy struggled around for ten minutes with a torch looking for his socks, only to discover that he still had them on.

One of the most popular camping places was Tayvallich, in Kintyre. Geoff would take one lot of boys home and pick up another group the same day. It was exhausting work and he would have to snatch some sleep in a lay-by. At night he would play the guitar and sing with the youngsters. Back in

Glasgow, he got the Gorbals young people together and recorded an L.P. called "Tayvallich Singalong". The youngsters were thrilled beyond words.

The camps were very tiring. Geoff got very little rest or time to himself. On at least one occasion he confided, 'I've had enough of this. I'm not cut out for it. I must do something else.' Geoff knew that the pace was taking its toll.

With the appointment of John Anderson, formerly chief instructor at an outdoor centre in the Lake District, the outdoors work expanded. Adventure training, skiing, sailing canoeing and orienteering, became part of a Gorbals boy's curriculum. (Archery had to be discontinued after a highland sheep met an untimely end).

In 1967, a deserted ruined village, Peanmeanach on the Ardnish Peninsula, 30 miles west of Fort William, came to light.

Geoff obtained temporary lease of the ruined village which was accessible only by boat or long hill track. It was straight out of "Highland River"! Roofing material from blown-down Gorbals houses was transported to Ardnish and a squad of boys put the roof on one of the cottages, making it water tight. An old lobster boat with a wheel house, the Og, was purchased.

That summer, Geoff organised a six-week school for some selected boys. They loved it. They learned about tides and weather boats and lobsters. They went for a sail in the Og under the command of one of their own number. They learned some Gaelic. They went fishing, using lobster pots. They climbed and walked. They found stags' horns on the hillsides.

They agreed: it was 'magic'.

Geoff was ecstatic. Seeing those Gorbals youngsters enjoying moments of "sheer unconditional delight" filled him with intense satisfaction. His imagination started to run riot. Why not have a permanent outdoor centre for Gorbals— a Highland University by the sea? He drafted proposals for a permanent outdoor centre at Peanmeanach. It was a visionary document.

His dream was of the setting up of a community of about forty children, which would provide education on a wide basis for as long as each particular child should need it. Caravan cottages would be developed, to allow parents to come for holidays and there would be facilities for week-long camps.

He envisaged the stages as follows: "The first stage, lasting perhaps two years, would be a stage of initial building. We would require to appoint a warden of the community—a man who combined knowledge of young people and their way of life in the city with some knowledge of agriculture. He would be accompanied in the initial stages by young people of over school age and by such other adults as might be necessary. During this initial stage a double development would take place; on the one hand the beginning of agriculture; on the other the building, by contract, of the necessary buildings— one large cottage to accommodate house parents, plus ten children, a simple school, the renovation of the existing school as a studio-pottery. In the meantime young people employed there would be assisting with agriculture, the renovation of at least one of the old cottages, preparation of water supply, jetty, etc.

"The staff would teach art, agriculture, forestry, building and fishing, and would start small industries in which the children would participate. Thus, when the community reached its full development it would be not so much a school as a renewed village community.

"Clearly formal education would require to play a major part, but in this setting it could afford to be flexible and to be closely related to the needs of the children. The sharing in the community activities would in itself be seen as part of education and of the socialising processes and it is hoped that the regime of the community would make possible a large degree of participation by the children. It is hoped also that it would be possible to introduce flexibility into the length of time for which children would stay in the community—some for weeks or months, others for years, depending on their personal needs, their home situation, etc."

He set about selling the idea with an enthusiasm which was fanned by further visits of Gorbals youngsters to Peany-

Meany, as it became known.

On one occasion the bus bringing the children up from Glasgow was late. They had the excitement of sailing in the Og in darkness, then stumbling over the rocks towards the cottage.

Geoff was in his element, like a child. He organised Highland games for the youngsters. The losing tug-of-war team were hauled into the burn. He joined in the games at night, creeping about the heather, flashing torches. He taught the boys to play touch rugger in the water. He watched with pride as Dennis Irvine displayed his newly acquired skill with the outboard engine.

Older boys came up for a week at the Glasgow Fair—some with wives and children. Geoff joined in the merriment as a wee boy in swimming trunks splashed uninhibitedly up the burn. He watched the excitement on the face of one lad spending hours examining stones at one of the sandy bays.

On Sundays a sympathetic priest, dressed in full regalia, celebrated Mass in the open air. Geoff in his scruffy old shorts also conducted worship. And at night, round the camp fire, he played his guitar for the singing and said some short, but obviously meaningful prayers.

Sarah Mason, a student at St Andrews University, had gone to help at Peanmeanach on placement, as part of her course in pastoral and social studies. She remembers: "When Geoff was present, there was an atmosphere of terrific fun—it was electric. When he left, the mood seemed to plummet and there was an almost physical sense of anti climax.

"The plans for the future of Peanmeanach were very exciting and Geoff's vision of what it might be is still for me one of the most memorable things about him."

He made plans to set up a trust to raise the necessary funds and was given a loan of £30,000 to make a bid for the Ardnish peninsula, which was due to go on the market. He sounded out a friend, John Webster, a missionary with agricultural experience, about the warden's position.

But it was not to be. The owner of the peninsula decided to withdraw it from the market and asked for the work done to be dismantled. Despite repeated and desperate attempts to have the matter reopened, it was made clear that the

Gorbals—Peanmeanach dream would remain just that.
Geoff was broken-hearted.

Chapter XII
Christ of the Dark Streets

Grace is insidous, it twists and is full of surprises.... when it doesn't come from the right, it comes from the left.... when it doesn't come from above, it comes from below; and when it doesn't come from the centre, it comes from the circumference.

— **Charles Péguy**

Prayer is a subversive activity.　　　　**Daniel Berrigan, S.J.**

Geoff's spiritual and theological pilgrimage in Gorbals had led him over the years to seek new ways of interpreting the secular realities of the world. As he suffered alongside rootless and hurting youngsters and as he became increasingly disillusioned by the Church's incapacity to address the realities of life as it was lived by so many people, he searched for a new spiritual vocabulary which would accord with his own experience.

In the early stages of the Gorbals experiment, when his thinking was much more church-orientated, he pleaded for change. In a BBC radio broadcast in 1962, he had called for a variety of experiments in church life.

"This willingness to be flexible—to break boldly through the old in order to discover humbly the new— depends of course, on a renewed understanding of the Christ of the Christian Church," he said. "We have forgotten that he weeps in compassion over the city as He did over Jerusalem; that He strides in anger through injustice and exploitation as He did in the Temple; that He is present to heal and to unite, that He is walking the dark streets long before his so-called followers ever do. Forget this and we forget that we can only blindly and in part enter into the torments of the city as he does. Forget it and inevitably His Church stands aside from the life of the people; the political, the social, the working life—indeed even from those very questionings and confusions which should be the Church's concern. It cannot even intercede faithfully, because it does not share in the life of the city which it holds up to God. Renewal of the Church in the inner ring must start at this point and be ready to take

139

seriously the radical changes in the Church's life and structure which the Christ of the dark streets commands."

Geoff never saw himself as a radical in theology, nor was he a follower of the latest trends. The Death of God theology came and went in the 1960s, and he was not much influenced by it. When a Glasgow church was being rebuilt and a new spire put on, he commented good-humouredly that it would be more in keeping with the spirit of the age to put in a crypt, to express God as Ground of Being.

He remained thirled to the Knoxian Scots Confession of 1560, and often used to quote from it. He liked the passage— "The notes of the true Kirk of God we believe to be first, the true preaching of the Word of God; secondly, the right administration of the Sacraments of Jesus Christ; last, ecclesiastical discipline rightly administered....wherever, then, these former notes are seen and for anytime continue (be the number never so few, about two or three), there without all doubt, is the true Kirk of Christ, who according to His promise is in the midst of them."

In a commentary on this, he had written in 1966: "The Word truly preached means that it must be spoken of, discussed, gossiped in such a way that it is heard; to proclaim it from the pulpit only is to preach only to those who go to Church. The sacraments rightly administered must clearly point to the death and rising of Jesus Christ, the ordinary man for ordinary men. The discipline of the Church—the caring, sharing Church—must again in our day take on a new significance, not as the discipline administered by a paternal authority so much as a self-discipline of time and money, freely entered into. Where the word is confined to the church building, where the sacraments are veiled in pomp and ceremony, where discipline is ignored—there the notes of the true Church are missing."

The same year Geoff was asked to prepare a study guide called "A Dead End Church?" along with John Harvey, for the Scottish Christian Youth Assembly. He agreed (provided the question mark was in the title!) and finished the draft at 3.00 a.m. at Tayvallich.

In the study guide, Geoff explicitly rejected the Church as a triumphalist, authoritative, powerful institution and pointed to what he saw as its true role—as servant, friend and prophet in the image of Jesus Christ.

On the role of the Church as a friend, he wrote from real experiences: "Here we are talking of the almost desperate need of the friend who comes at midnight; we are talking of the desperately lonely, of the alcoholic, of the mentally sick, of the neurotic; of the foreigner. We are talking of the people who have been shut up inside their own world and find friendship almost impossible, or make impossible demands in their friendship. We are talking of the need within our sick society that its saddest victims should be heard with patience until in time a bond of genuine affection grows. We are talking of the love which in time casts out the many fears of our modern society."

Turning to the Church and secular society, Geoff wrote a passage which provides clues for understanding his later political development.

"One of the grave tragedies of the Church in our modern society is that while it has lost the authority which it once had, for example after the Reformation, it nevertheless retains a meaningless status in public life and preserves the myth of a Christian society; and strangely enough, many non-Christians want it so.

"But to take seriously its place in our secular society, the Church may very well have to lose its identity. For the task of the real Church is to help the State to be a real State i.e. by its decisions, its actions and by the justice and equality and integrity of its legislation, to glorify God. The task of the real Church is to assist not only the political structures, but also the other secular structures of industry, trade, culture, leisure, education, welfare etc., to discover purpose and integrity and wholeness and truth. The Church has always known that it has the task of assisting the individual Christian to remain 'unspotted by the world' in his personal behaviour —with varying degrees of success. But now as never before, when in all these structures there is, on the one hand, self-seeking and corruption and callous deperson-alisation and on the other, a genuine search for purpose and truth on humanist grounds, the Christian must ask if he has anything to contribute, and must be helped by others to find

141

an answer and fulfil it—and he must not be put off if he finds that his closest allies do not share the basis of his faith. The task in our day is not to protect the Christian from the world, but to assist him in the sharing with all sorts and conditions of men in the shaping of the future."

Geoff concluded the study guide: "The subject of your study is vast, for it is no less than the story of God's love for His world. Our faith is that this is God's world; that Christ is abroad in the world—in the structures of all society, in the dark city streets, in the silent places of man's loneliness and his despair; and that there He summons His Church to reflect His love and the coming of His Kingdom."

His final sentence is a pointer to the movement of his thought—"Our certainty is that Christ will cleanse the world of its sickness and of its hatred; of war and of all enmity; of injustice and of destruction—if not with the Church then without it."

Powerful and moving words: the more poignant because they were not penned in a comfortable book-lined study, but in a tent surrounded by sleeping lads from Gorbals.

David Lunan remembers a sermon Geoff wrote after midnight at Tayvallich, and preached next morning in a local church. It was just after his visit to Fr. Borrelli in Naples. Where in Scotland, he asked, could one find sacrifice like that? The Church was dealing in cheap grace, not costly grace. He quoted the words of Bonhoeffer , "When Jesus Christ calls a man, he bids him come and die."

The night he wrote the sermon, various people were throwing in light-hearted suggestions. Then a woman asked him, if he had only one chance to preach to a congregation, what would be the theme of his sermon? His immediate answer was that there is only one thing to preach about and that is the love of God.

Geoff was regularly invited to preach at Cramond and he always went. His sermons were usually about wealth and poverty, or a theme like Jesus' cry of dereliction from the cross. The reverse of inspirational! He would urge his hearers to look around them for the poverty in their midst and to take responsibility for its victims. In one sermon on the story of Judah and Benjamin, he told the congregation that though they might on death be listening for the trumpet on the other side and the welcome "Well done, good and faithful servant", they might instead hear the question "Have you brought the boy?"

Geoff used to chuckle in a bemused kind of way as he said that he did not really know why the Cramond congregation kept inviting him back. The answer is that they were proud of him.

In his cell at No.74 and on the Gorbals streets, Geoff was developing a theology of the servant, crucified Christ, who was poor, had no status or power, was vulnerable and was totally available. Geoff believed it was more important to do Christ's will quietly and patiently and anonymously in the world, in the company of non-believers, than to preserve the status of the Church. The Church, he felt, was too quick with answers which its credentials gave it no right to give. Evangelism, he believed, should be 'gossiping the Gospel' when asked for one's point of view.

In a televised interview with Robert Kee about ten years after the formation of the Gorbals Group the man who was now titled Home Board Evangelist said the Church had a tradition of taking over people and of manipulating them. "This I think we have to fall over backwards in avoiding. We may have made mistakes in Gorbals by falling too far over backwards. But what we have always wanted to say is that this is something we are happy to share if anyone wants to share it with us."

In tape-recorded notes in preparation for the Kee interview Geoff acknowledged his debt to John Macmurray, Karl Barth and T.F. Torrance, but said that the only theologian who "at the end of the day I really light up for is Dietrich Bonhoeffer."

Dietrich Bonhoeffer had come from a wealthy academic home in Germany. He was a bright and up-and-coming young theologian at the time Hitler was taking over and Bonhoeffer was horrified by what he saw. He formed a little community of ministers-to-be. They believed that if Christian discipleship meant anything at all it must do so in the **world** as well as the Church.

Bonhoeffer, who had said in 1941: "Only in defeat can we

143

atone for the terrible crime we have committed against Europe and the world,' became involved in an underground plot to kill Hitler. He was caught, put in prison and executed in 1945 at the age of 39.

In his notes on Bonhoeffer, Geoff said that he had found him helpful in interpreting the significance of the secular and the loss of 'religion' and the 'hiddenness of Christianity'.

Appreciating Bonhoeffer's insistence that God must be found in the midst of the world's sufferings, Geoff added: "The problem of the institutionalisation of the Church is that, having separated off a place where God is, you have immediately posited places where God is not. By separating the professional cleric as a man of God you have immediately posited the supposition that the non-cleric may, in some way or another, be less a man of God.

"Ordination is ordination into a more participant, not a less participant life. Ordination is confirmation into the world , not into the Church and is the release to be entirely within the world, to be participant in the world."

On the question of appropriate modern Christian discipleship, Geoff said that the personal *imitatio Christi* in modern secular terms must be the acceptance of a bondage, for economic or other reasons, freely and consciously entered into for other people.

Bonhoeffer's *Letters and Papers from Prison* inspired Geoff, as they had others. In these letters, Bonhoeffer wrestled with the question of how to be a Christian disciple in a post-Christian world which did not particularly want to hear from the Church.

He rejected the traditional division of life into sacred and secular, the Church having dominion over the sacred. He opposed the view that Christianity has to do with the soul and not the body. The whole world was Christ's and faith was not just for Sundays and quiet moments.

He also rejected the common view that a space could be made for God at the point where science lacks answers. Such a 'God of the gaps' would eventually be squeezed out of the universe altogether.

Bonhoeffer promoted the idea of 'religion-less Christianity.' What he meant by that was not a Christianity without prayer and worship, but a Christianity which dealt with the centre of life rather than sniffing sanctimoniously around the borders. Jesus Christ was Lord of the whole world, not just the traditionally religious part of it. The Christian's duty was to serve Christ in the world.

He criticised the kind of religion which concentrated on man's weakness. He attacked the 'priestly sniffing' around the sins of men, which he described as religious blackmail. Man had come of age, said the German theologian, not in the sense that he was perfect, but because he saw through the 'God of the gaps' and the God who attacked man at his weakest points.

"When we speak of God in a non-religious way" he said, "we must not gloss over the ungodliness of the world, but expose it in a new light. Now that it has come of age, the world is more godless and perhaps it is for that very reason nearer to God than ever before."

The accepted ways of talking about God made Bonhoeffer uneasy and he often found it easier to talk about God with unbelievers than believers. He wrote: "I often ask myself why a Christian instinct frequently draws me more to the religionless than to the religious, by which I mean not with any intention of evangelising them, but rather, I might almost say, in 'brotherhood'. While I often shrink with religious people from speaking of God by name—because that name somehow seems to me here not to ring true and I strike myself as rather dishonest, (it is especially bad when others start talking in religious jargon: then I dry up completely and I feel somehow oppressed and ill at ease)—with people who have no religon I am able on occasion to speak of God quite openly and as it is were, naturally."

The words struck a chord with Geoff, who was uncomfortable in the presence of very religious people and yet could talk about God naturally with boys in Gorbals.

Bonhoeffer argued that God must be seen in the very centre of life or not at all. God, he said was 'the beyond' in the midst of life. Geoff gave his amen to that. Christianity, said Bonhoeffer, was a very 'worldly' religion: the job of the Christian was not to withdraw from the world and become a saint—God called us not to become **saints** but **men**, participating fully in the life and the struggle of His world. The 'saint' did not care much for the pleasures of the world, but this was ingratitude to God for his gifts. "It is improper," said Bonhoeffer, "for a man to long for the transcendent when he is in the arms of his wife!"

Writing in his prison cell, as he heard the bombs explode in the city, he went on: "During the last year or so I have come to appreciate the 'worldliness' of Christianity as never before. The Christian is not a *homo religiosus,* but a man, pure and simple, just as Jesus was a man, compared with John the Baptist anyhow. I don't mean the shallow this-worldliness of the enlightened, of the busy, the comfortable or the lascivious. It's something much more profound than that, something in which the knowledge of death and resurrection is ever present....Later I discovered and am still discovering up to this very moment that it is only by living completely in this world that one learns to believe. One must abandon every attempt to make something of oneself, whether it be a saint, a converted sinner, a churchman (the priestly type, so called!), a righteous man or an unrighteous one, a sick man or a healthy one. This is what I man by worldliness—taking one's life in one's stride, with all its duties and problems, its successes and failures, its experiences and helplessness. It is in such life that we throw ourselves utterly in the arms of God and participate in his sufferings in the world and watch with Christ in Gethsemane. That is faith, that is repentance and that is what makes a man and a Christian."

What Bonhoeffer was doing was to sketch the outlines of a new breed of "holy man" who would love and enjoy the world, plunge himself into its problems and sufferings, not talk a great deal about God to a world weary of religious talk, yet would be sustained by an arcane, or secret, discipline of prayer and worship.

This spoke exactly to Geoff's condition. He believed in God, he believed in prayer: yet he rejected the idea that Christians were better than other people and automatically had more solutions to the world's problems.

Bonhoeffer's ideas about the powerlessness of Christ and therefore of the Church also found sympathy with Geoff.

146

"God allows himself to be edged out of the world and on to a cross," wrote Bonhoeffer. "God is weak and powerless in the world, and that is exactly the way, the only way, in which he can be with us and help us. Matthew 8: 17 makes it crystal clear that it is not by his omnipotence that Christ helps us, but by his weakness and suffering."

As he sought to interpret his experience in the 'dump' of Gorbals, Geoff was moved by these words—"Man is challenged to participate in the suffering of God at the hands of a godless world. He must therefore plunge himself into the life of a godless world, without attempting to gloss over its ungodliness with a veneer of religion or trying to transfigure it. He must live a 'worldly' life and so participate in the sufferings of God. He may live a worldly life as one emancipated from all false religions and obligations. To be a Christian does not mean to be religious in a particular way, to cultivate some particular form of asceticism (as a sinner, penitent or a saint) but to be a man. It is not some religious act which makes a Christian what he is, but participation in the suffering of God in the life of the world."

It is not surprising that Geoff Shaw quoted Bonhoeffer frequently at Gorbals Group Communion services and meditated on his writings as he attempted to make sense of his vocation. For Geoff himself, though he was too conscious of his own weaknesses to see himself in that light, was an example of the kind of Christian the German theologian was talking about.

Geoff Shaw was not a saint—he was too immersed in the world, too complex, not untroubled enough, for that. But he was truly a "worldly" holy man—a profoundly religious man who found his life not by withdrawing from the world, but by plunging himself bravely into its pain and suffering. In so doing, he was drawn closer to the sufferings of the powerless and vulnerable Lord he sought, in his best moments, to follow.

147

Chapter XIII
End of a Decade

There is no expeditious road
To pack and label men for God
And save them by the barrel load.
—**Francis Thompson**

The new humility will never be recovered save in a body that is really
human, that can laugh at its failures and admit its ignorance. It is a
fellowship such as this that begins to be spoken of in the criminal
quarters of town as something worth looking into.—
George F. MacLeod.

Ten years after it had started the Gorbals Group was keeping
more than a few balls in the air.

Geoff likened the set-up to a wheel, with the Group at the
centre. Immediately round it were the many activities in
which Group members were involved through informal case
work, co-operation with other agencies and political action.
On the rim was a series of associations which had been set up
to deal with some aspects of the Group's work. The Group
had become so successfully overworked that it had needed to
set up a number of organisations to run its activities. At least
one member of the Group was on the committee of each
association and reported monthly at a Group meeting. The
Day Nursery, the Nursery School Association, the Gorbals
Adventure Playground, the Playrooms, the Crossroads
Youth and Community Association, *The Gorbals View,* the
Hen House, the Holiday Scheme, Braendam Holiday House:
it was an impressive list of Group-inspired activities. Where
the Group had not done so well was in recruiting local leadership. They were still dependent on a large number of
volunteers from outside.

The sheer pressure of demand had necessitated a change in
role for the Group. Originally everything had been discussed
and decided on in their homes. Now the Group itself had
become institutionalised and was involved in co-ordinating a
wide range of activities.

It had been pioneering work. Long before such things

149

were fashionable, or even known, the Group had started a pre-school playgroup, a day nursery, a community newspaper, an adventure playground and a community clothes shop. Such activities are commonplace now, but at the time they were unique. Much of the Group's philosophy on case work, on working in small numbers and on treating delinquents was also highly original, as was evidenced by the increasing demand for student training in Gorbals. Some of that philosophy was enshrined in the Social Work (Scotland) Act of 1968. Geoff and Walter Fyfe were, in fact, in on the discussions with Judith Hart and Kay Carmichael on the setting up of the Act. Several Group members were, from time to time, called upon by outside bodies to help with advice.

On the social and political front the Group had always adhered to the policy of working through existing bodies. John Harvey and Geoff still held office in the local ward and constituency Labour parties and the Group played a part in a wide variety of organisations—the Scottish Pastoral Association, Christian Action Housing Association, Glasgow Adventure Playground Association, Poverty Action Group, Institute for the Study and Treatment of Delinquency, Glasgow Area Union of Youth Clubs, CND, War on Want, Save the Children Fund, Association for the Advancement of State Education and the Scottish Churches Council. The Group was also represented on the committee which set up the Glasgow Community Relations Council, whose first full-time officer was Walter Fyfe.

As a result of the new flexibility, considerably more local people had become involved with the Group. Some were not particularly concerned about the disciplines of membership. A new factor was that Helen and John Anderson were agnostics and did not participate in the worship. New members who joined the Group were: John Atherton, a local Episcopal priest and his wife Vanni; Marjorie Laing, a social worker; Doreen Robertson, a voluntary worker in Lilias Graham's playgroup who had moved into Gorbals in order to join the Group; Norah Trundle, who helped Lilias with the Hen House and other projects, and a Gorbals housewife, Betty Malik.

150

On the left the house in Abbotsford Lane where the Gorbals Group began.
(From a painting by Anne Donald.)

Geoff, Elizabeth Fyfe, Walter Fyfe and Kirstie Wedderburn, with a group of Gorbals youngsters.

Geoff with a group of children in the junk playground in Nicholson Street.

John and Beryl Jardine after their son Mark's baptism, 1958.

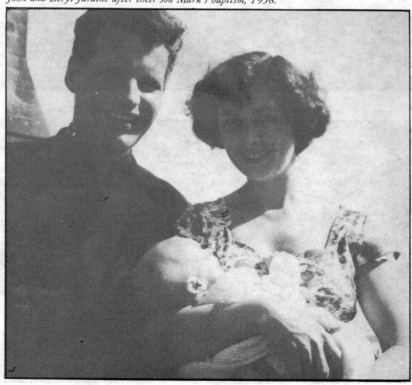

The Group had undoubtedly had immense success as a serving organisation in the community. Its record as an instrument of evangelism was a bit less impressive. The Gorbals Group report to the Home Mission Committee of the Presbytery in 1968 revealed that during the ten years of the Group's existence not one person had become a full member of the Church of Scotland and maintained membership over any length of time. Eight people had become members of the Scottish Episcopal Church.

In the report Geoff attempted to analyse the problem. He wrote: "In the light of accepted views of any undertaking of the Church, these Church of Scotland figures plainly require comment.

"The eventual nature of the Group has made it difficult for local residents to find a meaningful and permanent sense of belonging within the actual Group. Group meetings of twelve middle-class people have seemed strange to the several local people who have attended and some have expressed the feeling that 'they feel strange in the Group.' This plainly raises a question against the wisdom of having maintained one group over the period, when perhaps a greater participation of local people could have been achieved by smaller units of those Group members who have come to live in Gorbals from another area and background.

'The depth of the gulf between Protestant and Roman Catholic has been one of the most marked discoveries over the years. And yet this gulf only exists—except in the most bitter of either side—in regard to actual worship. All the Group's activities in other spheres have been deliberately open—all clubs, discussion groups, our homes, etc. have been entirely open to both Protestant and Roman Catholic. And Protestant and Roman Catholic families in normal circumstances get on without difficulty together. But the point of separation comes at formal worship. For example, a Roman Catholic member of the club marrying a Protestant girl was happy that one of the ministers of the Group should conduct the wedding, but not in Church. The same boy has talked at length of matters affecting the Christian faith, but states categorically that he could not take part in any regular

151

Protestant act of worship. There would, of course, be exceptions to this. The fact remains that the value of the Group within the area has been seen to be its willingness to be of service to the whole community, regardless of religion.

"Any action which might undermine this valuable emphasis, giving priority to a separating activity, would seem to the Church of Scotland members of the Group to be wrong. It is possible that, had such a step been taken at the beginning, the situation might have been different. It is possible also that if a Roman Catholic priest were to become a member of the Group again the situation might be different. At present we see it as right to stand, as it were, outside the doors of both denominations.

"It must be stressed that in the minds of the first members of the Group the winning of people into membership of the Church was never thought of as a prime responsiblity of the Group and this was clearly stated in early documents. The concept of evangelism was much more akin to some of the study of the World Council of Churches in which, stated simply, evangelism becomes a moving out towards the community without an initial demand for response. The love, caring and compassion of the Christian community is unconditional. Furthermore, we are faced in the present day by a widely recognised need to discover the nature of the Church set in the heart of the modern secular world and have resisted any pressure from outside to set up even the East Harlem Protestant Parish type of church community."

Trying to sum up the lessons of the previous ten years, he went on: "The Group has never at any point claimed to be providing an alternative to the parish church system, nor to be discovering the new pattern of the Church. It is not to be assumed, therefore, that the conclusions reached after ten years can ever be assumed to provide a blueprint for future developments elsewhere.

"The underlying conclusion after ten years' experience is that the basic idea of the founding of such a group was, and is, entirely right. As an approach to the kind of situations which the group method was designed to meet, there is unqualified agreement within the Group that much of what has been done could not have been done without the setting up of

152

some such structure. This is not to say that all the decisions which have been taken have been the best, nor that the Group has been outstandingly successful in any aspect of its work. It is to affirm that only by such a group could we ever have come to grips with the real situations of the area...

"The fact of living within the area of concern has always been held to be of supreme importance within the thinking of the Group. The value of this has been borne out in two particular aspects: first, the ready availability to people in times of crisis or simply at the times when people want to drop in on us to chat, or talk about important things; secondly, the ability to share with people the sense that Gorbals is home and that Gorbals and areas like it have their own validity and dignity. Traditionally, social workers, ministers, etc. do not live in areas such as Gorbals; thus they stand always as people coming in from outside to change the area or the people living there; right of access to homes is a one-way traffic only and there can be little element of mutuality in the relationship; the clue to the problems and pressures seems to be to get out. Yet there is a real pride and dignity in Gorbals which we believe that the Group has done a little to affirm.

"But we are well aware that living in the area would not have been particularly easy for any one individual in the Group and that the close relationship of Group members has been of invaluable support, not only in the pressures of living in Gorbals, but in the pressures of specific problems and crises...

"The most tragic aspect of our neighbourhood action has been the discovery of the unbelievable gap in knowledge and understanding which exists between the cultures of areas such as Gorbals and the middle-class areas. Partly this is the result of the inevitable distortion and half-truths of the mass media of communication.

Looking to the future, he concluded: "We believe that the partial successes of the Group have paved the way for a whole variety of experimental approaches on similar lines, not only in regard to geographical areas such as Gorbals, but also in regard to different functional areas of society, in particular, in regard to industry. The importance of the small group

153

structure; the value of the close relationship in a predominantly non-ministerial group; the residence within and the real belonging to an area of considerable social pressure; the vitally close relationship of concerned action with the interpretation of Christian faith; perhaps also the 'secularising' of the Christian community—all these seem to us to be important, to be valid and to present a challenge to the Church as a whole. We believe that it is in the willingness of the Church to re-form structures rather than to make marginal reforming alterations of worship or even doctrine that the future of the Church in the inner city lies."

The future of the Group itself was, of course, problematical. By the end of the decade, houses in Gorbals were being demolished and some members of the Group lived in East Pollokshields. Should the Group continue to remain where it was and help plan the new Gorbals, or should it move on to an area such as Pollokshields or Govanhill?

While the internal debate went on the Group continued to be active in the community. They helped in the formation of the Gorbals Action Group, set up to campaign for improvements during the redevelopment. Plans were prepared by Crossroads, of which Geoff was secretary, to launch an appeal for £386,000 to help provide youth facilities for the new Gorbals and to get the ever elusive outdoor centre. Changed days indeed from the times when the Gorbals Group put their assets on the table in Abbotsford Lane.

The old school in Nicholson Street was worn out and the Group rented a flat at 258 Nicholson Street as an arts centre. In February 1969 the actor Andrew Cruickshank opened Centre 258. In another flat upstairs a hostel for young people in temporary need of accommodation was opened. Surely there would be a few spaces on the floor at 74, Cleland Street now!

The crucial event came, however, in May, 1970. At the time it did not seem to be all that significant, but it was destined to change Geoff Shaw's life in a quite radical way.

For it was then that the quiet champion of Gorbals delinquents was first elected to Glasgow Corporation.

Part III: Breathing Life into Caesar
Chapter I
Compassion and Anger

As for you, I tell you what the epitaph on you Scottish dissenters will be—pure, but impotent. Yes, you will be pure all right. But remember, at the price of impotency. You will not influence the course of British politics by as much as a hair's breadth. Why don't you get into a nunnery and be done with it? Lock yourself up in a cell away from the world and its wickedness... I tell you it is the Labour Party or nothing. I know all its faults, all its dangers. But it is the party that we have taught millions of working people to look to and regard as their own. We can't undo what we have done. And I am by no means convinced that something cannot yet be made of it. —

Aneurin Bevan to **Jennie Lee**, 1931.

If there is a god I hope it is Jesus. — **Jimmy Reid**

The meteoric rise of Geoffrey Mackintosh Shaw is one of the most intriguing phenomena of Scottish political life. It is worth rehearsing the bare details.

In 1970 he was first elected a councillor. By 1973 he had become leader of the administration of the City of Glasgow. In 1974 he was elected first convener of the new Strathclyde Regional Council, covering half the population of Scotland. By 1976 he was being quoted as a probable first minister in a new Scottish Assembly. All in six years.

Behind this astonishing timetable lie some fascinating questions. How did such an inexperienced councillor shoot through the ranks of politicians who had been around for years? How did a man so apparently unambitious reach such high political office so soon? How did a Protestant minister rise to the upper echelons of a Scottish party widely acknowledged to be, in the West of Scotland, pre-dominantly Roman Catholic in its make-up?

To understand the more overtly political phase in Geoff Shaw's life it is important to realise that there was no sudden political conversion. Nor, on the other hand, was the move into public political life simply an accidental drift: in fact

155

Geoff Shaw had known defeat at the polls four times before being elected.

Although his Edinburgh background was fairly conservative, political discussion in the family did not follow any given line. His brother Vaughan was a keen Liberal and indeed contested Paisley as a Liberal candidate at the 1950, 1951 and 1966 General Elections. So for Geoff the move into Labour politics was a kind of natural progression. Questions at home, at school, at Cramond, at university and in Malta had contributed to a widening of political horizons; East Harlem had moved him in a more socialist direction; Bridgeton and Gorbals had confirmed his leftward stance, to the extent of being a card-carrying member and then office-bearer in the local Labour Party. It had been a psychological breakthrough for Geoff to vote Labour for the first time; after that, socialism was an integral part of his world view.

The roots of Geoff's political philosophy lay not in Marxism, but in his Christian faith and in his concern for individuals. As he saw what was happening to the casualties round about him he felt increasingly that society should be organised in such a way that fewer people started off life with the dice loaded against them in terms of housing, environment, education and jobs. He wanted the abundant life to be shared and he felt that socialism was the best way for this to be achieved, as well as being the political philosophy most consonant with Christianity.

But there were different forms of socialist vision and different channels of expression: why the Labour Party? The short and simple answer is because the Labour Party was **there.** It was to hand. With a broad power base in the country, it had the opportunity to translate dreams into something approaching reality.

Geoff was a democratic socialist. Sectarian, revolutionary socialism had little appeal for him. And the fact that the Labour Party was a coalition of leftward views of varying degrees suited his reconciling and tolerant temperament.

For Geoff, politics was part of a complete view of life. Care for individuals, theology, community work and politics were all of a piece and he refused to separate them. As with Bill Webber and Don Benedict in East Harlem, it was not enough for him to do ambulance work: real concern for individual people necessitated caring about availability of work, where they lived and the quality of life they had.

Typically, Geoff viewed politics, as he did theology, from the stance of the outsider. What he saw happening to youngsters in Gorbals angered him. Growing up in difficult circumstances, trying to cope with a widespread criminal sub-culture, having little hope of jobs, many of these youngsters seemed to be doomed to failure. Geoff often said that compassion and anger were two sides of the same coin. He loved to point out that Jesus wept over Jerusalem—then strode in to throw the money lenders out of the Temple. He conjured up the picture of Jesus weeping over Glasgow then striding in to deal with the economic and social injustices of the city. Anyone seeking to understand the Geoff Shaw kind of socialism must start with that imagery.

He was not a class-conscious person and he got on well with people from all kinds of backgrounds. He took people at face value. Some saw this as his weakness. When Gorbals boys were derogatory about 'toffs' Geoff would point to some of the Group members and helpers and insist that it was wrong to generalise in this way. He sometimes did use an 'us/them' analysis, though. 'Them' meant the manipulators, 'us' referred to those manipulated. But this was not a class division. Geoff reacted against manipulators—and pompous people—irrespective of their background. Sometimes at church committee meetings if he felt he was being patronised he would be reduced to monosyllabic utterances. Those who knew their Geoff could spot the tell-tale signs of internal anger—a reddening of the neck.

As we have seen, Geoff's political vision stretched well beyond Gorbals. He was concerned about international affairs and, of course, peace. He stood on the left of the Labour Party, because that was where the logic of his personalist views seemed to take him. His political friends, like Norman and Janey Buchan and Neil and Kay Carmichael, tended to be on the left.

He campaigned for Norman Buchan at election times. He spoke at several meetings for him and was a great success with the ladies of Kilmacolm, who found themselves

157

charmed and confused by this well-spoken socialist clergyman. On one occasion Geoff took Alice Cullen, the M.P. for Gorbals, down to Gourock to speak at one of Norman's meetings. The front seat of Geoff's van was broken and the honourable member for Gorbals had to make the journey sitting on a pile of rope in the back of the vehicle.

Mrs Cullen, a couthy housewife, told the Tory matrons: "Where I come fae, no' tae vote Labour is a sin against the Holy Ghost!"

Geoff used to borrow the Buchans' big van for flittings and their tent was used for Gorbals camps. They were part of a circle of people with common sympathies: they wanted to change society radically, by democratic means and their desire for change grew not simply out of ideas, but out of their experience. The heart of this Scottish 'New Left' was in issues like the H-bomb, peace in Vietnam, social justice, extensions to democracy and changes in the penal system.

Neil Carmichael, who was a conscientious objector during the war, was another who influenced Geoff's views on peace and politics.

CND protest and agitation for social change went hand in hand, often in a disorganised sort of way. They weren't always very successful. Geoff helped to organise a big demonstration at Rhu, arranging for a marquee and lots of food. Six people turned up.

"I'll never forget the look on Geoff's face," Janey Buchan recalls, "when he came into our spare room and saw the mountain of food to be disposed of! He always helped us laugh at a good mess and CND was often in a mess.

"His great contribution was that he was always sympathetic. He stopped you climbing the wall. He was able to laugh at things. And he was marvellous at coping with nutters and loonies."

He was also involved in the Vietnam protest movement. There were two main protest groupings in Glasgow—the 'Peace in Vietnam Committee', which was a broad coalition of groups. They sought an end to the conflict in Vietnam, and a negotiated settlement. The Vietnam Solidarity

Committee was more ideologically committed, largely Trotskyist, and they supported the Vietcong. Geoff was joint secretary of the first group. (The treasurer was Margaret Shaw, no relation. Nevertheless Geoff used to get a lot of mileage out of letters addressed to 'Mrs Margaret Shaw, 74 Cleland Street'). He was one of the delegates in a mass lobby of Parliament which hoped to change Government policy on Vietnam. He also took part in several demonstrations in Glasgow.

Geoff was happy in those days to co-operate with Communist Party members on certain issues. Though he rejected totalitarian Marxism, he felt that many Communists were more passionately committed to social justice than some of the Labour Party people. He had a great admiration for Jimmy Reid, then a CP member.

Jimmy Reid remembers: "I met Geoff quite a lot over the years—we had a common interest in Christianity and politics. We were on the same wavelength. He was on the left of the Labour Party, though not ideologically committed. He was very concerned about cultural deprivation and about racism. He was not one of those people who kept their purity by not becoming involved. I always admired him."

Thus, throughout his time in Gorbals, Geoff was involved in politics, both theoretical and active. The move into public political life was not a question of saying I've tried one way and that didn't work, so now let's try something else. Politics had always been part of the way for Geoffrey Shaw of Gorbals.

The only surprise for people was that, out of the Gorbals Group, Geoff was the one to emerge as a full-time politician. Walter Fyfe had always been the most politically active member. (Looking at the Group some people said that John Harvey was 'the minister,' Geoff Shaw 'the youth worker' and Walter Fyfe 'the politician'). Walter's political radicalism expressed itself not only in ideas, but in direct **confrontation**. He saw his political role as not so much reconciling, as exposing inherent injustices and taking action to remove them. A sharp analyst and a belligerent campaigner, he was a passionate political crusader who not only saw the necessity for political battle, but actively relished it. In local organisations, in trade union activities, in rent strikes, Walter Fyfe sought to unmask the oppressors and take the fight into the enemy's camp.

Geoff was too nice for that sort of thing. Too tolerant. Too willing to give the other fellow the benefit of the doubt. Too keen to persuade rather than to fight.

Thus it was never Geoff on the front line during the rent strikes. Direct action caused him anguish. Confrontation distressed him. Conflict was something to be resolved rather than welcomed. In times of political crisis he was not to be found at the political barricades, but at 74 Cleland Street, patiently spelling out his vision of Christian socialist utopia over lukewarm Nescafé.

Why Geoff, then and not Walter? Walter felt his role was to challenge the authorities and to stand on the side of the oppressed against the authorities. To join the local authority would be to become part of the very system which he believed was working against the people he stood with. Walter, who had been instrumental in Geoff's joining the Labour Party, sometimes despaired of the movement and felt it was selling out on its ideals.

Geoff was a very loyal person and once he joined the Labour Party he supported it through thick and thin. So when he was approached in 1967 about going on the panel of municipal candidates he gave it serious consideration. He consulted the Group. Walter's verdict was, it's not for me, but do what you think right. The others encouraged him. The local councillors were not very popular with the Group. They felt it would be good to have their own voice in the City Chambers rather than being dependent on others.

Thus it was that Geoffrey Shaw came to raise the Labour standard in Kingston in May 1967. Kingston, which is not far from Gorbals, had been a Labour stronghold in the past, but by 1967 it was a marginal seat. The Labour Party majority in 1963 was 1,701, but the figure had fallen dramatically each year since then. The building of the Kingston Bridge had cut the rented house population and the Labour vote. In 1967 Councillor Pat Lally, a Gorbals man and a friend of Geoff's, had held the seat with a majority of only 373. The swing to the Progressives (a coalition of Conservatives, Liberals and

Independents) was over four per cent, with no Nationalist candidate standing. There was a Nationalist candidate standing in 1967, so Labour's position was obviously in jeopardy.

The *Glasgow Herald* commented: "This is Mr Shaw's first attempt to enter the Corporation. It will surprise many if he succeeds. Kingston looks like returning its first Progressive councillor for many years."

Nevertheless Geoff campaigned hard. A team of volunteers, some from Gorbals, went round the doors. One of the canvassers, the Rev. Douglas Alexander, remembers their frustration. So many of the houses had peep holes and seemed barricaded. Geoff was more concerned about the fact that people felt they had to do that to protect themselves.

Then came an incident that changed the whole course of the election. Harry Dutch, then *Glasgow Herald* municipal correspondent, telephoned Pat Lally, Geoff's election agent. He asked where the Labour candidate could be found, as he understood he had firm views on the segregation of schools. Councillor Lally's political alarm bells started ringing. The implications were obvious to him. Roman Catholic voters tended to support Labour, but if Geoff made a statement condemning separate schooling, that would be any support out of the window.

He tried to locate Geoff, but couldn't. Harry Dutch did.

The story in the *Herald* the following morning ran as follows:

A Church of Scotland minister who would campaign for the integration of Roman Catholic and Protestant schools is seeking election as the Labour candidate at next month's municipal elections in the Kingston ward of Glasgow.

The Rev. Geoffrey Shaw, an Edinburgh man who has lived and worked in Glasgow for the past 12 years, sees the integration of the schools as the next logical step in the movement towards a fully comprehensive system of education.

"I believe the continued segregation of Roman Catholic and Protestant children at separate schools is one of the main contributory factors to the bigotry and intolerance in our midst", he says.

Mr Shaw, who is 40, has strong views on the integration question and is also a supporter of comprehensive education. He wants to see all fee-paying and selective schools abolished and would support any moves that would provide for the education for all children in Glasgow on a territorial basis.

The chairman for a number of years of CND in Glasgow—he has taken part in Aldermaston marches—Mr Shaw has no difficulty in reconciling his claim to be a left wing socialist with that of being a minister of the Gospel.

"My own particular basis for my socialist principles stems out of my understanding of the Christian faith," he says.

His work in Gorbals has given him first hand knowledge of the city's housing problems and as a councillor, he says, one of his main priorities would be to get people out of the slums and into decent houses.

That was it. The knives were out. The election was as good as over. One Labour councillor, who didn't care for this upstart minister anyway, told Dutch: "You have finished him." Another Labour councillor demanded that Geoff be dropped for ever from the panel of candidates. It became apparent that to vote Labour on this occasion **was** to sin against the Holy Ghost—one cleric went so far as to say that to vote for Shaw was to break the First Commandment.

A local priest preached against Geoff and those who were at worship that day were left in no doubt as to who **not** to vote for. A rather bewildered elderly man, emerging from the chapel, told one of Geoff's canvassers, "I wish they'd make up their mind. They tell us to vote Labour, now they're saying not to."

Geoff went to see the priest concerned to discuss the matter, but to no avail. The friend of Father Mario Borrelli was on the blacklist. Eleven years later the Roman Catholic Archbishop of Glasgow was to read a lesson at Geoff's funeral and go on to describe him as a "personal friend and a dedicated Christian, dedicated to the causes of social justice and to the wellbeing of the people of the Region."

The result of the election was as expected: A. Garland (Prog.) 1260; Rev. G.M. Shaw (Lab.) 1148; G. MacLean (SNP) 580; P. Devitt (Comm.) 80.

Five years later Harry Dutch, who had moved to Edinburgh in the meantime, was appointed Glasgow's first public relations officer. Geoff greeted him in the City Chambers with outstretched hand and broad grin. "My assassin!" he said. Mr Dutch subsequently became head of public relations for Strathclyde Regional Council.

So Geoff's first foray into politics ended in failure. It also pointed up a serious dilemma. To exercise political power on behalf of others you have first to be elected: but to state your views honestly on every issue may cost you the election. Is it right to compromise, to trim your sails in order to be elected? Or should you speak out on all issues regardless of the political consequences?

Refusal to compromise may mean abandoning the political arena to the unscrupulous and thus increase social misery, yet restraint in speaking out may be a denial of the very motivating force that takes a man into politics in the first place. Every politician worth his salt has to work out the issues he would go to the stake for: only purists and cynics find it easy.

The following year Geoff was adopted as Labour candidate in Govanhill, immediately south of Gorbals. That was 1968, the year of substantial Scottish National Party gains and in this predominantly Tory seat Geoff came third with 1820 votes, behind Derek Wood (Conservative) with 2722 votes and Unity Miller (SNP) with 2407 votes.

Geoff meanwhile continued with his other political activities. At a public meeting organised by the Glasgow Committee for Civil Rights in Northern Ireland he deplored the fact that there were people in Ulster deprived of their right to vote because they were Roman Catholics. Saying that he was thoroughly opposed to any form of religious discrimination, he added: "It is tragic that a man like George Wallace could point the finger at Britain in matters of religion and race."

Early in 1969 Alice Cullen, MP for Gorbals, indicated her intention to retire at the next General Election. Geoff, who was secretary of the Gorbals Constituency Labour Party, was approached to stand as a candidate for nomination and the Gorbals Group gave their consent. As constituency secretary Geoff had protested a few months earlier at a proposal by the Boundaries Commission to change the name of the revised Gorbals Constituency to Queens Park. He told the commission that the name of Gorbals had a long, glorious and honourable historical tradition. Their accusation that its only significance was derived from glorified gang fights was grossly unfair. He agreed that the name Queens Park did not have the pejorative overtones that Gorbals did. "Possibly it would have a snob overtone, but that is a different matter," he said.

There were several nominations for the Parliamentary candidacy, but it soon became clear that it would be a straight fight between two men—Geoffrey Shaw and Frank McElhone.

Frank McElhone, Labour councillor for Hutchesontown Gorbals, had a grocer's shop in Gorbals and was well known for his work in the area. People would come into his shop, perch themselves on fruit boxes and make their complaints. His campaign for the Gorbals nomination was managed by Jimmy Wray a local activist. Geoff's most active supporter was the Rev. John Harvey, at that time vice chairman of the constituency Labour Party.

The two clergymen were out-manoeuvred. New Labour Party members suddenly appeared and meetings were (legitimately) packed. The Ward Labour Party usually numbered about ten: suddenly many new people wanted to join.

What was more disturbing was the raising of the religious issue. Stirring up religious feeling was a dangerous business and there were those around who did not scruple to turn it into a Billy versus Dan battle—all the more ironic since Geoff was as much anathema to the Orangemen and the Church of Scotland loyalists as he was to extreme Roman Catholics. It was not the Labour movement's finest hour.

Geoff was saddened, but he refused either to pack meetings or to fight back on the religious issue. Some of his supporters wanted to mix it, but he gave explicit instructions that this was not to be done. He lost the nomination by a very narrow margin—and he remained loyal to the Labour Party.

Some of Geoff's friends were critical of his refusal to fight. Their argument was: either you want the nomination or you don't. If you want it go flat out to get it. Geoff and John Harvey saw it differently.

Govanhill, May 1969: failure again. This time Geoff moved into second place, polling 1559 votes against 2740 for the sitting Progressive candidate, W.C. Hunter. Unity Miller came third, with 1268 votes and C. Campbell (Communist) got 231 votes. Govanhill seemed even more of a Progressive stronghold.

In October 1969 Geoff was adopted as Labour candidate for a by-election in Whiteinch ward. He came third, behind Progressive and SNP. As in all his elections his opponents remember him as quiet, courteous and unflamboyant. Defeat was beginning to look like a habit.

But not quite. In May 1970, contesting Govanhill, Geoff had a stunning success, overturning the Tory majority of 1181 and winning by a majority of 582. The results were: G.M. Shaw (Labour) 3154, W. Shearer (Con.) 2572, R. Anderson (SNP) 865, D. Hardie (Comm.) 129.

Geoff's victory was part of a Labour revival which saw the socialists come nearer to breaking the Conservative/ Progressive hold on the city. It was also a personal triumph.

The new boy took his place quietly at the City Chambers. He was appointed to the General Finance, Social Work and Municipal Transport Committees. He set about learning the business of local authority procedures. He also began to establish himself in Govanhill and quickly gained a good reputation for his ability to deal with complaints.

After his first Kirkin' of the Council Service, at which the magistrates, councillors and officials were present in church in formal attire, Councillor the Rev. Geoffrey Mackintosh Shaw, minister of the Church of Scotland, was asked by one of the dignitaries what he thought of the occasion.

"Hilarious," he said.

Chapter II
Articulating the Fury

Be ye therefore wise as serpents, and harmless as doves.—
Matthew 10.16

Politics is about choosing between inherited blunders of the Fall.—
John F. Kennedy

God grant me the serenity to accept the things I cannot change,
Courage to change the things I can,
And the wisdom to know the difference.— **Reinhold Niebuhr**

At the beginning of the decade Gorbals was tumbling down.
The great Laurieston dispersion was well under way, with its
children being despatched to such promised lands as Castlemilk and Easterhouse—to what Walter Fyfe called the "new
socially controlled one-class areas, the Sowetos and tribal
homelands of Glasgow." Billy Connolly's phrase for the
housing schemes was equally apt—'deserts wi' windaes'.
There were those who found it impossible to sing the Lord's
song in a strange land and as they hung their guitars on the
standard verandahs they wept for their old familiar single
ends. A few of them found their feet standing outside the
familiar territory of 74, Cleland Street, Gorbals.

Demolition was beginning to affect Gorbals Group
members personally and was posing ever more urgently the
question of the future of the Group. And what was to
become of the youth programme? It needed to adapt to the
new Gorbals.

Geoff wrote in the 1970 Crossroads report:

"The policy of Crossroads Youth and Community
Association, in keeping with the thinking of the Gorbals
Group, has always been opposed to large, structured
groups and to the institutional type of organisation and
building. Therefore, looking to the future, we rejected
the idea of a large 'main entrance' youth centre. Instead
we hope, in time, to produce a series of smaller,
individual buildings—a recreation hall, an art centre, a
café club, a workshop, etc. We already have an option on
a piece of ground large enough to include all of these on

167

the same site. But we would like to be flexible enough to retain the possiblity that some of these might be sited in other parts of Gorbals or even in other parts of the city where need arose; and further to retain the possibility, which we have already discussed with the Planning Department, that some activities might be housed in for example, the basement of a multi-storey block.

In the first instance it was decided that we should proceed with the erection of an extended playbarn. The proposal has already been discussed with the Scottish Education Department and with the Education Department of Glasgow Corporation."

Geoff was as busy as ever with young people and 74 Cleland Street continued as a refuge. One problem which constantly agitated him was how best to help young people released from institutions.

In a paper on 'After Care and the Community', prepared for a day conference of the Scottish Association of Voluntary Child Care Organisations in 1970 he argued:

"The general thesis of this paper is to stress that the old-fashioned view that all we have to do is to channel the young person into some local youth organisation is not enough; that the tremendous strides taken in recent years in the improvement of purpose and method in the Approved Schools create corresponding new responsibilities in regard to community after-care; and that it is every bit as important that we should be looking very thoroughly at the supports which the young person is entitled to expect on release from Approved School.

"How best can we summarise the difference between life in the Approved School and life after the return to the community? Quite simply, the salient difference is that in school the young person knows where he or she stands: on return, life is suddenly more confused and more complex. It is the old difference between security and insecurity (and it is always worth remembering that much recidivism is due to an often unconscious need to return to the security of an institution and to the institutional freedom of not having to make all your own decisions.)"

Looking towards Abbotsford Lane.

Molly Harvey, Lilias Graham, John Harvey, Joyce Livingston and Geoff (in 'working claes') with the Group van in Cleland Street before setting out for a CND march.

Inside 74, Cleland Street after being elected convener of Strathclyde.

In approved school, said Geoff, a youngster experienced consistency, care, structure, facilities, self assessment, participation, support. On return to the community many of these things were absent and the youngster was faced with even worse problems.

He recommended that more information on the problems of after-care should be passed to employers; that police should be better trained in this field; that the courts should have a wider choice of disposal possibilities; that parents of young people on licence should meet in groups; and that voluntary help should be used by the Social Work Department.

He also suggested that youth organisations should contact schools and should accept young people on licence where possible; that voluntary youth clubs should consider a much wider variety of informal and open youth clubs and other experimental opportunities. He also advocated the development of experimental advice centres, the provision of unattached workers and the setting up of halfway houses.

On this last suggestion Geoff commented: "There is already growing awareness of the need for hostels for young people who, on release, have no family or proper home to go to. But it is possible also that with the provision of proper hostel accommodation it might be good for some young people to be transferred some months before full release to halfway house accommodation.

"Equally it seems necessary that there should be provision of some sort of training centres in cities. These could be additional alternatives both before and after approved school. This would give the courts another available place before having to commit a young person to approved school—i.e. a form of non-residential compulsory training. It would also provide a transitional period of training on release from approved school to live at home, perhaps thereby shortening the period of compulsory residential training. Finally, there is a case to be made out for some form of work centre which could be the first place of work for a young person released to live at home."

Not surprisingly, Geoff was a strong supporter of the new system of children's panels and he helped to train members of them. The replacement of the children's courts by the panels, which have more informal procedures and which involve members of the community, was a pioneering concept for Britain. It was part of the Social Work (Scotland) legislation of 1968.

Geoff took every opportunity to publicise the work of the panels and urged Gorbals people to become involved. He felt the community must solve its own problems. He wrote in the *Gorbals View* that he hoped the public would see the panel system as a new way of breaking through the old 'hard versus soft' arguments.

"What is important is that a child should get real help to realise his potential, a real discovery of creative freedom."

Creative freedom for youngsters was a constant theme, especially as he considered the new housing to which Gorbals children were moving. Again in the *Gorbals View* he wrote that most people agreed the slums of Glasgow had to go, that fine new housing was a first priority for every family and that there was a need for many more play spaces.

"But not enough of us believe that there is a need to provide, alongside the neat and tidy new houses and flats, places where children can invent for themselves; can dig and build and destroy for themselves; can use imagination for themselves; can experiment with the slightly dangerous height of a high pole or a walkway.

"Of course it could be an eyesore, but adventure and creativity are necessary parts of the development of a child. Take it away from our antiseptic new areas and we will create a generation of unimaginative morons from an Orwell novel. Or else we will produce an explosion of real destruction.

"...Glasgow needs ideas like the adventure playground and the Glasgow Festival. It needs to try new things in new ways. It needs even to make mistakes. Otherwise by 2000 AD it will have become a city without spirit—new, immaculate and dead."

Although he was still deeply involved in Gorbals, political issues began to take up more and more of his time. He was compelled to think through his attitudes on such matters as rents and education.

One of the first debates he was involved in as a councillor was on the proposal by the Progressive/Conservative administration to raise house rents. The motion was passed by one vote. Geoff told the readers of *Gorbals View* why he voted against it.

"Basically the Labour argument is this: there are four main human rights which must be made available to everyone— the right to eat, the right to learn, the right to have a decent place to live in and the right to be healthy enough to enjoy these three. All four should be provided free by the community,or at a price which will exclude no one. (Though everyone equally has the right to pay for what they consider to be a better service if they so desire.)

"Labour has always said that rents should be within the reach of the poorest. But the recent increase imposed by the Tories means that more and more people know that they are being priced out of the right to have a decent house. That is why I voted against the increase."

His views on education were also sharpened by the new Conservative Government's moves.

"Mrs Thatcher, the new Minister of Education, has already withdrawn the order to local authorities to introduce comprehensive education. In other words those authorities which have not yet introduced comprehensive education will not now be required to do so.

"Or will it be simpler if Mrs Thatcher dismantles the comprehensive system altogether? Few will really notice the difference. The end of comprehensive education will not plunge us into economic crisis or international war. It will only knock us back into the leftovers of Dickensian squalor with its jealous safeguarding of privilege, its callous indifference to the needs of the poor, the unintelligent or the slow starter."

Geoff began to find the political scene a relaxation. He appreciated the cut and thrust of debate and his membership of the Social Work Committee allowed him to use his expertise for the benefit of a wider community. He also enjoyed the camaraderie of the City Chambers.

In February 1971 the professionalisation of the Gorbals Group work took a further step forward when Barbara

Holmes was appointed to the Group with a special remit to provide supervision of students on community work placement and with some responsibility for tuition of Glasgow University students. Funding was by the Social Work Services Group. The pioneering work of the Gorbals Group had been recognised and their expertise was seen to be valuable in training a new generation of community work students. Geoff himself was responsible for the supervision of some students on placement from universities and colleges. The Gorbals Group had certainly come a long way. But was it in the right direction?

In May 1971 Labour made sufficient gains at the polls to form the administration of the City of Glasgow. There was a streamlining of the Corporation's committee system and the quiet, hard-working member for Govanhill became sub-convener of the newly-styled Social Work and Health Committee, which had resulted from the new legislation of the Social Work (Scotland) Act. Geoff was appointed convener of the sub-committee on community welfare. In addition he became a member of the Civic Amenities Committee, the Visiting Committee for Perth Prison and the Scottish Council for Health Education.

Within the space of one year Geoff had become sub-convener of a major Corporation committee. Most of his colleagues felt that he was an appropriate choice. Some felt it was time for the Labour Group to depart from the old principle of Buggins' Turn for the appointment of conveners and to give younger qualified people an opportunity to prove their worth. Another significant event was Geoff's election to the executive of the Labour Group—a clear indication of the high regard in which he was already held by his colleagues.

The 1971 session in the Corporation was a time when the new councillors were settling in to the new committee system. Labour had a very comfortable majority, holding 67 seats to the Conservative/Progressive 43, with the SNP holding just one. The major issue coming into the arena—one which was to have a tremendous significance for Geoff—was that of the reform of local government.

The first major re-organisation of local government since

172

1929 had been on the cards through most of the 60s. The publication of the report of the Wheatley Commission in 1969 made it clear how far-reaching and contentious the reforms were likely to be. Wheatley recommended a two-tier system of seven Regions and 37 Districts, to replace the existing 430 elected authorities in Scotland. The Regions were to have housing, education, social work, police and fire, strategic planning, roads and transport, water and sewerage. The Districts were to have local planning, building control, urban development, cleansing, parks, libraries and the other amenity services.

In 1971 the Heath Government published its White Paper altering these proposals by transferring housing to the Districts and it provided eventually for nine Regions, 53 Districts and three Island Councils. The West Region (later re-named Strathclyde), already criticised because of its size, was to be enlarged.

Geoff was soon to become deeply involved in discussion with county authorities which were, in effect, to be abolished under the proposed re-organisation.

But he was not simply concerned with matters of politics. In October 1971 the Gorbals Group was further weakened by the departure of John and Molly Harvey. John, who had latterly been minister of Laurieston Renwick Church in Gorbals, was appointed warden of Iona Abbey. The Harveys had been good friends and he felt a great sense of loss at their leaving. As when all close members of his Gorbals family departed he was very upset. On arrival at Iona John and Molly found the following note from Geoff:

"My dear John and Molly, I never was very good at saying goodbye, and I shall be hard put to it tonight not to make a fool of myself.

"So this is just a note to wish you well, but most of all to thank you. It doesn't seem at all long since you joined the Group, but all that time it has been great just to know you were there, even during the last couple of years when, through my own fault, I have not seen so much of you. Good, too, to share in so many of the Group things, and most of all a rare privilege to be allowed to share so much in your own happiness. And thank you for putting up with

173

the moods! I'll miss you an awful lot. Go well, stay well. With love, Geoff."

Geoff recognised that his involvement with the Group was less, due to his increasing political commitments. The political work was enjoyable and fulfilling and he could see the beneficial results, but he knew within himself that it was being achieved at a cost.

He continued to press on with the Crossroads work, pushing plans for the new Gorbals. His imaginative idea for using the space under the proposed multi-storey blocks was taken up by the Corporation. His proposal was that accommodation should be made available for an art centre, teenage café club, workshop and play centre.

The community work of the Group was increasing all the time. Geoff was asked to write his reflections on their activities in a paper for the Calouste Gulbenkian Foundation. Under the title "The Community Worker: what he does and the skills he requires", he attempted to assess the Group's present experience, skills and failures.

Dealing first with engagement skills he said that the essential element in Group membership had been residence within the area of Gorbals. This had required adaptability to sub-standard living conditions, acceptance of twenty-four hour availability and the ability to distinguish between participation in the life of an area and over-identification with it. Membership of the Group had required the ability to function within the fluidity and flexibility of the Group. There was no Group leader and chairmanship was on a rotation basis.

Turning to the organisational skills he said that the Group had never been very thoroughly organised. Twenty-four hour availability had often meant that the personal time of Group members had been organised by the demands placed on them. He was very conscious of his own failure to involve young people or parents in the organisation of the youth clubs—it was a skill the Group needed to learn.

He went on: "The Group has always considered communication to be perhaps the most important community work skill of all. Specifically, the role of the Group

174

or the Group member is to be the bridge between cultures, levels of education and points of view. This ranges from the simple explanation of a form or a statutory process to the interpretation of basic administrative policies or legal principles. It is true that good government is always seeking to improve direct communications; but there is still a very long way to go and the function of the Group has been to assist in preventing the system defeating the individual or the local community simply by being too complex to understand.

"Violence is often related to the 'fury of the inarticulate' and we have felt that the many conversations with groups or individuals in their own homes or ours have perhaps helped to extend the educational system beyond the school years and to enable people better to express their own thoughts, demands and aspirations. The many appearances with people in criminal court or civil tribunals have been attempts to be articulate on behalf of people; to express for them genuine concerns and even emotions which legal representation can hardly do and which so often are repressed not by intent, but by the weight of procedure and circumstances."

On the subject of political skills he wrote: "The Group has always felt that some members at least should be involved not only in assisting the community to function within society as it is, but to contribute to change through political action. Within the local Party the Group member is required to function as a full member, but to expect no special dispensation from normal political removal from office within a local Party; to accept the importance of the immediate local issues, but also to relate them to wider concerns. The Group has further seen my own election as a councillor as a direct extension of the Group's political involvement, made perhaps more effective by holding office within the present administration and in the Social Work and Health Committee. Plainly one of the necessary skills involved here is the ability to relate Gorbals' needs to the whole social work situation. There is, of course, some tension in this situation. It is perhaps easier to stand outside, but in close relation to, the decision-

175

making processes than to be identified with an administration in the problems and, occasionally, the necessary compromises."

From his new understanding of the difficulties of working from within the system, Geoff was seeing how comparatively easy it was to be part of a pressure group. The activist could press his own case vociferously without having the responsiblity of decision; the councillor, even if he wanted to press his own area's claims to the exclusion of others, was soon forcibly reminded by his colleagues that the world didn't end at the boundaries of his own patch.

Many of Geoff's associates and friends were people who distrusted the local authority and felt that, by and large, councillors were self-interested careerists who didn't really represent the interests of the people. He felt himself increasingly having to defend his position. This argument, he countered, was far too simplistic: if you wanted to change the system the thing to do was to get your sleeves rolled up, get your hands dirty and change it. He also had by now a lot more sympathy for elected representatives who, he now felt, were generally doing their best. At one Gorbals Group meeting he said, "To compromise is to be Christian." By that he did not mean that all compromises were Christian, but simply that in many situations, particularly where resources were being allocated, compromise was the only Christian option. The debate between the outside 'purists' and the inside 'compromisers' was one which was continually conducted not only at meetings, but in Geoff's head.

Although he was in the system, he did not see himself as being part of the establishment. He was not seeking the *status quo*; the point of working within the system was to make changes. What Geoff represented at this stage can best be summed up by the label 'community politics'; that is he felt strongly that communities should have more say in deciding their own destiny, and should have more participation in decision-making. He wanted to democratise politics. He was totally opposed to the idea of major decisions about Glasgow being made by a few unrepresentative people in private caucus. The other side of his community politics was that he wanted more money and staff to go direct to local communities, who would have the responsibility for them. This cut across the prevalent local government philosophy that the only people competent to employ staff and handle money were the local authorities themselves. Geoff was impatient to change all this.

One example from this period will illustrate. A minister in Easterhouse proposed a community project in which two full-time workers would be employed by a local committee to help meet the needs of the area. He approached Geoff, as convener of the Community Welfare sub-committee. Geoff was naturally very enthusiastic—it was right in line with his own thinking—and the proposal was passed by the committee. The first the local Ward representative, Councillor Tom Fulton, knew about it was when he read it in the Corporation minutes. When challenged about the matter, Geoff said that the decision had been made on the basis of a report by the Department, but the only report that could be produced was a letter from the minister himself.

What had happened was that Geoff, in his enthusiasm for the project and his fear that it would be stymied by the traditional philosophy, had out-flanked the local councillors and had taken a short cut. Councillor Fulton's argument at the time was that there were other projects in the area requiring money. Given full consideration, they might have been given priority over the one Geoff had taken an interest in. Geoff, on the other hand, felt that to delay would be to lose a valuable initiative by local people. He feared that the project would be vetoed in favour of something more traditional and less threatening to local elected representatives.

In a number of ways Councillor Shaw was making his presence felt. In May 1972 he was appointed to the Education, and Law and Procedure Committees. As part of his membership of the Education Committee, he served on the sub-committees dealing with further education and religious education. He also became sub-convener of the Social Work General Services Committee and a member of the sub-committee on residential and day centres. A further mark of his growing stature was that he topped the poll for the election of ordinary members to the Labour Group Executive.

This might have been enough for anyone to be getting on with, even for a man as patently capable as Geoffrey Shaw. But there was more to come. In July 1972 Lord Provost John Mains died and suddenly the leadership issue within the Labour Group was in the melting pot. Bailie William Gray, Leader of the Labour Group, elected to go for the provostship, and he won the nomination narrowly against a long-serving elder statesman, David Wardley. Councillor Richard Dynes became Group Leader, Geoffrey Mackintosh Shaw was elected senior vice chairman, with councillor Tom Fulton junior vice chairman.

Thus, in just over two years, the outsider from Gorbals had risen to the position of deputy leader of the administration of the City of Glasgow, over the heads of more senior colleagues. Was it too much, too soon?

Chapter III
The Lavender Hill Mob

The hour is great and the honourable Gentlemen, I must say, are small— **Thomas Carlyle**

When we win in this country, and win we will, one of the biggest changes that is going to come is there is going to be a big sweep-out of the Church. These political priests, the whole ragbag lot of them, will have to go. We want church leaders who will do the job they are supposed to do, which is to look after the morality of the people, and not the Third World.— **John Tyndall,** National Front leader

Here is a scenario. The Rev. Geoffrey M. Shaw, minister from Gorbals, enters politics. A saint among rogues, a politician with a halo, an incorruptible man among corrupt men. He is elected to high office almost immediately.

The person most likely to dispute this 'Jesus Christ, Superstar' theory would be the same Rev. Geoffrey M. Shaw. He never saw himself in terms of sainthood, and he never rated his political colleagues as anything other than good men doing their best—which was, on occasion, a weakness in judgement, if not in charity.

How then do we account for the sudden rise to political power, albeit only city-wide, of a minister of the Church with very little direct political experience? To find the answers it is is necessary to return to 1968. That was the year of the plague as far as Labour was concerned, when the SNP came down like locusts and decimated the socialist ranks. Experienced councillors found themselves out in the wilderness: some decided to call it a day. Thus by electoral defeat, or death, or retirement, or moving on, many of Labour's most able and experienced campaigners were not available. Sir Peter Meldrum. Bill Taylor. And now in 1972, John Mains. The giants of the Labour movement in Glasgow were gone.

At the 1971 elections all but one of the seats lost to the Nationalists had been won back, plus some from the Tory/Progressive administration, which had been in power from 1968 until 1971. A significant feature was that there was an influx of 22 entirely new Labour councillors. These, added to the six newcomers elected the previous year, including Geoff Shaw, meant that nearly half of the Labour Group which formed the majority administration from 1971 was composed of new councillors. And most were on the right side of 40!

This was a new phenomenon for the Labour Party. In the '50s and '60s there had been a dearth of talent coming forward to get on to the party's panel of municipal candidates, possibly due to Labour's dominance during this period and to lack of vacancies—once elected, the councillor of old tended to stay for ever. It is also a fact that Labour's quality of candidates was restricted by the difficulty working men had in getting the necessary time off work. Councillors tended to come from a narrow range of occupations: self-employed shopkeepers, publicans, trade union officials, insurance agents and railwaymen, who were somewhat rare and fortunate in having provision for leave of absence—without pay—included in their conditions of employment.

Thus, in 1972, there was something of a leadership vacuum. An able and articulate person was bound to catch the eye. Geoff's quiet but authoritative manner was impressive. 'Chairman, there is grave concern that...', or 'Many of us are worried...' He spoke the concerns of the back-benchers.

It would be misleading to present the new councillors as a homogeneous group, but the majority of them were young and inexperienced. Often disparagingly referred to as 'the Lavender Hill mob', they stood generally on the left of the Party. They were suspicious of the old guard. Who would be their standard bearer?

In terms of sheer ability Geoff Shaw seemed to stand head and shoulders above the others. He was outstanding. Too much deference is paid in the Labour movement to educational qualifications and he had these in abundance. He was known as a man of integrity and compassion and his track record in Gorbals needed no embellishment. He was a likeable, modest and charming man who actually listened to what other people were saying. He was known to be on the

180

left of the Party, but at the same time a reconciler and a unifier. He had no personal clique around him. He owed no political debts to anyone. He was an outsider. His inexperience was a help, in that he had not had time to make mistakes. His hands were clean and, of course, he was available.

The need to have someone incorruptible at the helm cannot be overestimated. Some Labour councillors and former councillors had recently been convicted on corruption charges. In a cynical climate of public opinion, it was widely felt that they had been unlucky rather than unique. It was a real bonus that Geoff would be immediately recognised as a standard bearer not only of the new left, but also of public morality.

But what of the Protestant minister in a predominantly Roman Catholic Party? Geoff did actually benefit from the traditional respect paid to the clergy. In any case the majority of Roman Catholic councillors liked and admired him and shared his general outlook, and his reconciling temperament helped. His ecumenical work in Gorbals was well-known and in post-Vatican II days, the closer rapprochement of the Churches was an encouragement to Christians of all denominations to make alliance in common causes.

Thus the rapid political promotion of Geoff Shaw was due to a combination of outstanding personal qualities and accidental historical circumstances.

How did Geoff see his own role in politics as a Christian and a minister? Did he regard himself as being in a privileged position, of having special insights? How did he regard the relationship between Church and politics?

In a broadcast interview at this time he gave some clues. He said there was no sense in trying to be of use to people without also trying to change the situation they found themselves in. It was wrong to help people to function in a situation which was basically unjust. What was needed was the **changing** of that situation itself—a process which carried one inevitably into the areas where decisions were made.

Asked about the role of the Church in politics, he said it

was to witness as a body to certain aspects of truth.

"I would question very much whether the Church has traditionally witnessed to what I would consider to be the fundamental aspects of truth—that is another question to look at," he said. "I think the Church as a body may do this in terms of general principles. What seems to me to be tragic is that the Church members assume that because the body 'up there'—the Assembly or the Archbishops or whatever it is— are making their pronouncements, this is the Church's whole function."

Saying that individual Christians should be involved in the decision-making process, he went on: "Politics always have to be concerned with what is possible. At the same time I think there is one function which many people have to carry on in politics, and that is the function of trying to press the limits of what is possible. In other words, to assume that the idea is just not possible and therefore to forget it, is wrong. In politics there is always the compulsion to be pressing as hard as possible to make the ideal possible."

Was there a Christian norm that could be applied in any kind of political deliberation?

"No, I don't think there is. I think it has been customary to say that the Christian ought to be the kind of person who functions in a certain way in politics, or the Christian is honest, or the Christian is nice, or the Christian is concerned, and so on.

"I don't think this is really so. I think some of the most honest people are non-Christian and some of the most concerned and capable people are not Christians. I don't think that Christianity really has much significance at this point. I think there is a Christian assumption that the Christian person is nicer than the others. This is sheer presumption. I wouldn't feel that it applied in politics. But what I think is important from a Christian point of view is to be able to get the **starting point** right. Thereafter you become, in a sense, 'lost' within the political process and legitimately lost. You are no longer saying, 'I am Christian and therefore my decisions are more likely to be right than yours.' You are saying, 'I become simply one part in a political process.' The extent for me to which my Christian understanding of things was relevant was in terms of **choice** of **party.** It was in terms of choice of the whole way in which the political process is going."

Asked in what ways he saw a greater correspondence between the politics of the left and the essential Christian outlook, Geoff said that on the basic underlying issue of economics there was an inevitable question mark against the whole system of capitalism, which seemed to him, from the Christian point of view, to be basically suspect. The concept of sharing could most effectively be introduced within a socialist system.

How could the Church and ministry be regarded as being objective and neutral if it supported one group over another?

"There is a difference, I think, which has to be drawn between the body as a whole and the individual member of it. I would question, though, the assumption that the Church has to be able to give an objective evaluation all the time, and it would be my view that there must be issues on which the Church as a body cannot stay 'objective.' I think there have been some issues outwith Scotland where we have been prepared to cease being 'objective'—Central Africa would be an obvious example. The tendency is for the Church to resort to objectivity at the point at which it is faced with a decision it doesn't like and that is a rather different thing. But I think that the individual within the Church should not be tied by the resolutions of the body as a whole.

"I'm not sure that there is such a thing as somebody who is neutral. I hope there is not. I think that inevitably by being committed to a position you may offend people, you may raise questions which they have not asked or wanted to ask before. But at any rate you are approaching them with some degree of honesty which, I would hope, has its own merit."

To meet all his commitments Geoff was working flat out. The new Social Work Department was in a state of flux and the new Director of Social Work, James Johnston, was, like

Geoff, something of a new boy to local government. It was a difficult period for all concerned.

In social work Geoff's concern for the underdog was very marked, to the extent that some officials felt that those who were not underdogs got less than justice. Geoff was made chairman of a working party on list D schools and he set to work on it with reforming zeal. His work for the Children's Panels was highly valued.

It is interesting to note that Geoff refused to become a magistrate. The seat of judgement, the dressing up, were not for him. He may have thought it likely, too, that he would know a lot of the people in the dock before him!

In BBC's 'Thought for the Day' in October 1972 he pleaded for imaginative understanding of delinquency and not to see the solution simply as birch versus social work.

"I think of countless young men, on the face of it brash and hooligan and violent, each with his own personal hankering for meaning and happiness, each seeing the carefully built edifice of his hope crumbling under the pressures which deep within himself he cannot understand.

"Violent and victim, conformist and law-breaker, all are bound together as human persons. And how do we know the despair of a boy caught in a culture he cannot escape or change and therefore perpetuates? How do we know the despair of a man trapped by a past he cannot undo? What do we know about the futility of counting for nothing? What do we know of fear that stalks the dark streets?

'So I am not pleading for sentimental excuses, for blind eyes, or soft soap. I am saying that unless in our judgements we can begin to imagine the heart of the other, we really were better to keep silence."

In the 1972/3 session the most important political event—and one which split the Labour Group—was the question of the rents of Corporation houses. This had been a sore point over the years, with a majority of the Group being against increases. There had been a desperate struggle in the Labour Group before they reluctantly put up the rents in 1967. Then the Progressive/Conservative administration had raised rents again in 1968, 1969 and 1970. Labour were again in control in Glasgow, but the

184

Conservative Government brought in the Housing Finance (Scotland) Act, 1972, which imposed a statutory review of rents on the Corporation. The Labour Group decided to oppose rent increases and were backed up by a steering committee of Scottish Labour-controlled local authorities.

Councillor Dynes, as Group leader, initially supported the anti-rent increase faction, but latterly, as the Secretary of State for Scotland brought pressure to bear on the Corporation, he bowed to the statutory rule. Geoff Shaw and the majority of the councillors eventually did likewise and the decision to implement the Act was passed after a long period of argument.

Despite his senior position, Geoff was never one of the Group executive 'insiders' and he became the focal point of support for the predominantly new councillors. There were rumblings of discontent with Councillor Dynes's style of leadership. Friends and associates kept urging Geoff to stand against Councillor Dynes at the elections for Group leader in May. Councillor Shaw wasn't so sure. He wondered if he would even win his own marginal seat in Govanhill and he felt he had more than enough on his plate.

In the meantime he pressed on with plans for an extension of local democracy, arguing the need for community councils with 'real teeth and power' once local government reform came into effect.

He told a conference of town and country planners that the pattern was already changing in Glasgow, with the submergence of the idea that a councillor was merely an administrator who resented local interference. The concept of the elected person as the people's representative must be strengthened. Opposing the idea that community councils should consist of 30 people in each area, Councillor Shaw said that the very areas where councils were most needed would be unable to produce 30 at the outset.

"They are most needed in the difficult and ghetto areas," he said. "If we are to get the fight and drive to change our society, then we must have efficient and powerful voices in those areas speaking to the local authorities."

And if he were the leader of the local authority administration would not voices from the ghettos have a better chance of being heard?

Chapter IV
Shaw's Glasgow

The philosophers have only interpreted the world in various ways; the point is to change it.— **Karl Marx**

As for the best leaders, the people do not notice their existence. The next best, the people honour and praise. The next, the people fear; and the next, the people hate... When the best leader's work is done the people say, 'We did it ourselves.'— **Lao-Tzu.**

Councillor Shaw need not have feared for his seat. The electors of Govanhill had found their hard-working representative very much to their liking and in May 1973 they rewarded him with a trebled majority.

A few days later, despite his own strong doubts that he would win the election, he became leader of the administration of the City of Glasgow. The vote was 39 votes to 36. Tom Fulton was elected senior vice chairman and Pat Lally junior vice chairman.

The controversy over the Rent Act had obviously played a part in the leadership contest. Those who were discontented with the Dynes leadership, or who had old scores to settle, voted for the untested Shaw. Many of the younger councillors wanted a change in direction, and a new style of leadership.

Dick Dynes was a shrewd and able politician whose leadership was more in the traditional style. He was blunt, forthright, glad-handing, support-promising and sometimes authoritarian. He had friends—and enemies.

The Shaw style of leadership would remain to be seen. How did he see the job? He wrote in the *Gorbals View.*

"The group leader is not a city boss with individual power. He is the chairman of a group of 83 Labour councillors (the largest group ever!). My main function will be to influence the group in the setting of priorities and to help the committees and conveners in putting through their programme speedily and effectively. At present so many things seem to be of priority importance that it would be impossible to put them in any kind of order, though I have already been involved in a number of talks which help to get the picture clear."

The group leader was, as usual, a man in a hurry to get things done. He went on:

"I hope very much that we will be able to improve our policy-making procedures, so that we in George Square know clearly the framework in which we are all working and can let the public know better what we are doing, and why. I hope too that we can become more sensitive to need on the one hand and on the other to the views and feelings at local level. I hope we can keep on improving the present services and especially we want to get things right in the staffing of the Social Work and other departments prior to the changes in local government in 1975.

I hope we can greatly improve the situation in regard to unemployment among the young; can work for the private tenant; can pave the way for a proper working of the community councils after 1975; can improve the quality of life in the so-called areas of need; can act constructively on the whole problem of homelessness in the city. All these and more will, I hope, be receiving our renewed attention.

Glasgow Corporation has only two years to run before the reform of local government. I shall be doing everything in my power as group leader to see that we prepare the way well for the new administrations which will take over."

By virtue of his position, Geoff became chairman of the Policy Committee. This Committee had been set up the year before, following the publication of studies criticising the way in which Corporation departments acted as independent empires. The Policy Committee was set up to attempt co-ordination of Corporation policy, though it had no real powers. Some of the officials feared the committee, in case it interfered with their own departments. Some councillors were suspicious of it, lest it take away the power that rested in the group meeting as a whole.

The Policy Committee consisted of the Labour Group executive, plus the chairmen of the major committees. Its great strength was that for the first time, the men with political muscle would be briefed together by officials on the costs and consequences of their decisions and get the necessary facts and figures before, instead of after, taking the decisions.

The remarkable thing is that the Policy Committee was the first Corporation committee of which Geoff was the chairman. Leaders of the administration tended to be experienced chairmen of at least one major committee. He found it stimulating to look at overall policy directions and to channel thinking towards the areas of highest need in the city. He also thought it was good that officials should have to justify their thinking and that councillors should have to air their doubts before officials. The Policy Committee was a revolutionary step for the Corporation, but at the end of the day its lack of powers meant that it was merely a nod in the direction which Geoff wanted to follow. He was keen to examine in depth the whole range of policies pursued by the various departments and to establish agreed directions. He also wanted to involve the Glasgow public in discussions of these new moves. The hard fact was that he lacked the experience—and the power—to make the changes he wanted and he underestimated both the intransigence of the departments and the innate conservatism of many of his Labour councillors.

What he did do, however, was to bring about a change in the public mood. His rapid rise to power brought hope to community activists and groups, many of whom were socialist in their thinking, but who felt George Square Labour to be both defensive and unimaginative. Geoff Shaw, with his integrity and his record of community service in Gorbals, had shown that it was possible for a man of fresh ideas to break what they saw as the static pattern established by the born-to-rule 'mafia' and to try to set a new agenda for Glasgow. It was cheering that someone who was so patently idealistic had reached a position of leadership—a man who spoke the language, if not of the common people, at least of the common activist.

But was there really a wind of change blowing through the corridors of the City Chambers? Was Geoff Shaw's elevation to the leadership of the administration really a victory for fresh ideas? Did the comparatively raw recruit from Gorbals have the necessary experience and political skill to formulate a new programme, choose his allies and push it through? It was one thing to articulate new directions, but could he deliver a new deal?

It was not long before some tests came.

In June 1973, the Corporation voted not to implement the average 50p per week increases which the Government planned to take effect from September. The Conservative Secretary of State for Scotland, Mr. Gordon Campbell, sent letters to the 59 councillors who voted against the increases, asking for their views.

Geoff Shaw said he had received one of the letters and was seeking legal advice.

"Some people might find it an attempt to intimidate those councillors who are opposed to increasing rents. I don't think this will work," he said. "Instead it will almost harden opinion."

Councillor Shaw warned that if it reached the stage of councillors being sequestrated the money received would barely cover the cost of the expenses involved.

Sheriff officers going to 74, Cleland Street would not have come away with much.

The Secretary of State set up an inquiry. The reporter was Mr. Kenneth Cameron, Q.C., son of the famous Scottish judge, Lord Cameron, and a former pupil of Edinburgh Academy. The Labour leader told his fellow Academical, there was no doubt that dealing with matters of fact, "the Corporation admit and, to a certain extent claim, they have not increased rents in terms of the present kind of hardship."

He added: "It may be questionable whether there is any value in a councillor addressing himself to a matter where the whole jurisdiction has been removed from the the council anyway and where we are little more than flunkies in the matter of how much rent should be charged. This important function has been taken away from us."

It was no small matter for Geoff to oppose the law. He had an innate respect for the law, but he felt strongly, along with his colleagues, that at a time of wages freeze, repeated rents rises were penalising ordinary people. He was dismayed when he saw tenants, unable to face extra hardship, moving into derelict properties. He had written earlier in the *Gorbals View*:

"No councillor can lightly vote against an act of Parliament, but this Act directly contradicts very deeply held political and social beliefs. I believe I had no choice but to vote No."

This view was not shared by everyone in the Labour Group. One by one, local authorities in Scotland which had resisted implementation, dropped their resistance in the face of surcharge threats and the possible withdrawal of Government subsidies.

With no unified tenant support in the city, the Glasgow Labour Group reluctantly bowed to the pressure of events and voted to implement the Act once more.

Another issue in which Geoff was deeply involved was the final stages of the abolition of fee-paying schools in Glasgow. The former Edinburgh Academy dux was firmly opposed to selective schooling, which he saw as a perpetuation of privilege. A committee of former pupils of Glasgow High School pursued plans to build a new school at Anniesland and there was a lot of acrimony over the Corporation's decision not to grant full and final planning permission after having granted it in principle.

Geoff got the Policy Committee to look at the matter and although two planning sub committees and the planning director had recommended approval of planning permission, the Policy Committee took a different view and instructed the main Planning Committee accordingly. Giving evidence at a public inquiry into refusal of planning permission, councillor Shaw said the Policy Committee, which had been set up to "establish priorities within the administration," was the only body which could look at city-wide needs in education and public open space as a whole. There were, he said six secondary and 21 primary schools close to the proposed new High School in Anniesland and there was a shortage of public open space in the area.

Despite his own background, Geoff felt as a Christian and

as a socialist that there were much greater needs in the city than the building of an independent school. Under the piecemeal Corporation system such a proposal would get through, but the Policy Committee's business was to look at the city's needs as a whole and to work out a system of priorities based on need.

His opponents accused him of deviousness, arguing that Shaw was simply using the land planning argument to mask his hostility to fee-paying schools. Despite disclaimers, they may well have been right. Even Labour's convener of planning felt the arguments were weak.

Much of Geoff's political activities at that time were set against the background of the Conservative Government's measures. Through the Policy Committee, he ordered a survey of the take-up of means-tested benefits. He knew full well from his Gorbals experience that many peole did not get the benefits they were entitled to because they didn't know about them, or they didn't know where to ask, or they couldn't read. Geoff made sure that more publicity was given to this problem.

The Corporation decided to extend the range of free facilities for pensioners in the city. Geoff stated : "We are not greatly impressed by the prime minister's offer of another £10 before Christmas, which will enable people to enjoy the luxuries of bread and bacon and mince without having to worry about the cost.

"Allowing for the fact that basic pensions are still too low, the Labour Group feel we should do everything in our power to make facilities available to pensioners free wherever possible."

Geoff enjoyed the use of political power when things like this could be done: when compassion and anger could find expression in constructive political action.

He even managed to persuade the Corporation to pass a resolution calling for the withdrawal of Polaris nuclear bases from Scotland. Glasgow might not be Calvin's Geneva, but people certainly knew that Shaw was in business.

December 21, 1973. "Councillor Shaw's motion passed

by 58 votes to 18. It criticised the Government, saying it should relax Phase 3 to allow fair wage settlements for miners, power workers and railway men; suspend recent increases due under the Housing Finance Act and withdraw restrictions on public capital expenditure for essential local government services."

By this time, some churchmen were wondering why this revolutionary was still on the payroll.

The firemen's strike in 1973, was an issue which caused Geoff enormous pain. Firemen's pay scales and conditions of service were negotiated nationally through the Fire Brigade National Joint Council and a commission of enquiry, the Cunningham Committee, had been set up to look at national pay and conditions of service. Because of the wage freeze, firemen could not be paid the kind of increase they wanted. Through the strike, the Glasgow firemen attempted to force the Corporation to agree to a local settlement.

As leader of the administration, Geoff was involved in talks. He had a great sympathy for the firemen and wanted to make a local settlement. A package deal, involving the continuance of a payment of 48p which was due to be discontinued, plus a £2 across-the-board "travel allowance," was rejected by the men, against the advice of their union leaders.

Geoff, appointed with Lord Provost Gray and Councillor William Harley to deal with the issue, had to agree to a decision which went completely against the personal grain—to call in the troops. It was anathema to him to bring in the armed forces to deal with a situation in which men wanted what he saw as a legitimate increase. The dispute drained him physically. He was literally grey with worry. Exercising political power could be very costly, especially when the only options were unattractive. Here he was, "blackleg" Shaw, the man who brought in the troops to "break the firemen's strike."

He was also closely involved in the strike by Glasgow Corporation dustmen. He had, not surprisingly, a warm rapport with Mr. Alick Buchanan-Smith (brother of old friends, Robin and George), by now an Under Secretary in

193

the Government. It was a case of Academical speaking unto Academical, on the issue of how to clear the mounting rubbish from the backcourts and streets of Glasgow.

Local Government reform was another pressing issue which needed a lot of attention. At first lukewarm in his enthusiasm, Geoff came to see the potential for good in the situation—new organisations would mean the opportunity for new priorities and new methods to be built in right from the start. His one big fear **was** that the new regions might be bureaucracies run by officials and he warned that back bench councillors must have more say in shaping policies. The Labour Group had largely supported the Government's proposals.

The new set-up was approved by Parliament in October 1973, after bitter arguments about the size of Strathclyde and the role of Glasgow. Geoff learned some hard political lessons in the process. Bearsden and Milngavie, two wealthy suburbs, had been due to be included within Glasgow District area. Councillor Harley warned Geoff about the strong lobby against this and advised him to go to London to keep the pressure on MPs. Geoff, however, had been assured that there was no need to worry and he took the assurances at face value. He was shattered when the vote resulted in the exclusion of Bearsden and Milngavie.

Nevertheless, he saw the new arrangements as a step forward. He said: "A more positive and imaginative stage has been reached. For many, including the Corporation, Strathclyde is not a disaster, but contains possibilities of a new approach to local government, with the region becoming more than just an amalgam of the authorities now in it."

By this, time he was begining to appreciate the difficulties of making radical changes through an established authority, with its own traditions and built-in resistance to change. Would the setting up of a big new authority not be a God-given opportunity to get back to the drawing board?

As leader of the administration, Geoff had been involved in many discussions on future local government plans. On December 4, 1973, the inaugural meeting of the Joint Advisory Committee of Strathclyde Region was held. It

194

consisted of leading political representatives and officials from the authorities covered by the proposed giant council. They elected as their first chairman the Rev.Geoffrey Mackintosh Shaw, a politician of some three and a half years standing, by now one of the leading figures in the Scottish Labour movement. Councillor Richard Stewart of Lanark County Council was appointed vice-chairman and Sir James Falconer, clerk. Sub-committees and working parties were appointed to make plans for the transition to the Strathclyde Region.

The plan was to hold the elections for Strathclyde Regional Council in May 1974. The council would then have a year in which to sort out its own organisation and plans, before taking effective control of its own functions in May 1975.

Geoff like other Councillors, had to make up his mind: would he stay with Glasgow District, or would he opt for the new Region?He might well have been a future Lord Provost in the District Council, but he was genuinely excited by the Region's potential. He decided to stand for the Region.

The next question was: should he try for a safe seat, since his own division of Crosshill/Prospecthill was reckoned to be marginal?He elected to stay put. It was an act of honesty and a political gamble.

The selection of candidates for Strathclyde caused a lot of ill-feeling. Some Labour stalwarts, including Lord Provost Gray, were denied nomination by local associations.

In a public statement, Geoff Shaw denied there had been any rigging or plot in the election of Labour candidates for Strathclyde, but he admitted there had been packing of meetings and inflation of local party membership.

He stated: "Many members of the party, including myself, believe that such inflation is unethical but it is constitutional within the party, it is legal within the law of the land and because it is a purely local matter it makes nonsense of the suggestion of concerted plots." He added that a team of good candidates for the Region was being built up.

The statement represents a subtle and potentially

195

dangerous transition from Geoff Shaw the outsider, the Left wing community representative, to Councillor Geoffrey M. Shaw, insider, public spokesman for the Labour Party.

Although Geoff was a very effective communicator and obvious asset to the Labour movement, there was discontent with his leadership within some of the sections of the Labour Group. Part of the problem rose from his determination to democratise local politics. He did not want decisions made by a small clique to be handed down for rubber-stamping.

This low-key, non-directive approach did not suit everyone. Some councillors were averse to thinking—they wanted to be told what to think. Was that not what a leader was for? All this talk about options was confusing—gimme it in black and white, tell me how to vote!

Geoff refused to be the Tamany Hall Big Daddy, putting his arm around a councillor in the corridor, asking him if he was interested in bailieship and telling him that he depended on him for the big vote on Friday. He was not a "fix-it" politician. He wanted to fix things **in the long term,** although he was not always sure how to go about it. Politics for him was about ideas and radical change and he was keen to promote public discussion of the main directions.

One of his weaknesses as a "political" politician was that he refused to see politics in terms of personalities. If a proposal came up, he would simply look at it on its merits. He would not ask who had put it up and what his motives might be. He invariably gave people the benefit of the doubt and took people at face value. These were good qualities in a clergyman, but they rendered a political leader vulnerable. He was not a political animal, instinctively sniffing out conspiracies and going for the opponent's "jugular". Political con-men and manoeuverers knew how to take advantage of his naivety—and his loyalty. To councillors used to the tradition of strong leadership from the front, Geoff Shaw was a disaster—a leader who could not lead.

Part of the trouble was also that Geoff could be and often was, indecisive. His ideas were clear, he knew the direction in which he wanted to go, but he was not good at quick

196

decisions. Local government is all about decisions. It deals with everything from the siting of a public lavatory to the allocation of millions of pounds. A local councillor is responsible for more decisions in a month than a back-bench MP might be in a life-time. But Geoff tended to vacillate, to play for time. When the options were few and nasty, he looked for ways round them, rather than through them. Sometimes it was due to his imagination and his compassion; he was always searching for fresh ways of avoiding hardship. But some of it was due to a temperamental inability to make decisions speedily. Another factor was that he was by nature a reconciler and a gentle person; he found it difficult, in fact, impossible, to bawl people out or to show someone the door. And he would always make a last-minute attempt to find a consensus.

Geoff's inexperience also showed in the organisation of the office of the Group Leader. Papers accumulated and his office began to resemble 74, Cleland Street! He was not good at delegating work. So things piled up, as more and more choices had to be made. He wanted to be accessible to all members of the Group, some of whom played on his tremendous loyalty. All of this, combined with his legendary conscientiousness, meant that the job was more of a burden than it should have been.

Quite a number of councillors found this very frustrating. A leader who appeared to sit on the fence, who did not make quick decisions, who insisted that they think through the issues for themselves and who refused to use patronage as a political weapon, was no leader. Others were unhappy because after nearly a year in office, he had not been able to make any great changes in the system, even though his personal contribution had been enormous. The millenium had not come. And now that he was Group Leader, Geoff was himself part of the establishment, someone to be rebelled against!

He had also clashed with some of the senior members over the Group's policy towards the ill-fated Clyde Fair. This attempt at a Glasgow festival was very much in line with the kind of thing Geoff believed in. He wanted the Labour Group to support it. But the Fair's internal administration

197

had not been very efficiently run and the Group decided to withdraw support. Geoff stubbornly dug his heels in, arguing that there were always risks with imaginative ventures. His attempts to have the matter reopened and pushed through caused antagonism. Needless to say, disciplining errant members of the Group was also something which Geoff found very distasteful.

The criticisms came because Geoff Shaw was no longer a new boy. He was the standard bearer, the leader and had to be judged accordingly.

The complaints have to be seen in the context of a widespread recognition of Geoff Shaw's immense strengths as a person and a political leader. Even those who disagreed with him admired him for his fairness, his tremendous ability, his integrity and his compassion. He had the capacity to rekindle flames of idealism in tired politicians and the ability to make sense of things to the man in the Glasgow street.

What was easy to forget was that the leader under scrutiny had been in public life for less than four years.

Chapter V
A Week in Politics

The gates of hell will not overwhelm the Church; it has opened its gates to hell too often. It zealously inveighs against the harm done to Joesph and the sheep, but it has made its arrangements with the upper classes and serves as their spiritual defender. It bristles at see-through blouses, but not at slums in which half-naked children starve.—

Ernst Bloch.

A week in politics is a long time.— **Harold Wilson.**

With the increasing intensity of Geoff's political commitments, it was obvious that something had to give. There were not enough hours in the day to do political work, to work hard in Gorbals, to be fully involved in the Group and to be on call for delinquent youngsters.

The life of the Gorbals Group had changed. With the departure of the Harveys to Iona and the Andersons on a round-the-world yacht trip there was much less sense of permanence and continuity. Everything seemed provisional and day-to-day. Only two of the old-stagers were left—Lilias Graham and Geoff. The other members of the Group were Norah Trundle, a retired insurance secretary who worked with the Hen House; Marjory Laing and Hilary Hendry, social workers; Joyce Livingstone, nursery school teacher; Anne McPherson, leader in charge of Glendale centre in East Pollokshields; Doreen Robertson, a teacher at Hayfield Primary School; Betty Malik, a housewife involved in the Glendale Playgroup and Christian Action Tenants; and Peter Ives an American Congregational minister and his wife Jenny. The majority of the group now lived in East Pollokshields or Govanhill.

Although there had never been a formal leader of the Group, Geoff was looked up to as the leader and things tended not to happen till he arrived. But because of the pressure of political work, Geoff was often not able to come till half way through the evening.

Not surprisingly, the worship of the Group had been weakened by the regular presence of people who saw no point in praying.

Communion, once the central, unifying act of the Gorbals Group, had been switched to the end of the evening, at which point the non-worshippers left. Putting Communion to the end was perhaps symbolic of what was happening. Lilias Graham felt it was the beginning of the end when someone asked at a Group meeting, "Are we having Communion tonight or aren't we?" Even though the Gorbals Group had often argued about worship, Communion had always been at the heart of a Thursday evening meeting. It was now becoming an afterthought.

The Group—and Communion—still meant a great deal to Geoff, but he knew within himself he wasn't giving enough time or attention to the life and worship of the Group.

Nor was he able to give enough time to work in Gorbals. *The Gorbals View,* which had been subsidised by the Group to the tune of several hundred pounds and which had survived several crises, was now published from Barbara Holmes's office in Crown Street. Miss Holmes's work was proving effective. She was involved in advice and representation of Rates Valuation Rent Appeals, support for tenants associations, provision of information on welfare rights, **assistance** in the setting up of a day care centre for the elderly and a new pre-school playgroup and the training of students.

Crossroads was going strong and Geoff was still engaged in running summer camps for youngsters. In June 1973, the Playbarn, costing £37,000 was opened. Ian Ferris who had been a member of the Group for two years, was appointed to run the Playbarn programme, with another leader, Andrew St. John, responsible for conducting an informal programme amongst younger children.

In September 1973, Ian Ferris was tragically killed in a climbing accident in Switzerland. Geoff conducted two memorial services, one in Community House and the other at the top of Buchaille Etive Mor. At the Community House service, Geoff was overcome and asked everyone to close their eyes in memory of Ian while he recovered. At the mountain top service, he put everyone at their ease by saying "Ian's probably sitting on top of that cloud laughing at us!"

Gorbals, by this time, was a mixture of derelict houses, gap sites and rising multi-storey flats. Geoff's proposals for the community use of spaces under the "multis" were accepted—the first venture of its kind in Scotland. In one of the spaces, accommodation was provided for a further extension to the community work training programme under the direction of Richard Bryant.

But where was the Gorbals Group going? No new ideas were coming forward. Much of the dynamism had gone. Some of the work was now happening in Govanhill and East Pollokshields.

In the Group report to the Home Board, Geoff wrote: "The Group believes it has a considerable contribution to make not only in the changing area of Gorbals and in the gradually deteriorating areas of East Pollokshields and Govanhill, but also in the wider world of social and community work.

We appreciate the continued interest of those few church people who have been concerned with the work of the Group and many of the people in the field of social work whose support and interest have been of immeasurable value."

Recalling the foundation of the Group in 1957, he went on: "The Gorbals Group continues through its life and activities to attempt to implement its original purpose—"to provide in the area a caring Christian presence." This service is summed up by the repetition, during the Communion service at the end of the weekly Group meetings, of these words—"The Spirit of the Lord is upon me, because he has anointed me to preach the Gospel to the poor; He has sent me to heal the broken-hearted, to preach deliverance to the captives and recovering of sight to the blind; to set at liberty those that are oppressed and to proclaim a year when men may find acceptance with the Lord." The Group has always believed these words to join to join together the responsibility both to express, usually in the privacy of our own homes, the grounds of our faith and work out in practical detail the requirements of service to the exploited, the delinquent, all those who have brought their needs to our door."

Geoff drew strength from the Group—whenever he could. It was still his family, the place where he could be himself. From time to time, especially when the political pressure was on or when he was feeling impatient about the lack of effect he felt he was having, he was not the best of company. One of the members said, "It may be that he can rely on our support, however depressed or frustrated he was in his pursuit of progress in the change of minds to a better understanding of how best to achieve happiness, or satisfaction, or a better life, or what everyone is really looking for—perhaps the Kingdom of God on earth."

No wonder Geoff was moved to tears when Lilias Graham, whose house was in danger of imminent collapse, announced her retirement from Gorbals. Her plan was to work for a spell in South Africa, then to return to Scotland to run a house for families from deprived areas who need a holiday, at Thornhill, near Stirling. Lilias had been a much loved friend and support.

A revealing glimpse of Geoff and the Group at that time comes from Rev. Peter Ives, the American minister who was a member for three years. He had the opportunity of reflection with Geoff about what the Gorbals Group experience meant.

"Whenever Geoff spoke to us about the Gorbals Group and he did so often during the years 1971—74, he used the term "Christian presence" frequently in the discussion. Geoff had other ways of describing the work and the purpose of the Group, but none that seemed so meaningful to him as the idea that it was a 'presence' in the heart of the Gorbals. Once I asked him if the term "presence" wasn't too passive a concept to describe the dynamics of Christian diakonia. "No" he said, "I use the term intentionally, to emphasise the importance of living in the community one is serving." For Geoff, this meant a total involvement in the life of the neighbourhood and it was his commitment to this principle that explains why he resisted leaving his apartment in Cleland Street, even long after he had become a city councillor.

"Ministry was expressed in secular form as social work, group work and community organisation. Rarely was the

Gospel proclaimed in explicit language during daily conversations and there was no proselytising for the institutional church. Yet most people, both within and outside the Group, were well aware that the Gospel was implicit in all that was said and done. Geoff himself struggled with the tension inherent in Christian witness of when to speak explicitly about one's faith and when to remain silent.

"At the same time, let no one doubt that Geoff did a great deal of theological reflection on a day to day basis. One only became aware of this insight when one listened closely to his words and the readings selected during the Thursday evening Group meeting and Communion service. Before Communion was served, it was Geoff's custom to read selected passages from such books as Bonhoeffer's *Letters and Papers from Prison,* Alan Paton's *Instruments of thy Peace,* and Bonhoeffer's *Ethics.* These passages were not simply selected at random; he had obviously spent some time thinking about the readings, for they always spoke in a meaningful way to some concrete problem of concern that the Group was facing.

"What about the future of the Group? Geoff did speak to us at great lengths about the future during informal chats in his living room. Basically, he had two thoughts in mind. The first option was to take seriously the fact that the new Gorbals would no longer live in tenements, but was about to to occupy large high-rise flats. If the Group was to be a "presence" in this new community, it needed, also to occupy apartments in these buildings, in much the same way that Group members had lived in proximity within the tenements.

"But it was also becoming apparent to Geoff that many of the Group's members were already moving to other parts of Glasgow (Govanhill, East Pollokshields) and that perhaps, it would never be possible again to talk about living in close proximity within one building or neighbourhood. In other words, the Group of the future would simply be those who continued to identify with the on-going work of the organisation and met regularly on a Thursday evening for fellowship and Communion. One option projected the vision of the Group's earliest goals, only now within the context of the high rise apartments; the other option was more tailored to the changing nature of the Group itself. My own feeling was that Geoff deeply hoped a younger generation within the Group would commit itself to the first option, much in the way that Geoff, Walter and John had committed themselves and their work to the old Gorbals. Not only would he have liked to have seen a new Group moving into the Stirlingfauld Towers, but I'm sure he would have joined the move also."

All of the Group spoke warmly of Geoff and with great admiration for him as a person and as a Christian, as they remembered him in the good times and the bad. Let Peter Ives' words sum it up for them—"His presence was so powerful, his commitment to his work so great and his compassion so all-encompassing that it will be impossible to think about the Gorbals and Glasgow without Geoff. He taught Jenny and I, by his example, more about the nature and meaning of the Gospel and Christian ministry than any other person we have ever known. We feel so fortunate to have been able to know him and to have lived and worked for a short item with the Gorbals Group. There was something about his goodness, his warmth and his vision that we never want to forget. We would have loved to have had our children know Geoff as we knew him, but since that won't be possible, perhaps we can pass on to them the something of what Geoff gave us, in the way we live our lives in the days ahead.

"One of his favourite prayers was St Francis of Assisi's "Lord, make us instruments of thy peace." Surely, his life was such an instrument. He was a wonderful man who expressed his faith in the way he lived. How much we will miss him, and yet how fortunate we all were to have known something of his love and his love of life, there in the heart of the Gorbals."

In the heart of Gorbals—a Christian presence. None more so than at 74 Cleland Street, where Geoff continued to act as host to waifs and strays and drunks and despairers. Political and CND colleagues knew that the best time to phone Geoff was between one and two in the morning—

they would be sure to get him then. Rab Hyland, who stayed at No. 74 for a spell, and who used to sit up at night talking with Geoff about politics and peace, said: "Geoff was a father figure to all of us. He would never let anybody down. He even refused to go ex-directory in case someone was in trouble and wanted to get in touch with him."

As always Geoff drew strength from the warmth of the Gorbals people like Mrs Roseanne Irvine. "Geoff was a good, good friend, the best I ever had. He could sit down at the table with you. He was a personal pal—he was at all my daughters' weddings. My children went to his clubs—he would never shut the door on anybody.

"I had a job at Bedford Street Nursery and when the bus strike was on Geoff went and got my pay for me. That's what he was like. He used to say to me: "You and me's the same Roseanne." When he buried my man, he wept."

At Rose Irvine's wedding to Jimmy Donachy there was a mix-up, with the priest not being present on time. Mrs Irvine ran up to Geoff and to John Harvey at the back of the church and said: "Tae hell wi' this, wan o' youse'll have tae marry her!"

The Christmas Eve service at No. 74 was an annual event which everyone enjoyed. Geoff would read some scripture and a passage from Bonhoeffer and would ask everyone to remember friends who had gone away or were in prison. They would all sing carols, then have sherry, cake and coffee. At one such service, when the carols were being sung, a boy who was staying in the house came staggering into the crowded room drunk.

"Why don't you go to bed?" suggested Geoff. "Because you're standing on it," was the response.

All this time Geoff continued his 24-hour availability. Whatever else might need to be cut from his programme, time for those in need was not.

He took a group of Gorbals youngsters to see Billy Connolly at the King's Theatre and enjoyed the lads' excitement when they went backstage to meet the comedian. Geoff had known Connolly long before he was a star and he could repeat some of his Glasgow sketches word for word.

He also appreciated Billy Connolly's so-called blasphemous sketches. Geoff himself was always ready to poke fun at religion or even to parody it, precisely because he saw how near to idolatry religious attitudes could be. Nevertheless, his willingness to do so, and to 'take off' the Authorised Version, brought raised eyebrows. There was a similar reaction to his enjoyment of Connolly's Glasgow street humour. Geoff liked the quick repartee and the bawdy humour of Gorbals, a fact which disconcerted Christians of a more conventional stamp. His view was that the Church had too much to say about what he felt were comparatively trivial matters, while remaining silent about the 'obscenities' like the build-up of nuclear weapons.

He once borrowed a book by an American friend—an academic treatise called *The Rationale of the Dirty Joke*. When it went missing from the City Chambers there were endless jokes at Geoff's expense. He never seemed to mind.

As time went on he found the days exhausting and fulfilling, frustrating and exhilarating. He was helping to make political changes which he felt would bring future benefits to people in Glasgow—and yet, there was always self-doubt. Was it really worth it? Was he achieving what he wanted to achieve? There were full days in the City Chambers, evenings in Gorbals, nights with despairing people, telephone calls, more letters to type at 2.00 am, or even 6.00 am. It was at this time that Geoff left letters in his desk marked 'To be opened in the event of my death,' giving instructions about his funeral and the disposal of his meagre property. Did he have a premonition that he could go on at this pace for ever?

May 8, 1974. Elections for Strathclyde Regional Council, Crosshill/Prospecthill Ward. G. Shaw (Labour) 4,508; L. Dorfman (Conservative) 2,748; D. McKellar (SNP) 2,546; A. Stewart (Communist) 139. Majority: 1,760. The *Glasgow Herald* described it as a 'surprisingly comfortable' majority in a seat which had been regarded as 'somewhat marginal.'

It was a good campaign. The constituency party chairman, John Kilmartin, remembered how Geoff had got angry when someone suggested he canvass through the churches.

"He refused to use his status as a minister in any way. Nobody could corrupt Geoff Shaw. He had tremendous strength of character.

"As you get older and mellower, you look around for people without personal ambition. Such people are rare. Geoff Shaw was a genuine giver. He didn't exist for himself—he was a man with a mission. I liked him and respected him.

"He was not flamboyant at all. He could sit quietly at a meeting, but you'd know he was there. When he did stand up, he had something worthwhile to say. The Labour Party won that seat because of Geoff Shaw.

"He was in politics because he had a social concience. He really cared about people. I remember him going at two o'clock in the morning to bail someone out. I said, "that boy's a lost cause." Geoff said, "No.""

"I miss him for what he stood for. He was a giant among pygmies."

May 13 1974. *The Scotsman.* "Minister is chosen to Head Strathclyde."

"The man who will eventually become almost as powerful in Scotland as the Secretary of State was named yesterday by Strathclyde Region's ruling Labour group as Councillor the Rev Geoffrey Shaw of Glasgow.

"He will be Labour's nominee for the post of Convener of the Region, which takes in half of Scotland's population, at the statutory Regional Council meeting next Monday, 20th May. His confirmation in office is a formality, as Labour hold 71 out of the 103 seats on the new council.

"....He is fairly far "Left" within the Labour group—he led the Corporation's defiance of the previous Government over implementation of the Housing Act right up to the end; he takes part in anti-nuclear protest marches and as sub-convener of Glasgow social work committee he has initiated some sweeping reforms.

"But equally he enjoys the friendship and respect of most of the Conservative councillors in Glasgow."

Some churchmen didn't know whether to cheer or cry. "Involvement in politics" (meaning statements at church assemblies) was one thing, but political chairmanship of

207

half of Scotland was another matter altogether. If there was anything worse than a politician, it was a successful politician, particularly when he was a Left wing socialist to boot.

Geoff told Jack Webster of the *Daily Express*: "The Church has been far too silent in terms of the exploitation which is still there in our communities. I don't think it is necessarily the function of the Church to attempt to give the answers, but I do feel it has a strong responsibility to make the public aware of the pressures under which many people have to live."

Councillor Shaw's electoral triumph was sweeping. He had gained the convenership outright on the first ballot—polling 38 votes, as against Councillor Dick Stewart, deputy leader of the Labour Group on Lanark County Council, with 21 votes, and Councillor William Paterson, Convener of Ayr county Council, with 11 votes. Councillor Stewart was elected Labour Group leader, Councillor Charles Gray vice convener, Councillor Paterson depute group leader and Councillor Ronald Young, group secretary.

So at the age of 47, exactly four years since his entry into local government, Geoffrey Shaw was political head of two and a half million people.

Why? Mainly because of his record and his known personal qualities. Strathclyde was a new venture and most of the new councillors, from many different parts of the West of Scotland, only knew a handful of their colleagues. Geoff Shaw was known not only through his public appearances, but also through his work on the Regional Advisory Committee. He had no personal clique around him. He was a reconciler. If he was politically ambitious, it was not obvious. Strathclyde was a brand new venture and one which was not popular in the public mind—there were fears about its size and its possible extravagance. What could be better, in terms of a brand new public image, than appointing as front man, a clergyman with a simple life style, widely known to be incorruptible, Mr. Clean himself? His very inexperience was seen as an asset. He would not be hidebound by old systems, or owe political debts to too many people. Shaw was the obvious choice.

There had been fears that Glasgow would dominate Strathclyde. The election of the main office bearers showed a desire for geographical spread and Geoff Shaw, Glasgow's main representative,was known for his fairness: he would not promote Glasgow's interests at the expense of other areas.

But if some of the representatives had seen the Rev Geoffrey Shaw as a mere front man, they were in for a disappointment. Geoff was not in politics to be a figurehead. In considering whether to stand, he had rejected the role of Convener with ceremonial powers only. The Lord Provost of Glasgow represented the city at functions, but took no part in the political process: Geoff was not interested in that kind of role. He had not moved into political life to be a talking head on television. He had given up the possibility of the chairmanship of a major committee,such as Social Work, in order to influence the political choices of the giant Region. So he would only be convener if he were also chairman of the powerful Policy and Resources Committee.

In his time at George Square, Geoff had seen the potential of the Policy Committee as an instrument of change. A central co-ordinating committee which could review the whole range of policy and set out priorities would be a real asset for the new Strathclyde Region— provided it had powers to make enforceable decisions. That was exactly what was envisaged in the new Policy and Resources Committee.

The Labour Group agreed, by a narrow majority, that the Convener should be chairman of Policy and Resources. It was to prove to be a fateful decision.

Commenting on the choice of Geoff Shaw, Claude Thomson of the *Glasgow Herald* wrote of the man he first met in Malta. "No one is more conscious of the responsibility of leading the Strathclyde Regional Council in their task of improving the quality of life within its boundaries than Geoffrey Shaw, the Glasgow minister who within four years has shot from being virtually unknown to the general public to becoming one of the most familiar names in Scotland.

"......Geoff Shaw cares deeply about people, particularly those requiring a helping hand from the community. While he appears a rather academic political figure, he is highly articulate and has a penetrating ability for formulating policy.

"Whether he has the iron in his soul to lead the administration in Strathclyde has yet to be proved. As chairman of Glasgow Corporation Labour Group, by no means an easy body to control, he has irked his colleagues at times by a reluctance for incisive intervention and decisiveness in settling disputes."

May 13, 1974. *Glasgow Herald* "Dynes Beats Shaw by Two Votes."

"Councillor the Rev Geoffrey Shaw, who at the weekend was chosen to lead the Labour administration on the new Strathclyde Regional Council, was yesterday defeated in a bid to remain leader of the ruling group of the Corporation.

"......Mr. Shaw said that while he would very much like to have continued the work he had been doing in the Corporation, he would now be able to devote even more time to the work of the Region. The important thing was to get full co-operation between the Region and the District."

The pro-Dynes faction had lobbied hard and had pulled out the votes of the firm and the infirm. The campaign had been able to capitalise on a certain amount of anti-Strathclyde feeling, as well as on Geoff's weaknesses as a leader.

As in the case of the Parliamentary nomination, Geoff had known about the campaign against him, but he refused to fight. Given his Strathclyde election, the 37—35 vote against him was by no means discreditable. Councillor William Harley, a close friend, who had advised Geoff not to stand for re-election, was pleasantly amazed by the size of the pro-Shaw vote. And Geoff had the personal satisfaction of topping the poll in the elections for the group executive.

As it was, the result was no bad thing. He was able to direct all his attention to the working of the new Strathclyde Council. He was determined that it should not be just a piece of reorganisation, but a far-reaching democratic experiment in Scottish political life.

Chapter VI
Present at the Creation

I have a dream today—that freedom will reign from every hill and molehill in Mississippi—from every mountainside, let freedom reign—and when this happens, when we allow freedom to reign, when we let it reign from every state and every city, we will be able to speed the day when all of God's children, black men and white men, Jews and Gentiles, Protestants and Catholics, will be able to join hands and sing in the words of the old negro spiritual, 'Free at last, thank God almighty, we're free at last.'—　　**Martin Luther King.**

I was to learn later in life that we tend to meet any new situation by reorganising; and a wonderful method it can be for creating the illusion of progress while producing confusion, inefficiency and demoralisation.—　　**Petronius Arbiter,** circa A.D. 60

Strathclyde Regional Council was officially inaugurated on Monday May 20, 1974 amid a mixture of cynicism, apathy, hostility and not very much optimism.

Rev. Geoffrey Shaw was formally elected Convener by 70 votes to 22, the other candidate being Councillor Leonard Turpie, leader of the Conservative Group.

In his first speech as convener, Geoff spelt out how he saw the tasks ahead.

After welcoming the new members and insisting that important executive decisions would be taken in the forthcoming year, Geoff went on:

"A host of questions about Strathclyde Regional Council itself are in the minds not only of members of the Council but of the public as well. Where will we meet? How often will we meet? What sort of committees will we have? What traditions of local government will we follow? The answer to these and many other questions are quite simply this, we do not know. The reason that we do not know is that it lies in our own hands to decide the answers. The Act has laid down a certain number of provisions but with the exception of these it is open to us as a council to shape our own future. I personally hope that we will move in some ways beyond some of the traditional formalities which may have

211

become with the passing years a little meaningless. I hope at the same time we will create for ourselves a structure which makes for clarity of thought and decision and which lets us all understand what we are doing, how we are doing it and how the other person is acting within the council."

Pointing to the need for more democracy and accountability, the Convener said he looked forward to a wider degree of co-operation with representative bodies of the public, with the universities, with the trade unions and with the community councils to which he personally looked as major sources of information and public opinion in the conduct of council affairs.

"Of course there may be difficulties with the community councils when they are set up," he went on. "Of course at all times they will not be patting us on the back and saying that we are doing a good job, but it seems to me that they can be of enormous significance within the whole process of local government provided we take them into our confidence at an early stage and ask them for their assistance in some of the decision-making process in which we will all be involved. I firmly believe that the more sensitive we can be to local opinion, the more effective will be our government of Strathclyde."

Turning to the problem of corruption, he continued: "This is at a time when recent events have cast a long shadow of suspicion across the conduct of local government affairs. I have no doubt whatever that the honesty and integrity of members here present provide the one perfect safeguard against any misconduct within our council. I have no doubt also that while I hope that there will be tolerance and understanding of each other in all other aspects, in this one regard the council and the various groups within it will be resolute in their action towards any breach of faith with the public, but it is my belief that it is not enough to ensure that the conduct of all our affairs is above board. I believe the public has a right to know that it is so and I hope that together we will very shortly set our minds to devising a machinery of scrutiny, particularly in regard to the matter of contracts, in order that the public may know for sure that we have taken every precaution to prevent any misconduct such as has appeared in other parts of the country over recent years. We owe this to 2½ million people."

Saying that local government was all about caring for people, the convener warmed to the theme which was to stamp his years in office. He recalled that a few months previously a useful piece of research had been published by the National Children's Bureau about disadvantaged children; those who belong to a family which either had only one parent or had five or more children, was badly housed and had a very low income. It had been found that in Britain as a whole, six percent of children were disadvantaged and that in Strathclyde the corresponding figure was 12 percent. Glasgow was higher still. What this meant in more obvious terms was that in the average British classroom, two children in the class lived in very poor circumstances. In the average Strathclyde classroom there were four and in the average Glasgow classroom there might be up to eight.

"We need to realise that these children live, too with their families and the figures mean that in Strathclyde as a whole, there are twice as many families in proportion to the population who are poor and badly housed and in one-parent or large families, as there are in Britain as a whole," he continued. "These are not just figures to play around with for fun, because the report also proved that what actually happened to these children is very serious. As compared with other children, the disadvantaged children are less healthy, do badly at school, are more likely to be delinquent, are smaller and have parents who are much more often unemployed. It is quite right that the title of the report asked the question 'Born to Fail?' It will be our responsibility to take note of reports such as this, to make sure that children in Strathclyde are not born to fail. It will be our responsibility in the council to care profoundly about the needs of the people who live here."

So Strathclyde was officially under way, pointed by its convener in the direction of the needy. Geoff's life was soon meetings, meetings, meetings; looking at committee structures, working out procedures and appointing officials at salaries several times higher than the convener had ever earned.

Many of the meetings and seminars had to do with organisation. In 1973 the government had set up a committee of local government officials in Scotland to study and make recommendations with regard to the committee and management structure which might be adopted for the new Regional Council. This became known as the Paterson Committee and Geoff had some misgivings about their recommendations. They advocated a system of corporate management, designed to end the competing empires of the old authorities where Housing warred with Planning and Highways ignored both in drawing up its roads programmes. Corporate management meant, in brief, that heads of departments must combine and not compete, to ensure the objectives of the council were achieved. In theory, it would be a new and sophisticated clutch, ensuring smooth and economical performance, responsive to the driver's pressure and changing gear quickly and cleanly. But what if the clutch dictated the driving?

Geoff, influenced by Ronald Young, a lecturer in local government studies at Paisley College of Technology, was worried about the new set-up becoming a large bure-aucracy, with elected members not having a very formative role. They wanted more democracy at the grass roots. Geoff was keen to delay the establishment of the traditional committees which parallelled the departments and produce a new kind of political structure which would have more control over policy. Geoff wished to set up more and more working parties to study this problem, but decisions about structure and staffing were urgently needed. He had not thought out the alternatives clearly enough and lacked the political and administrative experience to formulate a structure which would be both democratic and efficient, to tell anxious and impatient officials to keep on waiting and to line up supporters and to get the programme through. The Paterson proposals were more or less adopted—after delays which officials found frustrating—although some significant changes were made later, in the shape of an informal group of members and officers who produced the Multiple Deprivation report, the setting up of two Policy Review

214

groups and five Social Work member-officer groups.

Geoff conscientiously cultivated good relationships with the 19 Districts in Strathclyde Region. He held regular meetings to deal with matters of co-ordination and his low key and reconciling manner defused some potentially explosive situations. A few of the District heads were rather prickly and pompous and Geoff, as convener of a huge Regional authority, appeared rather diffident and self-effacing beside them. Some District authorities laid on big lunches when Geoff came. He made his feelings known these were working lunches rather than state visits and pie and tea would be just fine!

Perhaps the most potentially explosive relationship was that with Glasgow. Feeling in the City Chambers about Strathclyde was mixed, ranging from mild approval to paranoia. Some councillors and officials had never approved of the giant region; others were resentful because of their failure to get nominations or jobs. The fear that Big Brother would dominate was fanned by press descriptions of Strathclyde elected members as 'super councillors.'

The combination of professional jealousies and personal rivalries could have disrupted the whole Glasgow-Strathclyde relationship, but convener Shaw won not a few admirers by the good-humoured way in which he handled the situation. Indeed, one of his outstanding successes during his period as convener was the skilful and assiduous way in which he cultivated good relationships between himself and the provosts and chairmen of the 19 new district councils. His natural charm and his straightforward decency made him more a friendly colleague than an overpowering threat.

The Campaign for Nuclear Disarmament had begun to be a bit more active once more, and Geoff spoke at a rally at Custom House Quay in June 1974. He promised to continue his personal support for CND policies in his new post. He maintained this line throughout and one of the first clashes at the council was over an invitation to Strathclyde to be represented at a Scottish CND rally. The convener and three others were appointed to attend.

Devolution was the current hot national political issue

which had to be faced. Geoff was by this time a member of the executive of the Scottish Council of the Labour Party, bringing him into close touch with the Secretary of State, Willie Ross, and other leading Labour Party figures in Scotland. On Saturday June 22 1974, at what was to become a historic meeting of the Executive, a decision had to be taken as to the Council's attitude to the recommendations of the Kilbrandon Commission on the Constitution. Only eleven out of a total of 30 members of the Executive were present. They voted, by six votes to five, to turn down the various proposals on devolution. Geoff voted with the majority, most of whom could be categorised as the left and far left of the Executive. (He voted on most of the issues with the left). London, ever mindful of the Scottish National Party threat, sent the decision back "hameward tae think again." Think again they did. The Executive committee's decision was overturned at a special conference of the Labour Party in Scotland in August 1974. Devolution and the formation of a Scottish Assembly became party policy.

Not before Strathclyde Regional Council had its say, however. On June 24, 1974, the council decisively rejected an elected Scottish Assembly in response to the Government's request for their views on their discussion paper on devolution.

In their first major debate, the council, meeting at Hamilton, accepted a motion by Geoff Shaw which recognised "the sincere desire of the Scottish people" to see an effective decentralisation of power by the Government, but rejected "a separatist or federalist solution."

Councillor Shaw's motion said the problems of the West of Scotland could best be resolved by strong and effective action at Regional and District level. The motion urged the Government to ensure that the new councils were given enough time and independent power to establish themselves.

In the debate, Geoff said that whatever was ultimately decided by Parliament, the council must emphasize their awareness of the Region's problems and declare their belief in themselves and in the possiblity of greatly improving things in the Region.

The convener's motion received 66 votes, with 22 votes going to a motion by Councillor Leonard Turpie, leader of the Conservative Group, calling for the setting up of a Scottish Assembly on the basis of direct elections by proportional representation.

Councillor Gordon Murray, leader of the Scottish Nationalist Group, gained four votes for his motion criticising the Government proposals as inadequate. He vainly sought to have the matter re-raised at a subsequent meeting, saying that the council had had "naive, parochial and short-sighted leadership from their chairman."

The most important national influence at the time of the emergence of the infant Strathclyde was the economic plight of the country. With inflation rising rapidly and the Government working under the strictures of the International Monetary Fund representatives, all local authority spending came under the Treasury's axe. It pained Geoff, because, he was by temperament and philosophy a New Deal politician. He would have liked to expand services and create new jobs. Instead, he was forced to warn: "Over the next year at least, our policy will be one of retrenchment rather than expansion. We are going to tighten our belts, because I do not believe the public at this juncture wish an expansion of services that would lead to greatly increased rates."

Fed up with the high cost of public services, people tended to regard Strathclyde as an additional financial burden. Their hostility was fuelled by press stories about junkets and officials' high salaries. While insisting that local authorities must look carefully at areas where they were not making the best use of resources, the Convener hit back. "There is overstatement in the press and the public mind that if we cut out a trip here and there the rates will come tumbling down, which of course, is just rubbish."

So as the day drew near for Strathclyde Regional Council to assume power, Geoff Shaw found himself having to take on a defensive role. The economic retrenchment which was already taking effect did not augur well for the fulfilment of his political dream.

217

218

Chapter VII
You in Your Small Corner?

Render unto Caesar the things which be Caesar's and unto God the things which be God's.— **Luke 20.25**

The marginal person, the monk, the displaced person, the prisoner, all these people live in the presence of death, which calls into question the meaning of life.— **Thomas Merton.**

There can be no radical division between civilisation and what belongs to the interior being of man.— **J. Danielou.**

When Strathclyde Regional Council took up the reins of power on May 16, 1975 its convener was, for the first time in his life, technically unemployed.

The Church of Scotland had withdrawn his salary. The decision to take Geoff off the payroll in 1975 had been made a year previously. The Church of Scotland's Home Board felt that to continue to pay an Evangelist a salary, when he was engaged in full time politics, was wrong. Geoff, called to Edinburgh to discuss the matter, was annoyed because he felt he was being carpeted. He argued that at a time when the Church was extolling the virtues of being "involved in politics," it was important that he should remain an employee of the Kirk.

He did not want the money for itself. He could get by where no one else could, or would, on the allowances payable to a convener. But he was hurt by the implications of the decision. He felt it symbolised the Church's lack of commitment to the real world of politics. He was also made aware of a lack of sympathy, even hostility, on the part of a number of Church leaders. ("Imagine Shaw leaving the ministry to become chairman of some County Council or other," said one.)

Racked by the dilemmas involved in political choices, he knew at least where he would not find much support or encouragement.

Geoff always resisted the view that secular politics was sordid, whereas the Church was an arena of sweetness and light.

In a *Scottish Field* interview he was asked if he was not conscious of a conflict between his ministerial and political interests and duties.

His reply was a model of lucidity and commonsense. "I think if being a minister is an escape from so-called sordid decisions then it's a wrong kind of ministry. I think it's a kind of ministry which has been exercised by some people, but it is wrong.

"Anyway, the ministry is not unrelated to the whole question of politics. By appearing to live within a status quo, one is, in a sense, giving approval to a status quo, which is imagining that we can stand outside without taking part in one way or another.

"I don't believe there is such a thing as a non-political person. (There are, of course, plenty of non-party political people.) Any decisions we make regarding the place or nature of our employment and the way we live relate in some way to our values and priorities and these have a political significance.

"Certainly, I question the assumption that politics is a dirty game. A vast number of people I could mention, who are closely involved in politics, possess a considerable integrity; and after all, no minister or other particular individual in our society has a monopoly of this virtue. Who can claim this section of our community has integrity and this other has not? You suggest that politicians are intent on self-aggrandisement. Were, I wonder, the great divines devoid of self-aggrandisement? I wouldn't want to judge on that, but I don't think there's any sphere of human activity which is not open to precisely the same temptations and indulgence in personal pride and arrogance as one finds in politics."

At around the same time, Geoff wrote an article for the Rev. Douglas Alexander's parish magazine, in which he discussed Christianity, politics, central government and Strathclyde. He wrote. "In many ways it seems for me a far cry from the small world—the "microcosm"—of Gorbals, to Strathclyde's big world—the "macrocosm". And of course, the fundamental question mark against Strathclyde is just that—is it too big? Is there a danger that the many,

many small worlds will be lost—whether Gorbals or Bishopton or the islands of the West? Indeed, is there any sense in which realistically we can say that Strathclyde is one unit, one big world, one sensible "macrocosm"? Or to put it a different way, has local government ceased to be local?

"I have always thought it to be a mockery that we in the churches should claim belief in a Christ who came "that they may have more life more abundantly" when, for so many people, the physical conditions—at home, in the street and at work—made it so very difficult to live life to the full. The Christian faith can of course flourish in adversity. But it is profoundly hypocritical to accept or to ignore conditions of adversity for this reason, particularly when it is the other person who has to endure such conditions.

"Government, whether local or national, cannot create fullness of life. It can and must, seek to create conditions— to set the framework—in which people can achieve whatever to them is fullness of life. Christianity is about relations between man and man as well as between individual man and his God. And if that is so, the Christian must concern himself with the conditions under which relationships between individuals and communities are formed. The role of central government is to set the legislation and the policy through which a just framework can be created. The major role of local government is to administer such policies in the local situation—to create the local framework. In creating this local framework, the community, through and with its Council, seeks to husband its resources in the best interest of all, tries to focus the overall needs and possibilities of the total large community; and if it is a caring community, pays particular attenti on to any geographical areas or groups of people which have special needs and problems."

After giving a personal view of the history of the ancient kingdom of Strathclyde, he continued. "The present economic climate means that the Regional Council requires to husband resources perhaps more rigorously than ever before and clearly to establish priorities for areas of spending in the provision of services. Glasgow itself

221

must, of course, claim much of our attention. For many years it has struggled proudly to meet the problems of the aftermath of Industrial Revolution—and that in a period when it was seriously denuded by emigration from within its boundaries—through overspill, the new towns and particularly, the movement of many of the wealthy middle class to the outer suburbs or further afield. Much of the life of the west focuses on Glasgow and it is right that people of all Strathclyde can share its future.

"But—and it is an important "but"—it must never be thought that Strathclyde exists only for the sake of Glasgow. There are many areas throughout the Region where special attention must be directed in terms of improvement of services. But more important still, it is my firm belief that the fulness of human life demands a real sharing of a city, town and country—that the interests of all three are closely linked economically and culturally. The concept that we are bidden to shine "you in your small corner and I in mine" is all very well. But what if my small corner is very comfortable at the expense of yours? Or what if my small corner should be greatly enriched by a greater sharing with yours?"

Geoff Shaw was a unique kind of political leader in that he was able to articulate political ideals, based on a theological foundation which was in turn rooted in reflection upon the situation of individuals in the light of the Christian message. One does not have to agree with all his political views to see that this is so.

There could not have been many powerful political leaders at that time who lived up a dank tenement close, had only two suits (yes, he had got another one) and who drove a battered Hillman Husky. At least one official who called at Cleland Street to collect him for a conference was horrified by what he saw.

But the day Geoff had dreaded was at hand. Cleland Street was to be cleared. He had to leave. The Convener of Strathclyde Regional Council was the last tenant left in the block, although there were squatters above him. He hung on till the last possible minute. He had loved his cell, and did

With Councillor Dick Stewart at launching of concessionary travel scheme for pensioners.

The Convener auditions a young musician.

Geoff, best man at brother David's wedding, 1960.

not want to be parted from it. There had been so many, many good memories and associations.

When Geoff left 74, Cleland Street he was a kind of displaced person. The house had helped to define his life and his Christian calling. It was so much more than unsalubrious bricks and mortar. So, the old tin bath would no longer be needed. The stairs would cease to resound with the cries of drunks on their way for help. Never again would the tip-tap of the typewriter be heard there at 2.00 a.m.

Seventy-four Cleland Street and its neighbour on the corner were nearly the object of a preservation order. Geoff was very proud. But in the end, both were demolished. When it did eventually come down, it was an emotional moment as he stood watching with Rab Hyland. He arranged for a stone from his former house to be taken up to Barlinnie Prison. There in the Special Unit, life-term prisoner Jimmy Boyle carved on the stone the wizened face of a Glasgow man with a bunnet. It was for Geoff a treasured possession.

Thus, at the time Strathclyde was getting under way, Geoff Shaw had to leave his loved home, his salary had been cut off by the Church and he was without the effective support of the Group, which was dying with the old derelict Gorbals.

Where was he to live? One possibility was in one of the multi-storey blocks, but Sarah did not fancy that prospect very much.

Sarah Mason, from Cumberland, had first met Geoff in 1969, when she was a 19-year-old student. As already indicated, she had been involved in the summer camps at Peanmeanach. She loved working with the Gorbals youngsters and she helped with the cooking, as well as with outdoor activities.

When she finished her studies at St. Andrews, she took a job, on Geoff's advice, with Stirling Social Work department. She kept up her voluntary activities in Gorbals and visited Geoff at Cleland Street. The romance blossomed from there. She moved permanently to Glasgow when she took up an appointment with the Iona Community in Clyde

Street, working much of the time with dossers and down-and-outs.

Geoff wanted to continue to live in his division, so the choice of housing was limited. He decided to buy a three-room-and kitchen house up a stair in Queen Mary Avenue. He was never particularly fond of the house. He was distinctly uncomfortable in middle class territory and feared that his friends from Gorbals might not feel at home. Most of them did manage to find their way.

Not far along the road was the house of Lord Provost Peter McCann, with the two traditional ornamental lamp standards outside. The only regular sight outside the home of the Strathclyde Convener was the slumped body of a despairing Gorbals youth.

On the evening of Friday December 12, 1975 Sarah and Geoff were married in his home at Queen Mary Avenue. It was marriage Gorbals-Group-style, with worship in the house and Gorbals friends and lots of children present. The service was conducted by John Harvey. The best man was the boy Geoff had virtually adopted—now, of course, a grown man, with a family. One of the readings during the service was Geoff's favourite poem—"Everyone Sang" by Siegfried Sassoon:

Everyone suddenly burst out singing;
And I was fill'd with such delight
As prison'd birds must find in freedom
Winging wildly across the white
Orchards and dark green fields; on; on;
And out of sight.

Everyone's voice was suddenly lifted,
And beauty came like the setting sun.
My heart was shaken with tears; and horror
Drifted away...O but everyone
Was a bird; and the song was wordless; the
Singing will never be done.

There was no honeymoon, life was too busy for that. It had been hard enough trying to get free time for the wedding! That same evening Geoff and Sarah were on duty at an old folks dinner. (They did manage to get a holiday together a few months later, when they went to France to meet John and Helen Anderson. Geoff was very fond of the Andersons and he had followed their round-the-world sail with excited interest. He and Sarah had a relaxing time sailing in the French waters and hearing stories of the voyage.)

So Geoff who had been teased so often about getting married had done it at last. He felt much safer! He was no longer vulnerable to misunderstanding or pursuit. The defensive mechanisms were not needed any more. (A woman member of the Group observed, "Even though most females fluttered around Geoff like moths round a flame, he managed to charm them, yet remain distant.") One social worker friend treasured the night she was called out to help during a big fire at a block of flats. When she was telephoning on behalf of a client, Geoff appeared, put his arm around her shoulder and gave her a kiss on the cheek. The place was crowded, but Geoff no longer needed to be worried now that he was unavailable.

Sarah knew what she was taking on—a husband of whom she would see very little. Strathclyde was a huge area and Geoff felt an obligation to get around it. It was as if he was a parish minister, with two and a half million people in his parish! He was concerned that people in outlying areas of the Region should not feel left out and he was prepared to travel and talk with them. It was hectic and exhausting.

His visits to the islands were no holidays. His schedule for a trip to Islay reveals a ceaseless round of meetings and consultations. Local people who raised issues, however trivial, soon found that the Convener had taken the matter up.

Sarah accompanied Geoff on a visit to Tiree. On the first night on the island, a dove alighted in the window sill of their bedroom in the Scarinish Hotel. According to the local Councillor, Alex Hector MacPhail, doves were virtually unknown on the island. Could it have flown over from Iona? At any rate Geoff and Sarah were delighted.

Geoff had a particular love for Argyll, especially after all the camps there, and he asked to serve on the Argyll-Strathclyde Liaison Committee. He had a warm personal

225

relationship with Councillor Ford Spence, chairman of Argyll and Bute District Council, who said, "I well remember a few years ago walking in mid Argyll with Geoff Shaw when he expressed his hope for the success of Strathclyde and the manner in which he proposed to undertake the onerous and challenging duties he had so willingly and enthusiastically accepted when elected convener. One could not fail to be impressed by this man of conviction and sincerity whose vision was both far and wide.

"His skill, dedication, boundless energy, efficiency, personality and friendly manner did in fact ensure that Strathclyde was and is a success despite its size. No man could have made a greater contribution to the wellbeing of the people of Strathclyde than Geoff Shaw, who put persons before politics. He was well received by the people of Argyll and Bute and their respect and admiration for him transcended political differences."

Political differences there were. The Scottish National Party was committed to breaking up Strathclyde. The Nationalist M.P. for Argyll, Mr. Iain MacCormick, challenged Geoff to a public debate in Oban. He took up the gauntlet and won admirers with his fairness, charm and debating skill.

But he was not in politics just to debate and impress. He wanted power to push what resources there were in the direction of the areas most in need. On December 17th, 1975 came evidence of this determination, which was shared by some, but not all his colleagues. Settling the guidelines for the Regional Report to be sent to the Secretary of State for Scotland, Strathclyde Regional Council argued that plans for a further new town in Scotland, namely Stonehouse, should be abandoned and the resources set aside channelled to existing areas of deprivation.

Convener Shaw commented: "This is a hard decision, but if we are not prepared to take such a decision, we might as well abdicate all strategic planning responsibilities to central government." He went on. "For months now we have listened to the clamour of those who have called for the dissolution of the Regions. Today we can say loud and clear: "You are wrong."

"We who live in the West of Scotland have here the opportunity to debate the future of the West of Scotland, to draw together the various interests of its greatly divergent parts, to formulate the main issue on which coherent plans can be based which will in some cases replace, in other cases take over, the piecemeal and disparate policies of the former authorities."

Should central government, in whatever form, at some later stage bow to the voices of those who wanted to break up Strathclyde, it was his sincere belief that they would at least set in motion plans which would create a new future for the West of Scotland.

Major points among the 23-item list of policy guidelines for strategic development of the Region, which was approved by the Council, were the need to reduce unemployment and tackle urban deprivation.

In October 1975, he said, 74,310 people in the Region were unemployed—a rate of 6.9 per cent, compared to 3.2 per cent in 1966. It was estimated that from 1978—81 the Region would need 170,000 new jobs—120,000 in terms of job replacement, 40,000 to reduce unemployment to 3 per cent and a further 10,000 in terms of changing age/sex structure. Strathclyde's urban deprivation statistics were not good, he added, and the Council must devise a strategy which could make the Region a better place to live and work. And that must be done within the tight resources available.

Geoff argued that in a time of limited resources, it was obvious that the continuation of such a high level of expenditure for new towns would go against the prime objectives of stemming the flow of population from the inner conurbation and the expansion of jobs in the inner conurbation.

Not everyone agreed with the logic. There was a strong countervailing philosophy that what resources there were should go to the growth areas and that the inner city areas and housing schemes should go the way of the weak—to the wall. The reversal of this thinking was part of the "positive discrimination" policy adopted by the Region; that is,

227

instead of handing out resources on an equal basis, priority should be given to areas and groups which were most in need. The policy had its roots in the pre-reorganisation West Central Scotland Plan, which underlay much of the thinking in the Regional Report. It was pursued with particular vigour by Geoff Shaw and Ronald Young. Their opponents argued that it was a lame-duck approach, which would eventually drag the Region down.

Studies were made of the whole Region and priority deprivation lists were drawn up. It was agreed that any extra resources, such as Urban Aid, should go primarily to projects in these areas and that future planning should be based on such considerations.

Speaking at a conference on 'Deprivation in Glasgow', Geoff said the Region would channel money and resources on the basis of positive discrimination. Despite industrial and social change in West Central Scotland which local authorities could not control Strathclyde Regional Council would "make all the resources work to the greater advantage of the disadvantaged."

For Geoff Shaw it was Christianity and socialism at work. And it was to help implement such policies that he had insisted that the convener must have political power.

As chairman of the Policy and Resources committee, Geoff also insisted that there must be more democratic control of the formulation of Strathclyde's capital and revenue budgets. This involved the committee meeting in almost continuous session for four days under his chairmanship. He had helped to formulate the procedure whereby every department had to present various policy options on expenditure in order that the committee could make choices according to a proper order of priorities. It was a formidable enough task for a departmental committee chairman to take on for his own department. To tackle it for the Region as a whole, with a £600 million budget, was a colossal task. The meetings were exhausting and Geoff worked tremendously hard reading documents, interrogating chairmen and officials and trying to guide choices.

Along with some of his colleagues, Geoff Shaw was trying

to initiate a revolution in local authority policy and procedures so that the elected representatives had much more say on policy and detail. This went hand in hand with the agreed policy of 'open government.' He applauded the fact that under the new legislation all committee meetings had to be open to the public. With others, he insisted that councillors' surgeries be more frequent and more widely advertised. A further change was that this great authority was compelled to state, clearly and in public, what its overall priorities were and how it arrived at them.

The new democracy was very demanding—and what some councillors and officials had to say about it was not printable.

Geoff was distressed by the fact that economic cut-backs necessitated restriction rather than much-needed expansion. He vigorously defended the Region against allegations of extravagance, pointing out that in some departments there were fewer staff than under the old system. He wrote in the ill-fated *Scottish Daily News:* "Government restrictions, however necessary, have led to agonising decisions by people whose first instinct is to concentrate resources in those areas which have, over the years, fallen behind the rest of the country. In spite of this the Regional Council has attempted to express in budget terms the implications of the clear commitment contained in the Strathclyde Regional Council report—resources will be concentrated primarily on the lengthy process of resolving deprivation problems."

As the first full year for the Region drew to a close, the end-of-term reports were mixed. Bill Hyndman of the *Daily Record* called Strathclyde a "soulless monster of bureaucratic machinery," citing rates increases, cutbacks in services and a feeling of remoteness.

Claude Thomson's end-of-term report in the *Glasgow Herald* was: "Diligence—exceptional. Behaviour—beyond reproach. Success—better than most expected in a cruel financial climate. Prospects—potential for doing better as experience is gained and the economic situation improves."

The Strathclyde convener could look back on the previous two years with a great deal of personal satisfaction.

Strathclyde Region was well and truly in business. More open government had been established. The Region was now firmly committed to positive discrimination in favour of the areas of greatest need. Good relations with the district councils had been built up. And at a time of hostility towards Strathclyde, Geoff's own public performance had established a remarkably positive image for the Region.

But how was the new convener doing from the insider's point of view?

Chapter VIII
Pastor of Strathclyde

A liberal is a Communist with a mortgage.— **Adlai Stevenson.**

Adlai Stevenson... was too busy making up his mind whether he had to go to the bathroom or not. — **Harry S. Truman.**

He had black moods, but was all for life. Sentiment was subdued in him; astringency and buoyancy were always breaking through.—
Michael Foot on **Aneurin Bevan**

The trouble with Geoff Shaw as a politician was that he was a very good pastor. The man who was 'brilliant' at one-to-one relationships with delinquents and dropouts in Gorbals, and whose philosophy had always been to work in depth on a small scale, had been willingly propelled into the position of political head of half the population of Scotland. He cared deeply about his two and a half million charges. He agonised over economic cuts and the effect they would have. He worried at nights over decisions that had been taken that day.

Geoff's style had always been to listen carefully to what people were saying, to take personal responsibility for any problems, to mull over ideas and test them out with this friends, then do what he felt best. Organisation and efficiency were never his strong points. Now as political convener of Strathclyde he was expected to know who not to listen to, to make up his mind quickly, to delegate matters to others, to make hard economic decisions ruthlessly—then go to bed at night to sleep. He could not.

He was always on duty on behalf of the people of Strathclyde. Sometimes that duty delighted him, sometimes it wore him down. Many of the internal problems sprang from the original decision, advocated by Geoff, that the convener should be chairman of the Policy and Resources Committee and exercise substantial political influence. This decision meant that there were two sources of political power in Strathclyde—the convener and the leader of the Labour Group. And that meant trouble.

Councillor Dick Stewart, six years older than Geoff, had

been in politics nearly all his life. Brought up in Lanark-shire, he went to work in the pits at the age of 14 and served a long political apprenticeship. His early enjoyment of political discussion and activity led him into local government as councillor. He became agent for Peggy Herbison, MP, and was appointed full time secretary of North Lanark Labour Party. Despite more than one spell of severe illness he was, at the time of local government re-organisation, deputy leader of the majority Labour Party in Lanark County Council. He was therefore steeped in political life— a man who knew how to make political systems work.

Dick Stewart seemed to be everything Geoff Shaw was not. He was experienced, shrewd, tough-talking, hard-swearing, blunt. When decisions had to be made he took them and moved on to the next business. He was a political power broker, a manager who could get things done.

It would be easy to present the ensuing power struggle— for that, despite disclaimers, was what it was—as Idealism versus the System. But it was not quite so simple.

Geoff was certainly suspicious of Councillor Stewart at the beginning. He seemed to epitomise much of the authoritarian style of leadership that Geoff wanted to get away from. Dick Stewart, in turn, was not over-impressed by this greenhorn's naive approach and his obvious lack of experience. The two men, however, came to have a high regard for each other and developed a warm and even affectionate relationship.

Had Dick Stewart simply been a political operator looking for results, Geoff would not have had much time for him. But the Labour Group Leader's moral commit-ment and honesty impressed the convener, who also admired his colleague's political skill. After all, politics was about getting things done and Dick Stewart knew how to get things done. Councillor Stewart, on the other hand, had a high regard for Geoff's idealism and concern. His only regret was that he had not had him under his wing for the past few years!

Geoff was not always sure whether he wanted to be closely identified with Councillor Stewart or to be independent of him. He was in politics to do something new—to open things up, to set a new agenda, to develop a new style. He was therefore wary of many of the senior politicians and officials, whom he saw as representing the traditional West of Scotland establishment. He wished to ensure that Strathclyde was not the old Mafia writ large. He passionately wanted the Region to represent a new, open, socialist initiative in Scottish political life and he feared being swamped by the system. At he same time, he desperately lacked political and administrative experience and this made him very vulnerable. In his short political career, Geoff had never been part of the normal political and administrative machinery of local government. He had not served an apprenticeship. He had not learned the ropes slowly under the tutelage of a senior politician; even his short spell at the City Chambers was abnormal in that much of the political activity in his time there was geared to the approaching organisational changes. But this very inexperience and lack of identification with traditional politics was part of the attractiveness of Geoff Shaw as a politician and in any case was compensated for by his innate ability. Nevertheless, faced with the huge problems of Strathclyde, he could have done with more experience of the political and administrative machinery—and he knew it.

Thus, Councillor Stewart was both a source of political wisdom and a threat. Geoff was a bit like Jimmy Carter in his early presidency—desperately keen, indeed impatient, to make changes which would benefit the people, wanting to show his independence of the old politics, and trying to cover up his inexperience and uncertainty; at the same time realising that if ideas were to become projects in this cruel world, votes would have to be gathered in.

One way in which he could have tackled the problem would have been to work in close liaison with those who shared his views and do a bit of persuading and arm-twisting himself. But the formation of a Geoff Shaw group within the party was not his style. He had no stomach for intrigue and secret meetings and his strong party loyalty ruled out cliques.

Two sources of political authority presented problems for officials and councillors. Which one should be consulted? Sometimes people would approach the convener, then finding him busy or indecisive, would go across the corridor to the group leader. Councillor Stewart was always able to talk realistically about the political implications of a given matter and turn out a quick and accurate assessment of how the majority group would view it.

It would be true to say that, especially in the first two years of Strathclyde's operations, Geoff Shaw as Convener and Chairman of the Policy and Resources Committee was never quite so much in command of his situation as was Dick Stewart in his position as Chairman of the Labour Group. One experienced councillor observed: "More often than not, Geoff, when pursuing one of his own personal ideas or schemes before the group executive or full group meeting, appeared to be in the role of supplicant rather than as leader."

Geoff had the reputation of consulting too many people. He wanted to listen to all points of view before making a decision, but when the decision had to be made in a hurry, that caused problems. Councillor Stewart had a clear idea of who he would listen to on a certain issue, but sometimes the person who was shown the group leader's door would make his way over to the convener's office.

Geoff wanted, above all, to be available. He was afraid of losing touch. He did not want to consult a limited range of people about the same old tired options. He wanted his door to be open, not just for officials or chairmen, but for ordinary councillors—and even members of the public. He wanted people to have access to him. Highly paid senior officials were sometimes asked to leave the room while Geoff dealt with a complaint from a member of the public. And rather than delegate the matter to someone else, he would follow it through personally.

All this time, the Strathclyde convener was still making himself available for Gorbals youngsters in trouble. They not only turned up at Queen Mary Avenue, but at Melrose House, the Strathclyde headquarters in Glasgow. He insisted that no one be turned away, much to some peoples' dismay. On one occasion he was called out of an important

234

meeting to see a boy who had just been released from prison. Colleagues and officials were dismayed by the appearance of dishevelled youths at Melrose House, asking for "Geoff" and getting access to the convener. Willie Quail, personal assistant to the convener, would on occasion take a blood-stained suit to the cleaners, or a transistor and some books to Barlinnie Prison. Geoff also had an arrangement with his office that calls from any of the Gorbals youths would get through to him. He was determined never to let go.

Nor would he let go of problems. It was Geoff's tragedy that he became Convener of Strathclyde, with all the potential he saw in it, at a time of economic austerity and restraint. He kept trying to find new ways round difficult decisions and would repeatedly come up with last-minute proposals to avert hardship. Even when the necessary decision had been made, he continued to worry about it and sometimes tried to have the matter re-opened. He was concerned about individuals affected by decisions. For instance, it had been decided, after much discussion and lobbying, to close down the three-year-old educational television unit. Geoff lay awake worrying at night about the unit's director, whose career and earnings prospects might be permanently blighted.

Geoff's democratic inclinations, his insistence on availability and access, his willingness to look for new options, his persistence in dealing with matters personally rather than delegating and his unwillingness or inability to decide quickly, not surprisingly led to something of an organisational guddle. Willie Quail, whom Geoff had admired for his work in City Chambers and whom he had brought over as his personal assistant at Melrose House, suggested having a daily staff briefing, but this never happened. When his staff sought to protect the convener from some of his visitors, he refused. The last thing he wanted was a Haldeman guarding the door to his office and controlling his diary. Consequently the piles of paper on the desk grew higher and decisions were often left till a crucial stage. It was more than once that the convener rushed from Melrose House straight on to the television set to talk "live," without preparation. Despite the urgings of his public relations department, he insisted on writing all his own speeches. He often spoke at meetings 'off the top of his head'. He could do it apparently effortlessly.

It is not surprising that Geoff Shaw came to personify Strathclyde. He believed passionately in the Region, and on television his commitment and concern came through strongly. His ability to speak commonsense with a minimum of political cliché and his willingness to say that he didn't know all the answers created an enviable rapport with many people of all persuasions. People felt they had a "hot line" to Strathclyde so long as he was there. They had confidence in his ability and his accessibility. The soulless monster of Strathclyde could not be that bad if Geoff Shaw was in charge.

But was he in charge? Or was Dick Stewart? The system certainly wasn't working smoothly. Geoff resented the attempts of some of his senior colleagues to 'put him right' and he sometimes dug in his heels.

The fact is that the set up could easily have exploded before Strathclyde had been going for two years. If there had been a public bust-up, it could well have spelt the end for the infant Regional Council. That it did not is due to the personalities of the two men, their mutual affection and the fact that they both believed in the future of Strathclyde.

Dick Stewart, the political father figure, sometimes bawled Geoff out. "You're a silly bugger, Geoff," he would shout and tell him off for listening to too many people. When Geoff came up with an idea which had not been thought through practically, he would hear, "Christ, Geoff, that's a bloody silly idea!"

Geoff's own sense of humour helped keep things in perspective. At the Labour Group social he gently took the mickey out of the group leader by way of an Old Testament lesson—

"And it came to pass that the Lord spoke out of the whirlwind unto His Chosen One. And he said unto him— Rise up, you and your people and take possession of the land to which I have called you—a land of hills and rivers and fine fields yielding much grain; a land with a great city in its midst and many towns and much people. And the Chosen of the Lord said "Amen, so be it"— or words to that effect. And he took his people and he became their leader and the name of that land was Strathclyde and the name of the Chosen of the Lord was Richard. Now Richard was a mighty man of valour. His stature was like the stature of a sparrow and the locks of his hair were silver as the moon—yes even as a very small new moon. His voice was as the tender ripple of a mountain stream or as the gentle singing of a dove and words of sweetness flowed from his lips.

"And the Lord said unto Richard, "In fourteen days thou shalt make Strathclyde into a land of great happiness and prosperity." And Richard said "Bloody Hell!" And the Lord said: "Then in twenty eight days thou shalt make Strathclyde into a land of great happiness and prosperity." And Richard bowed his head and he said: "It shall be so." And it was not so. So the Lord summoned Richard to enquire why it was not so. And Richard replied "Christ I'm good but I'm no a bloody marvel."

"So the Lord was sore displeased and he visited Richard with many afflictions of the body and he took Richard from out of his people and he papped him into Law Hospital. And they languished sore and longed for his return, for they were all raving masochists. And in due course the Lord returned Richard to his people....."

Geoff Shaw's personal style as Convener caused some disquiet within Melrose House. He hated pomp and ceremony in politics as much as in religion and he disliked dressing up. Functions and dinner parties had little attraction for him, though he and Sarah attended many. The man who had dined so regularly on soup in Cleland Street showed little interest in exotic menus. He sometimes left functions early to be with his Gorbals friends.

There were many within the Strathclyde Council who were unhappy about the lowkey image of their leadership. Politics has to do with egos as well as decisions and there were those who hated to be outshone by their District counterparts. They wanted Strathclyde to flex its corporate muscle, even if only now and again.

But Geoff was not interested. During his term of office, Strathclyde Regional Council organised only one function which required dinner jackets. He preferred informal functions and even had to be persuaded against his will to retain the loyal toast at dinners. One colleague commented that Geoff was surprisingly gauche socially on big occasions. (He once took Prince Charles to the wrong end of the reception line and started with two old ladies instead of the dignitaries. But was it really a mistake?) He claimed the minimum expenses and fought attempts to have the convener's very modest allowance upgraded. His 1976—77 claims for attendance allowance totalled £2,460 gross £1674 net. Other years were similar.

He absolutely refused to have ceremonial lamp standards outside the door of his house. That kind of thing meant nothing to himself, or to Sarah. This austerity disturbed a lot of his political colleagues. Some of them had, in their own local authorities, got used to the lunches and ceremonial dinners and a style of political life whose attractions included free drink and social contact with important people. They were rising upwards and they were dismayed, confused and challenged by this strange, well-bred outsider who seemed intent on moving downwards. Others simply felt that a political organisation as massive as Strathclyde should display signs of its status and not act like poor relations at the feast. This discontent was fuelled by some of those on the right of the party who were suspicious of intellectuals in politics and who were disturbed by the convener's egalitarianism and socialism. In fairness, though, it has to be said that many applauded Geoff's style and had great admiration for his integrity.

When Geoff was first appointed, he did not want to have an official car at his disposal. He was afraid of becoming the kind of political leader barricaded in an office and only seeing people through the coloured glass of an official limousine. In discussing the issue with a friend, he said, "I don't want someone carrying my briefcase for me," and resisted the argument that it would be better for his energy to go into doing his job well, than into carrying bags.

He used to drive into the official car park in his battered

old Hillman Husky. It was something of a public joke. But it soon became obvious that the convener could not travel the length and breadth of the West of Scotland, finding parking places, attending meetings and rush back to Glasgow, using his own transport. He had to concede that an official Strathclyde car was necessary, especially after the Husky was stolen. He declined a Daimler and settled for a more modest Austin Princess.

The advantages of the car became obvious. For one thing, he could prepare for meetings en route or have a much needed sleep. He usually sat in the front, his head on the headrest. Sometimes a lad from Gorbals would be in the back. His driver, Jimmy Semple from Drumchapel, would wake him up just before the arrived.

Jimmy Semple found the convener a good friend and a kind boss.

"He treated me as one of the family. You always got him the same. He lived by his teaching—there'll never be another like him."

Mr. Semple knew just how hard Geoff worked. He was the one who would drop him off at his home late at night, with a bulging brief case full of papers. When the convener had the constituency business to deal with after a Strathclyde meeting, Jimmy would be told to go home once Geoff had been dropped at the house. Geoff would then get into his own car—by this time a second hand Marina with starting problems. If the car didn't work, Jimmy would get into the Marina while his boss pushed.

Jimmy Semple has many fond memories. On one occasion, Geoff had to go through to Edinburgh for the General Assembly of the Church of Scotland, then rush back to Glasgow for a dinner. When they got back, the chauffeur was amazed to see Geoff step out of the car in evening dress. He had been wearing a kilt when they left Edinburgh.

At the Police Benevolent ball, Geoff won a carpet in the £1 charity raffle. Jimmy and Geoff carried it from the car to the house in Queen Mary Avenue in the early hours of the morning. (It would have been interesting if he had been stopped by the former Gorbals policeman wanting to know where he got the carpet). When they got upstairs there was the familiar sight of the body of a drunk Gorbals youth slumped outside the house. They stepped gingerly over the boy and put the carpet in the house. As he went down the stairs, Jimmy turned round to witness the unforgettable sight of the Convener of Strathclyde Regional Council, in full evening dress, gently gathering up in his arms a drunken and desperate youth and taking him into the house.

Mr. Semple won't forget either the time he went to pick up the convener for a function. Geoff had received a note from a boy saying by the time the letter arrived he would be dead. They rushed up to Castlemilk with Willie Quail and got no reply at the house. The glass door was already broken and access to the flat was easily obtained. Willie found the boy dead behind the kitchen door. He had committed suicide. Geoff was distraught and angry. Angry because he knew of the suffering the boy had experienced—his mother and brother had died in separate tragedies—and because he had not been able to get to him on time. Needless to say, he didn't go to the function that night. The minister who conducted the boy's funeral, attended by crowds of teenagers, was the Rev Geoffrey M. Shaw.

Jimmy Semple observed, "He would never give up on anybody, even when his house was broken into. He would never believe that there was no hope—and he would let you know it."

The convener's staff loved him, even when he maddened them. Being personal assistant to Geoff Shaw could not have been easy, but Willie Quail was devoted to him.

"One couldn't help but be affected by the obvious warmth and sincerity of the convener", he said. "Certainly none of the staff ever considered it an imposition to stay on late, or go out of their way to do something for him. He treated the staff as friends. He laughed with us, joked with us, listened to our problems and ultimately left a lasting impression on us all."

Geoff was always appreciative of the work of the secretarial staff. On one occasion he took them out for Christmas dinner to the Albany Hotel. The girls expected Geoff to be late as usual and took the precaution of turning

Geoff and Sarah at the time of their engagement.

Acknowledgements are made to the Glasgow Herald, *Strathclyde Regional Council,* The Scotsman, *members of the Gorbals Group and other friends for permission to reproduce photographs in which they hold copyright.*

up well after the agreed time—to find that their boss had been, for once, on time!

Practical jokes went down well, too. Two of the girls left a fake Mars bar on the convener's desk. He outjaped them by putting teeth marks on the plastic and pretended he had had difficulty eating it.

There were so many things about political life that Geoff Shaw enjoyed, particularly the sense of being able to influence events. But the dilemmas troubled him. As with the Gorbals Group, he got very frustrated when his colleagues in the Labour Group failed to see things his way on major issues. When chairing meetings, he could be stubborn, persisting in asking support for a motion which it was obvious nobody was keen about. Sometimes he would psychologically "leave" the meeting. He was accused, on occasion, of not consulting the right people on a proposal, or of giving the impression that there was agreement when there was not.

It was all a part of his impatience—he felt time was limited and changes were crying out to be made. He got annoyed when colleagues seemed to refuse to act on the logic of the situation as he saw it, yet he did not like conflict and wanted to avoid head-on collisions. This undoubtedly led to a great deal of personal frustration; Geoff did not have the Dick Stewart capacity to bawl people out and be done with it. After one stubborn disagreement which looked like dragging on, he was moved and chastened when the senior colleague concerned took a reconciling initiative, quoting the Biblical injunction not to let the sun go down on one's wrath. He tended to internalise his frustration and anger and this, as has been observed already, sometimes affected his normally even temperament. (In East Harlem, he was working with a group of youngsters. One black boy gave him bother. "Hey Teach" the kid shouted, "Why are you so angry with me?"

—"I'm not angry."

"Then why is the back of your neck red?")

Further frustration came from his having to go along with Group policy at all times. He had to lead a Strathclyde delegation to a session on the big new £120 million Glasgow

Eastern Area Renewal Project, at the Scottish office. The strategy had been agreed at a pre-meeting, though Geoff himself dissented. The other members of the delegation were angry when at the meeting he propounded his own ideas.

"We forgave him for his immaturity and told him not ever to do it again. He had to be brought to heel," said a senior colleague.

Being 'brought to heel' wasn't what Geoff Shaw was in politics for and he wondered whether it was worth it. He continually suffered anguish at being party to decisions he did not agree with. There was, for instance, a proposal in the GEAR project to transform a car depot in Bridgeton into a big sports centre. Strathclyde's policy was to use it as a garage. Geoff, from his own Bridgeton experience, knew what he would chose, but he had to abide by the group decision.

A favourite sign at his home was a notice which said.

> 'Out of the gloom a
> Voice said unto me
> "Smile and be happy;
> things could get worse."
> So I smiled and was happy,
> and behold things did get worse!'

Geoff Shaw had to ask himself the question. Despite the smiling, were things getting worse?

Chapter IX
Shaw The Politician

*There are two tragedies in life. One is not to get your heart's desire.
The other is to get it.—* **George Bernard Shaw.**

*I've got two kids, I'm almost bald, I've got grey hair and my politics
have become refined.—* **Elridge Cleaver** former Black
Panthers' leader.

The newspapers were begining to suggest that for Geoffrey
Shaw, politician, things could only get better.

The *Evening Times* of August 5, 1976, under the banner
heading, "Who will be Scotland's first prime minister?"
profiled various candidates and cautiously put their money
in the direction of Shaw. The article argued: "Geoff Shaw
already 'rules' half the people in Scotland as Convener of
Strathclyde Regional Council. As such, the 47-year-old
lergyman, who is known to have Assembly aspirations, must
be a serious contender in Labour's ranks for the top post.

"When local government re-organisation was going
through he gave up the possibility of wearing the Lord
Provost's chain of office by staying a Glasgow District
Councillor and opted instead for a seat on the Regional
Council.

"Since the S.R.C. came into being, he has entrenched his
position as a foremost figure in Labour politics.

"Geoff Shaw also has the vital attribute of coming across
as a middle-of-the-road moderate, while attracting considerable support from the Left wing of his party.

"If any local government politician emerges at the top in
Assembly Labour ranks, he must be favourite."

Geoff Shaw's national political star was rising fast, but the
domestic political problems were piling up.

Evening Times again. October 21, 1976, front page banner
headlines—"It's Crunch Now for the Region. Savage cut in
jobs, or massive jump in rates."

The story began. "Strathclyde Region's political leaders
are today facing a shattering jobs v. rates dilemma. The
Government is pressing Scotland's biggest Region to slash

243

spending. The local authority is being forced to choose between massive redundancies among the 110,000 workforce, or a soaring rates increase next year to maintain services at even a minimal level."

The Policy and Resources committee were in a huddle for days, assessing all the options. The document containing the alternatives was half as thick as the Glasgow telephone directory. None of them was palatable. They could not be, when £14 million had to be lopped off the Region's budget.

Convener Shaw was distressed. He commented: "To demand, as the Government is now doing, reductions of a large scale in a very short time, is to demand what is virtually impossible."

He said it was unfair for councils to have, on the one hand, a continual clamour for more effective treatment of delinquency, the employment of more teachers and improved police and fire services and yet to be denied the finance to make these things possible.

Geoff hated to see cutting back in services and he had disagreements with Councillor Charles O'Halloran, chairman of the Finance Committee, over what could be saved.

Glasgow Presbytery's newspaper, *The Bush,* deplored cuts in the community education budget affecting the youth programmes in the Region and attacked the minister at the head of Strathclyde.

"Sadly, one sees the passing of a radical Geoff Shaw, loved by the few, and the appearance of Shaw the politician, no doubt admired by the many."

It was hard to take. Geoff replied: "The only thing to be said is that the paper is no more distressed about the cuts than the councillors forced to make them. We faced the dilemma of whether to abide by the Government's decisions, or ignore them and have the ratepayers foot the bill."

There were problems everywhere. The unemployment figures issued by the Government were the worst since the war.

Geoff flew to London as part of a delegation to discuss the effect of more cutbacks on jobs. He commented at the time: "You simply cannot say you will cut off so many

244

million pounds involving inevitable redundancies without going through a proper consultation process. You cannot cut off thousands of people at the stroke of a pen."

With spiralling inflation, big cuts in public spending and rising unemployment figures, the Strathclyde programme to deal with multiple deprivation looked pretty small beer.

Presenting a report which identified 45 areas chosen for priority treatment, Convener Shaw said that it did not pretend that deeply intractable problems could be solved by massive injections of finance, but pointed to certain immediate steps as the first stage in the long haul towards regeneration. He said the Regional Council was trying to avoid the 'hideous trap' of supposing there were easy and simple solutions.

Although Geoff worked almost single-handedly to present the report to all the Districts within the Region and to agencies like the Scottish Development Department, the dream of imaginative and effective initiatives solving the problem of deprivation in the West of Scotland was beginning to recede.

Something was happening to Geoff Shaw, too. He was reacting more and more defensively—like some of the old-style politicians, in fact. In the old days of Gorbals politics, he had insisted on the truth being told, even though it hurt the local authority.

A report by Professor Gordon Stewart, of the chair of Public Health at Glasgow University, described Glasgow as a "city of decay" and as the "unchallenged leader of the league of bad statistics." He implied that his report had been approved by the Strathclyde Convener. He proposed a controversal 10-year-plan to help the city's health and living standards and wipe out violence and vandalism.

Councillor Shaw replied: "I wish to make it clear that I very much regret that Professor Stewart appears to be using my name to imply approval by me of the contents of his report, of the publication of it and of statements which his has made in its support.

"The use of highly emotive language to describe Glasgow's situation is totally unacceptable and contributes nothing to the well-being of the city. I do believe it is useful

245

that people concerned with the well-being of the city should make their views known constructively to the authorities. I think it is extremely unhelpful to embellish constructive viewpoints with emotional exaggeration.

"The publication of Strathclyde's Regional Report, constructed in consultation with Glasgow District Council, makes it plain that both councils are fully aware of the problems which exist and the need to take firm action to remedy the situation."

A trifle over-sensitive perhaps? The *Gorbals View* in its time, even under the editorship of Geoffrey Shaw, had said much harder things and more emotive things about the state of Glasgow. Was Geoff becoming more of a political politician, over-reacting in the accepted ways and becoming more rigid? Or was it simply the maturing of a leader who, appreciating the actual constraints of power, had begun to see the limitations of criticism without responsibility?

He was involved more and more in defending the giant Region against criticism—and in bashing the re-emergent Scottish National Party.

Speaking at a meeting of the Council of Social Service at Tiree, Councillor Shaw said it was not good enough for the press or parliamentarians to suggest that money was being frittered away by irresponsible local authorities.

He said that Regions could not simply be scrapped. Any further reorganisation would mean functions going to Districts, which were too small to deal with transport, social work, roads, education and water, or to the Assembly, which was central government.

Glasgow might seem remote enough, but could Edinburgh really administer in detail the whole of Scotland?

"Of course it is nonsense, a bureaucratic centralisation of power which only the SNP is daft enough to advocate," he added.

Some people began to notice how Geoff was reacting in more overtly party political ways. Keith Bovey, a lawyer who had defended some of Geoff's boys in Gorbals and who was Geoff's predecessor as chairman of CND in Glasgow, recorded a change in Geoff around this time. Mr. Bovey, who was active in Nationalist politics, had led a deputation

246

of parents from Garscadden. The issue was that of cuts in the education budget and how they would affect the community centre in Drumchapel. When sometime later Geoff arrived to speak at a CND meeting which Keith Bovey was chairing, he immediately rebuked his old associate for having turned the deputation on cuts into an SNP issue.

The context in which this was happening is important. Geoff had spent a long time in Gorbals, caring for people. He had had there an inner detachment, a spiritual freedom which defined his purpose. In this he had been supported and challenged by a close-knit, critical group of people to whom he was accountable. He had been used to free-ranging discussions of new ideas, with all kinds of interesting and stimulating people dropping in to see him. He was a free spirit, who, could, within wide limits, do what he felt was right.

Now, as Convener of Strathclyde, there were all kinds of constraints on him. He had grave responsibilities. He faced very difficult dilemmas. He was daily under political pressure. And the Gorbals Group was, in effect, no more. That weekly centre of worship and reflection and critical support, which had sustained him for so long and had nourished him spiritually, was gone. He no longer lived and worked in the Gorbals he loved. People didn't drop in as they used to, because he was so busy and because he was married. Some of his friends regarded his move into local government a mistake and he was fair game for attack from churchmen, politicians and community activists. Few people really understood the lonely and painful path he had chosen. He was in daily contact with a narrow range of people, making decisions about fewer and fewer real options. And he had to toe the party line.

There was a grave danger that Geoffrey Shaw, increasingly isolated, would allow something of a spiritual vacuum to develop in his life, to be filled by, of all things a concept. Strathclyde. A functional unit of local government. To Geoff, of course, it was much more than that. He believed passionately in Strathclyde and what it could offer and travelled its length and breadth to help weld a unity

247

from many diverse elements. He cared for and yearned over Strathclyde as many a minister or priest does over his parish. He took great delight in the road signs, "You are now entering Strathclyde," and rejoiced when a shop in Hamilton changed its advertising slogan to "Strathclyde's leading sports shop." From platforms all over the West of Scotland, on television and in newspapers, he argued the Region's case. Self doubt was not allowed to enter in. If it had, the Region might well have foundered. But when all is said and done, Strathclyde is Strathclyde is Strathclyde. A big unit of local government which will be judged in strictly functional terms. For the convener, it was in danger of becoming a mystical entity.

Much of the public criticism of the giant Region was undoubtedly unfair.Local government in 1970—74 had been on something of a spending spree, knowing that reorganisation was coming back. Strathclyde had to pick up the tabs. Mounting inflation and cuts in government grants meant that rates were soaring, even as services were being held back or cut. The Regions were criticised for paying big salaries to officials, but in fact the appropriate levels were outside Strathclyde Regional Council's control. Staffing, contrary to public mythology, did not increase dramatically—in fact, some departments were less well staffed than their predecessors had been.

Since Watergate, almost every investigative reporter worth his salt has had a secret desire to bring down the government, however local, with one great exclusive revelation. But despite blazing headlines about 'junkets,' the scandals failed to materialise.

At first Geoff was sympathetic to public criticism, then amused by it. But latterly, he became irritated by it. He began to feel it personally. Words like 'misunderstanding', 'alarmist', 'sensationalist', 'distorting'—the stock-in-trade of the political spokesman—became more frequent in his public utterances. He had in fact a good relationship with the press. Reporters liked him because of his decency as a human being and because of his straight-forwardness. The man from Gorbals who had always avoided publicity like the plague, was often, because of his job, in the public spotlight. He came to appreciate the value of good publicity, without using it for personal glory.

As 1976 moved into 1977, Geoffrey Shaw was also finding it much harder than he thought to make substantial changes. Much of this had to do with the economic retrenchment in the country at large. Many of Strathclyde's decisions were being made for it by the Government, which in turn was having its decisions made by the International Monetary Fund. But it was also true to say that Geoff's passionate commitment to the areas of deprivation was not shared by all his colleagues, even though it was Labour Group policy.

If Geoff Shaw's election as Convener had been a victory for ideas, things might have been different. But he had been chosen for his personal qualities, which were so much needed both by the Labour Party and the new Region. He was there because he was useful, not because his ideas had convinced everyone. This realisation frustrated Geoff. He also found that to make radical changes, a politician needed to be absolutely sure that he knew what he wanted, had adequate support and was able to outmanoeuvre more conservative colleagues and officials. The Convener was convinced enough of the shape of what he wanted—justice for the underprivileged—but was less clear about the practicalities of realising it. This uncertainty was shared by bewildered officials, some of whom were unsympathetic to the general approach in any case.

Geoff was criticised because he trusted officials too much and relied too often on the appointment of social or community workers. The much-needed emphasis on deprivation and justice led to the development of a kind of deprivation industry, with masses of reports and the growth of a new and unattractive vocabulary. The language was only part of what Claude Thomson called "Parliamo Strathclyde"—citing such phrases as 'holding operation; ongoing situation; inherited commitment; inbuilt vacancy factor; realistic inbuilt vacancy factor; at this point in time; spin off from the estimates.'

It would be cynical in the extreme to suggest that the new focus on deprivation had produced only a change in vocabulary. In fact it reordered the Region's priorities and provided a screen through which all new programmes had to pass. Many deprived communities are only now beginning to reap the benefits in terms of extra resources, buildings and staff. Had Geoff Shaw not been a political convener, these things might not have happened, though of course it would be wrong to present it as his own single-handed achievement. It was, after all, Labour Group policy.

Nevertheless, the deeply-rooted problems of the West of Scotland, the lack of public resources, the extremely complicated nature of the interlocking causes of deprivation and the strength of "the way things are always done" lobby, all in the face of untried and uncertain alternatives, made sure that the gains were more modest than Geoff had hoped for. Often the convener would present proposals, after hours of examination and debate, with the characteristic phrase, "We have got this just about right." But in his heart of hearts he knew that something much more radical was required.

What he was discovering the hard way was that the convener's powers were somewhat limited. By the time proposals landed on his desk, they had generally been through the committee process and sifted by the chairman, who knew more about the subject matter than the convener did. Geoff was often like the man, who, when asked the way to Doncaster, replied "If I were going to Doncaster I wouldn't start from here."

The room for public manoeuvre was not always too great either, as Geoff had found to his cost. A demonstration in Glasgow outside Kingston Halls where the National Front were holding a public meeting, had led to the arrest of a number of prominent people. Geoff was angered by the arrests, feeling that the police had done less than justice. He wanted to rush out a statement condemning the police action—until he was reminded by his colleagues that he was the official head of the police authority.

He did not enjoy the rough and tumble of political life either. He was too sensitive and even too thin-skinned, to relish it. Intrigue and plotting were not part of his make-up. The world of politics is a bit like the arts, with malicious gossip being immensely enjoyed by the participants. Geoff had no time for either malice or even high-class, privileged, gossip. Frustrations, then, were not hard to find. Yet there were compensations.

The intellectual stimulation and challenge of seeking new solutions and trying to implement them was stretching. (He told Sarah he was most emotionally fulfilled in Gorbals and most intellectually fulfilled in Strathclyde). Travelling round the Region and talking with people was taxing, but enjoyable. And as convener, he had he had the opportunity of publicly backing everything from new ways of dealing with crime, to programmes supporting the arts.

Convener Shaw was still able to look at things from the standpoint of a Gorbals delinquent. He defended the privacy of people coming before the courts. Protesting about the terms proposed for social background reports, he demanded that only relevant information be recorded.

He said: "A lot of information is gathered for no apparent reason. It is imperative with these reports that a person involved realises precisely what is happening and is shown that there is no unnecessary interference with privacy.

"As a small example, I cannot for the life of me understand why one of the basic questions is about the offender's religion.

"The amassing of non-essential information about people is an unnecessary intrusion into their privacy. It is imperative that the offender should recognise that the information recorded is relevant to the disposal of his or her case."

Geoff had never forgotten the time a boy had come to him in tears. He had been humiliated in court by hearing his social worker seek to exonerate him by vilifying his parents and his home.

"Ah don't get the chance to see **his** hoose, an say whatAh think o' his mither and faither," said the lad.

He defended the new children's Panel System against its critics. Scotland should be proud of it, he said and should seek ways of making it work to its full potential.

"Sadly, sane and objective criticism of the Panel System is all too rare, because the objective critics understandably fear to be identified with the growing bandwagon of criticisms, sometimes, alas, coming from police officers."

Critics of the system, he said, seemed to suffer from an unrealistic nostalgia for the old days. The new Panel system he thought was likely to produce more constructive encounter between the child and his parents and the representative of the community than the courts ever did.

He also defended the practice of allowing people with court convictions to serve on the Children's Panels. He argued that there were many people who, having gone through the mill, were fully capable of adding value to the work of the panel. Justice must not be dispensed only by the co-called 'pillars of society', he said.

On the subject of the arts, Shaw criticised local authorities which failed to make grants to cultural and recreational bodies in proportion to their population. He also looked forward to the day when the economic situation was easier and councils could employ artists to work on sculpture and other projects.

He and Sarah were able to attend more concerts than they had been used to. Geoff had always loved music, but had not given himself a great deal of opportunity to indulge this pleasure. Attending a fiddlers' rally in Largs he was handed the baton and found the orchestra more readily responsive than he sometimes found the Labour Group. To cheers from the audience the former Edinburgh Academy music prize winner guided the orchestra through a Latin American number. It was almost as if some parts of his personality which had been suppressed in Gorbals were finding delayed fulfilment.

The former lawyer-to-be was appointed a member of the Royal Commission on the Law and he soon took up cudgels on behalf of young people who found difficulty in buying their own house. Opening a legal advice centre at Provanmill, the convener said that Scottish law needed to be reformed to protect people at the mercy of the housing sharks.

"Even here in Scotland the individual is often at the mercy of a massive system which in fact if not in theory is able to exploit and oppress those sections of our society which do not have ready access to the processes and procedures of the law," he said. He added that this oppression was particularly evident in the field of house purchase in many of Glasgow's older tenemental areas, where people had been 'grossly exploited' by the activities of the least scrupulous housing agencies.

On February 15, 1977 a small but significant item of news appeared in the papers. It was to the effect that two civic leaders in the West of Scotland, Councillor Geoffrey Shaw and Lord Provost Peter McCann, had been nominated to the Labour Party's panel of candidates for the Scottish Assembly.

On April 9, 1977 Geoffrey Mackintosh Shaw celebrated his fiftieth birthday. He was going to have to decide whether to press forward to the proposed Scottish Assembly, possibly to become first Scottish 'prime minister,' or perhaps even to give up political life altogether.

Chapter X
Tae Think Again

There is a storm coming that shall try your foundation. Scotland must be rid of Scotland before the delivery come. —
Robert Renwick on the scaffold, 1668.

Your responsibility is indeed terrifying. If you fail, it is God, thanks to your having betrayed Him, who will fail mankind. You fancy you can be responsible to *God; can you carry the responsibility* for *God?*
Dag Hammarskold.

Geoff Shaw had never been particularly keen on the idea of a Scottish Assembly. He had voted against it on the Scottish Labour Party Executive and he argued repeatedly that the new Regions needed to be given time to work. He was, of course, totally opposed to the Scottish National Party proposals to scrap the Regions and concentrate decision-making power in Edinburgh. He felt that ordinary working people in Scotland had more in common with the Yorkshire miners than with Scottish landowners and was sceptical of claims that a Scottish Assembly would find a new formula to solve Scotland's problems.

Much of this scepticism came from his own experience at Strathclyde. At a consultation on 'The Scottish Churches and Scotland's Future' at Dunblane in July 1976 he had asked the question in what sense were the new goals politically possible? In the reorganisation of local government, he pointed out, the structural **continuity** had proved more significant than the structural **change.** This would still be true with a Scottish Assembly. Nor must one over-emphasise the extent to which political decisions could change people's attitudes; the influence of the media was perhaps far greater. A key question would be the relation of community-action groups to the local authorities through the new community councils, which might also monitor the work of other public bodies which were not directly accountable.

It was a sober statement by an idealistic and able man who had learned through experience how entrenched were the

255

old ways of working and how heady talk about a new future needed the discipline of close attention to the political realities.

Why, then, was he now on the panel of candidates for the Scottish Assembly? There were a number of reasons. First, devolution was now official Labour Party policy and the Party was, with great difficulty, pushing a Bill through the House of Commons. Geoff was a Labour Party loyalist. He did not, of course, agree with everything the Party said, but approving as he did of the main shape of its policies, he felt obliged to give his support.

Second, he came round to the view that the Scottish Assembly and the Regions need not clash. The Assembly's main business would be legislative—it would be an extension of central government and would still need local government to implement its legislation. This, of course, still fell far short of enthusiastic endorsement. Third, the hard facts of the matter were that if the Scotland Bill became law, the Scottish Assembly would be there whether Geoff liked it or not. It would be making decisions affecting the people of Scotland. Would it not be better to be in there influencing decisions rather than standing aside?

Fourth, and more personally, he might not be re-elected to Strathclyde Regional Council. He had strong fears that he might lose his seat. In May 1976 the Nationalists, who were riding the crest of a wave, had made big inroads in District Council elections—to the extent that the Labour administration felt compelled to give up the reins of office. the SNP gains had come in largely working class areas. Geoff's own Govanhill seat, despite his personal victory, seemed marginal. If he wished to remain in political life, it might have to be through the Scottish Assembly.

Fifth, he might not be re-elected convener of Strathclyde Regional Council, or he might find the convener's powers drastically reduced. He had learned a great deal about political decision-making and had gained a lot of exper-ience. Was it right that this should go to waste when so much was still crying out to be done?

Finally, might not the Scottish Assembly still turn out to be an arena of more actual power from which to get things done? Aneurin Bevan had related how he sought power in his local council in the Welsh valleys, but did not find much there. He went to Westminster to seek this elusive power to influence events, but did not find a great deal as a back bench MP. So he came a member of the Cabinet. And so on.

Another explanation might be that Geoff Shaw had simply become politically ambitious and enjoyed the exercise of power so much that he wanted more. This is a possibility, but evidence is unavailable. Some political colleagues have argued that he must have been ambitious to have risen to the position he did. Yet they are bewildered by the fact that the usual signs of an ambitious and ruthless politician were not there—no outsize ego, no corpses strewn on the battlefield. Geoff struck most people as a man who was genuinely unambitious for himself, but who was ambitious to make change for the benefit of the people. At the same time it must be said that he was an intensely private man, despite all the publicity. There was a deep, personal inner core which made him an enigma to some of his colleagues. He kept his private thoughts to himself. A Machiavellian schemer he certainly was not, but beyond that who knows what conscious or sub-conscious thoughts were, or were not, there? Geoff himself wrote an intriguing sentence: "The modern Jewish philosopher Martin Buber used to talk of the innermost secret person. And all of us know that what lies deep in our own heart is often unknown to ourselves, let alone to the other."

What can be said is that the decision to go on the Assembly panel of candidates did not spring from a certainty of mind or a plan. In fact he was very, very uncertain about future directions. The Assembly decision was a provisional one, which would at least keep another option open. (It is interesting, incidentally, that during the referendum debate in February 1979 Geoff's name was invoked by both the 'Yes' and the 'No' campaigners to gain support for their positions.)

In the meantime there was a great deal to be occupying his time. The Glasgow Eastern Area Renewal project, for instance. Geoff was on the governing committee of the project, which had been established by the Government

257

with a view to regenerating the old East End of Glasgow. It fitted the Strathclyde policy of concentrating resources on areas of need, rather than putting them into more new towns. (The Secretary of State for Scotland had, by this time, agreed with Strathclyde's reasoning and had halted the development of Stonehouse New Town.)

Writing in the *East End Forum,* the convener declared: "As a Regional Council we have taken the quite firm political decision to concentrate as much as possible of our effort in those parts of Strathclyde Region which most demand priority treatment. Many of these are, sadly, within the city, but not all, by any means. Wherever they are, including the East End, they will clearly be making priority demands on the resources and attention of the Region."

Pointing out that the new towns, valuable though they were, had been successful largely at the expense of the older areas, he went on: "It is a bit too simple to say that the East End Project is a new town. But clearly some of the resources which would have gone into Stonehouse must be directed to the East End and clearly also much of the expertise and skill which has gone into the creation of the new towns should now be available in the East End. The main difference, of course, is that there is already in the East End a fair amount that is new and a great deal of the old which will stay. And most of all there are lively communities of people. So it is not a question of building a whole new town from scratch, as in Cumbernauld or East Kilbride, nor of grafting a new town on to the old, as in Irvine. It is a matter of taking away what cannot be kept and weaving the new into the old."

After referring to his own experiences in Bridgeton twenty years previously, Geoff urged local groups to work hard at the underlying questions—"What kind of East End do we really want? What were the things which made a 'good dump' even out of those parts where the physical environment was at its worst? What sort of work should we try to plan for? Do we want the old haphazard mixture of work and housing close at hand to each other? What sort of initiatives can communities take by themselves to make the East End a better place to live and work in? These and a

258

hundred others, demand the careful and imaginative thought of the local communities. After all, neglect could never totally destroy a community, nor can all the good planning in the world create a new community. Only people do that, and people who care enough to make it work."

Geoff pinned his hopes on 'the people' rising from apathy to change Glasgow's future. In an article in the *Evening Times* he wrote: "It is not difficult with hindsight to see some of the tragic errors of judgement and administration which marred the magnificent intentions of the City Fathers. No one doubts now what only a few were saying fifty years ago—that the huge perimeter schemes would throw up serious problems if they were seen only as dormitory suburbs on the outer rim of a vast wheel. They should have been towns within a city. No one doubts now that greater efforts should have been made to retain intact community structures of neighbour and family. But perhaps too little attention has been paid to changes which were taking place in society anyway—the desire for greater mobility, changing patterns of entertainment, etc. And perhaps, too, we have paid too little attention to the fact that Glasgow is only now really awakening from the fearful apathy which seemed to accept that change could only be effected by 'them'—the Corporation, the officials, the 'other people' who seemed to make decisions for the future behind closed doors."

The quiet man from Edinburgh went on: "Glasgow is a city of the gut reaction—spontaneous generosity; swift and fleeting anger; sudden bursts of pride; instant surges of wildly ill-informed criticism of what appears to be the blunder of the day. Without its intense emotions Glasgow would die. But more and more the gut reaction is being disciplined by the hard lessons of those who are prepared to engage at the local level in the long slog of putting things right. This is the hope for Glasgow's future."

But Convener Shaw was concerned about more than Glasgow. Ambassadors paying their respects came to Melrose House, perhaps somewhat doubtfully, and found their meetings with the convener lasting much longer than they expected. Some who came to scoff remained to tea.

259

They were impressed by the sincerity of this man who listened carefully to what they had to say and who was so knowledgeable on such a wide range of subjects. The US Ambassador Mrs Anne Armstrong was very complimentary. (Even a Miss World, Miss Cindy Breakespeare, came by to say hello.)

Ceremonial occasions with the Royal Family. Lunches with foreign dignitaries. Consultations with national political leaders. All were part of the convener's remit. He had to have more suits. Appearing at a ceremony in Govanhill he was chaffed about his smarter appearance by a friend from Gorbals days. Geoff replied: "If it's good enough for Her Majesty, it's good enough for the people of Govanhill."

Geoff and Sarah were good ambassadors for the Region in such company. Yet, incredibly, his first priority was still total availability for people in trouble. The phone calls and visits to Melrose House continued and he took time out to go to Barlinnie. When Colin Johnston, a 15-year old Easterhouse schoolboy apparently destined for the dole queue had a book of his punk rock drawings published, Convener Shaw immediately wrote him a note of congratulation.

Total availability was not easy for Sarah. Still doing social work for the Iona Community, she was worried about the day-to-day pressures on Geoff, plus the demands by youngsters. But total availability was too much of the bedrock of Geoff's existence for him to change, even if he had wanted to.

There was one boy in particular who needed a lot of help. He had a severe drinking problem and Geoff was the only one he could rely on in times of stress, which were often. Geoff and Sarah would often find him slumped on their doorstep like a stray and unwanted dog at weekends. Geoff didn't have it in his heart to turn him away: he knew he was the boy's last hope. It got so wearing that sometimes Sarah had to have weekends away just to get some sleep. On one occasion, after an exhausting day for Geoff, the lad came in a desperate state at 3.00 am. He jangled the bell repeatedly, but this time Geoff had decided he had had enough. He didn't get up. The tense silence was broken by the shattering of glass as a brick came through the window above the door. Geoff, tired and strained, talked to the boy through the door, explaining that though he still accepted him, he could not continue in this way. The lad eventually went off and Geoff suffered agonies wondering about his fate. He was almost relieved when he continued to come back.

The cost of discipleship was dear for every one involved. But Sarah never expects to see again in her lifetime the dimension of patience and love her husband showed that broken and demoralised lad.

Geoff's colleagues at Melrose House knew little or nothing of all this. They simply saw that the convener sometimes looked a bit the worse for wear and warned him about his overworking.

Overwork he certainly did. A typical day looked something like this. Rise 8 am. Switch on Radio 3. (He seemed to know all the classical music played, and would often sing along to it). Telephone calls. Leave home at 9.15. Melrose House at 10.00. Mail. Dictate letters. Committee meeting. (As convener he was an ex-officio member of every committee on the council). Lunch with visiting dignitary, or pie and pint with Willie Quail at a pub around the corner. 2.00 pm, presentation of prizes at Ayr Community Centre. 3.00, meeting with District Council chairman at Ayr. 4.45, record television interview. 5.30, home for a quick meal with Sarah, then feet up for a quick snooze, usually interrupted by the telephone. 7.00, out to Castlemilk for presentation of prizes. 8.30, on to community council meeting seminar in Govanhill. 10 pm, home with briefcase. Papers to read. Telephone calls. Midnight, the door bell...

'Who will save the world when I am gone,' was the caption on a cartoon he kept at home. Geoff was existing on five hours sleep a night, with naps at lunch or tea time and in his official car. He told Jimmy Semple: "I like the Oban runs—I can get a good sleep on them."

Observing on several occasions how tired the Strathclyde Convener was, Ford Spence invited Geoff and Sarah to

261

spend a few days with him in the quiet village of Benderloch.

"Each time pressure of duty prevented the invitation being accepted, although I knew that both Sarah and Geoffrey would have dearly liked to spend a few quiet days together. But it was not the nature of the man to place self before service to others," said the Argyll and Bute chairman.

He responded to many requests to speak at local community meetings. He acknowledged that he found difficulty in saying no and he felt it very important to stay in touch with grass roots feeling.

This availability and the desire to serve continued to spring from his Christian faith. Conventional church worship meant little to him; so much of the language failed to speak to his situation and to the dilemmas he was facing. He used to say that God was kicking Christians out into the world where hard decisions had to be made. He never saw his role in politics as being to convert other people, and he fell over backwards to avoid being the representative 'minister in politics.' He recognised the difficulty of his position and he never believed all ministers should be involved in party politics—he simply felt it was his particular vocation at that particular time. He was always afraid people would think he was taking advantage of his political position to advance religious causes and because of this bending-over-backwards, some people thought he was anti-religious!

(He certainly felt disillusioned with the Church at times and could not abide the jostling of church leaders for privileged positions. "Cut out the 'Rev.' ", he snapped at one such time when a printed invitation to a function was going out in the name of Councillor the Rev. Geoffrey Shaw.)

Even in his worst moments, however, he was a religious man in the Bonhoefferian sense—seeing the whole world as Christ's and understanding his present vocation not as the imposing of religious externals, but as grappling with the central issues which affected the life of the world.

A statement by Geoff, "Man the political animal", was

recorded by the BBC in their *Christ and Caesar* series in November 1977. He said:

"I always doubt the word of those who say they are non-political—the one who says something like "I'm not political, but it's time theyabolishedthe trade unions!" Or "I'm not political, but I think the price of cabbage is outrageous," or even, "All politicians should be shot."

"Each of these—and thousands of statements like them uttered in every house and pub and office—each of these is highly political. They are statements about the way mankind lives in our modern society, the way priorities of spending are decided, the people who make political decisions for us. Behind them lie countless assumptions and from them flow countless implications for our local communities, our work, our national and even our international relationships. They are indeed statements about the very stuff of politics. It's my belief that the Christian least of all has the right to say that such matters are irrelevant. For the conversation of God with his people is about his world—its peace, its prosperity, its poverty, its reconciliation, its mercy, its love, its suffering, its caring, its hate and its love.

"The Church may, though in our day rarely does, make its voice clearly heard on the directions it believes contemporary society should move; the voters may combine to express their corporate majority or minority views; but it is elected politicians, representing their Party at national or local level, who are entrusted with the responsibility to frame legislation, to establish priorities, to use or to control those external forces which so profoundly determine the lives of us all. The Christian cannot ignore or deride the actions of politicians. Indeed, the Christian most of all knows that he leaves human beings in the lurch if he neglects the political scene.

"History bears witness to countless thunderously evil actions and policies perpetrated in the name of religion; sometimes indeed by men whose private lives were, and are, lives of impeccable Christian virtue. History also, of course, bears witness equally to countless actions and

263

policies which have sought to interpret the living, loving angry Word of God within society.

"The Christian therefore does not stand back from the contemporary Party political scene, his holy hands unspoiled by the supposedly distorting influence of politics. He does not bay to the moon for a Christian utopia. In the light of his understanding of the love of God, the Christian can only throw in his hand with those who seem to be travelling a similar road through all the human aspirations and conflicts of our time."

"For my part I'm a socialist—not a very good or a very consistent socialist, but then I'm not a very good or a very consistent Christian either. I share this political creed in one form or another with immediate colleagues and with millions of socialists throughout the world. But underlying and underpinning the political creed is an even deeper and prior faith which for me dictates my allegiance to socialism. That faith, my understanding of the Christian faith, is based on what the Biblical Word of God declares to me. Let me state it as simply as I can.

"For me the Word of God is cruelly distorted by a system in which the capital wealth of the world is concentrated in the hands of a few. For me, the Christ who wept over a city and in violent anger drove out the extortioners from the Temple, commands a continuing compassion and anger over injustice and exploitation. That God is on the side of the poor commands a 'corresponding allegiance'. That the Word of God was made flesh and dwelt among us commands that we share in those truly secular decisions which ensure the equal dignity of all men and women.

"Casear cannot replace the Christ. Caesar cannot bring into being the Kingdom of God. Rather Christ breathes life into Caesar, into government, into affairs of State, into the stuff of politics. To turn your back on the political reality of life is to desert the world for which Christ died."

Thus spoke the worldly holy man who was travelling a lonely road. He had said in a previous interview that the Christian had no special revelation so far as specific political choices were concerned and had to become lost, legitimately lost, within the political process. The options he faced daily did not come to him marked 'Christian' and 'non-Christian.' There were times when he did indeed feel lost, and wondered whether he was travelling the right way: the sadness was that he did not have around him a group who, from their own experience, understood the painful dilemmas well enough and could reflect on them from the same kind of standpoint. There was—and is—no one else involved in day-to-day Scottish political life with the same capacity to articulate in a sophisticated, yet clear way a theological understanding of the political process. What Geoff desperately lacked was time for such reflection.

In terms of political ideals, he remained on the left. The gentle, open, reconciling style which gained him the respect and affection of political opponents remained linked to a desire for radical change. The British politician who made most sense to him was Tony Benn. Geoff recognised a kindred radical Christian spirit. After conversations with him, his admiration was confirmed.

An incident which Geoff's friends recall as making him very angry involved the Prime Minister, James Callaghan. When Mr Callaghan had gone to visit an old people's home in Easterhouse he was met with a noisy demonstration over rising unemployment figures. Geoff was present, and the Premier's dismissal of the young demonstrators as 'empty vessels' incensed him. He had seen too much of the effects of unemployment on teenagers in Gorbals to appreciate that remark.

When angered by things like this, Geoff wondered whether he should get out of politics. Political life had many attractions and compensations, yet it was costly, even in simple ways.

Colin Morris, a friend from Gorbals days, met the convener at the Open at Turnberry one day. Geoff, who was there on duty, asked him to come and eat at the reception he was holding. Colin declined, saying he intended to go

265

and paddle in the sea. "I'd give anything just to be able to do that," was Geoff's wistful reply.

In some respects Geoff was becoming boxed in. He had discovered how strongly entrenched the political system was and how difficult it was to make substantial changes. In 1977, for example, the Region abandoned the exhaustive and exhausting system of examination of the budget proposals and reverted to the old-style procedure whereby the convener, the group leader and the Finance Committee chairman looked at each department's budget options separately at a short session and reported in broad terms to the full Policy and Resources Committee. He had been able to make some significant changes, but he had found that it was not so easy to stride into the temple and scatter the money changers.

At the same time he believed strongly in the possibilities of Strathclyde and felt that only the Labour Party, conservative though it might be at times, had the necessary vision and machinery to bring about change. Gradually and imperceptibly he became more and more of a public apologist both for Strathclyde and for the Labour Party.

Friends observed a harder note, a more rigid party stance. On television he was doing the things expected of party spokesmen—saying that bad election results were not really so bad and blaming most things on the opposition. He was afflicted by the widespread Labour paranoia about the SNP and took most opportunities to attack the Nationalists. He was at a danger point for any politician who wishes to remain a human being—when natural charm can degenerate into mere technique.

He was beginning to do some of the things he had always stood out against—categorising and labelling, and looking for conspiracies. This traditional spokesman role pleased some of his colleagues, but dismayed many of his friends. He was now silent on issues such as segregated schooling. (And on segregated housing, too. He used to compare the new towns with selective schools, since they were able to 'cream off' Glasgow residents. The grading of local authority tenants was also anathema to him.)

He had learned some political lessons since the Kingston

days. But was he being true to himself? Had the man who had gone into politics to make radical changes simply become a cheer leader for the status quo? It was one thing to breathe life into Caesar. What if the insatiable and ungrateful Caesar were devouring the Christ?

These were questions Geoff asked himself repeatedly. The internal debate intensified towards the end of 1977 as he was forced to consider the various options open to him. By this time some straight talking had been done on the internal Strathclyde problem of the two sources of political power. It was clear that the convener's job was likely to become more ceremonial in the future, with political leadership the prerogative of the group leader. Geoff was good at the ambassadorial and spokesman roles—he had undoubtedly given Strathclyde the best possible start. But had he come into politics to become an after dinner speaker, or a television spokesman?

Further questioning came with the offer of a knighthood in the New Years Honours list. It created a genuine conflict. Geoff did not want the honour for himself. He felt the system was archaic and conflicted with the Christian understanding of man. But should he not see it as a political honour for Strathclyde? He was under pressure, particularly because of the rivalry with Glasgow District Council, to accept such a sign of status. He consulted with Sarah and his close friends and took their feelings into account.

It has a curious feel about it—Sir Geoffrey Shaw. Would it not have brought him full circle: the Edinburgh Academy boy, born to lead? Sir Geoffrey Shaw, second-term Convener of Strathclyde Regional Council being whisked away in a limousine to propose a toast to the Japanese ambassador. Sir Geoffrey Shaw, freed from the troubles of internal politics, presenting road safety awards at Melrose House. Sir Geoffrey Shaw, mixing with the best of Scottish company, renowned for his witty after-dinner speeches.

Get thee behind me, Satan! He knew in his heart of hearts that it wasn't him. He understood that there are, literally, fates worse than death. He turned it down.

But what should he do? He expressed to Sarah on several occasions his misgivings about continuing in politics. He felt he was best and happiest at the Gorbals kind of thing. He continually debated within himself whether personal individual service or wider political work was, for him, the best way of fulfilling his Christian vocation.

Jimmy Semple drove Geoff on a number of occasions to Priesthill, a deteriorating housing scheme in Glasgow. The convener said several times he would like to live and work there and he mentioned it as a possibility to Sarah.

He told some of his Gorbals intimates that he would like to give up politics and return to the kind of work he had been doing in Gorbals. At the opening of a new youth club in Calton he remarked to friends there, "When I'm finished this job I must get back to this."

In conversation with Sarah he said more than once that he envied his brother David, professor of clinical neurology at Newcastle University, since he was engaged in medical work which was providing straightforward benefit to people. And once—how nice it would be to be a lawyer!

Geoff was at a very difficult crossroads in his life. It was complicated by offers made to him. He was asked about doing a lecture tour in North America and he was also sounded out about taking a prominent position in a Scottish new town. He had been approached about being a candidate at two Parliamentary by-elections.

He yearned to go back to youth work: at the same time he had learned a lot about the machinery of politics and his experience ought not to be thrown away. And the Scottish Assembly, with all its uncertainties and all his misgivings, beckoned him.

Supposing he lost his seat at the next election in May 1978? Political prophets were going so far as to suggest that the Nationalists might take control of Strathclyde. He told close friends that if that happened he would like to go away and write a book, drawing some lessons from his experiences. And what if he won his seat, but declined to become convener under the probable new terms, or what if he was not re-elected? Since he had become personified as Mr Strathclyde life would be rather difficult for his successor.

All these were racking questions and Geoff felt rather isolated as he faced them. He was afraid of losing touch with his Gorbals friends, some of whom didn't want to bother him because he was so busy. He would phone Mrs Irvine to ask her to come over and he made her son, Denis, promise to come and see him more often. He was very glad when friends from Gorbals continued to turn up for the Christmas Eve service at Queen Mary Avenue.

For Geoff, the Gorbals Group had never quite come to an end. There were a few parties, usually when people who had been part of the Group left. On one occasion he asked John Harvey to celebrate Communion: every gathering of Gorbals Group people was, for him, a kind of Group meeting.

As 1978 dawned, despite the apparent certainty of the spokesman on television, Geoffrey Shaw was a man with deep and searching questions in his inner being. He was trying to re-locate his spiritual roots, without having the peace and quiet and setting in which to do so. Whatever else it was, Melrose House was no monastery.

"Willie, Willie," he would say to his personal assistant, shaking his head.

Politics sometimes sickened him. Yet was his duty not to stay there, amid the exhaustion, the calculations, the advantage-seeking, the half truths, the erosion, even, of his own ideals? Was this not precisely where God's action was? If people like himself were not prepared to make changes from within the system, was the violence which he abhorred not inevitable?

He had never grabbed the cup of political leadership, nor had he manoeuvred for it, yet he was not sure in his own soul whether he wanted to let it pass or not. The man who had never been called to a charge by the Kirk had answered a call from the people of the West of Scotland. He would never give up that charge, even if it broke his heart.

Chapter XI
As Prison'd Birds Must Find in Freedom

Ministers of good things are like torches, a light to others, waste and destruction to themselves.—
Richard Hooker, 16th century Anglican divine.

Come, now, solemnest feast on the road to freedom,
Death, and destroy those fetters that bow, those walls that imprison
This our transient life, these souls that linger in darkness,
So that at last we see what is here withheld from our vision.
Long did we seek you, Freedom, in discipline, action and suffering.
Now that we die, in the face of God himself we behold you.
Dietrich Bonhoeffer (Stations on the Road to Freedom)

The firemen's strike which had begun in November and dragged on through most of January, added to the pressures on Geoff Shaw. It brought back all the memories and feelings of the 1973 strike and it showed in his face. Again, he had a great deal of sympathy with the men and was frustrated—as he often was by this time—by being hemmed in by the system. He felt powerless, despite his apparently powerful position. The troops came in again and the convener often appeared at the scene of late night fires looking drawn and anxious.

He was obviously run down and it affected his powers of concentration. He was operating well below par and when he was exhausted he felt tired of political life. Friends such as Len Turpie, leader of the Strathclyde Conservative Group, privately urged him to get out. Tom Fleming bumped into his old friend at the television studios and seeing how tired he was said, "Take it easy, guid folk are scarce." Geoff just laughed and shrugged his shoulders. Later, when Tom saw him go out to the official car the actor mimicked a chauffeur saluting. Geoff laughed.

The endless negotiations and meetings took their toll. Geoff was smoking heavily: a colleague passed a note to him

271

during a meeting pointing out that he had just lit up his eighth cigarette. He knew himself that he wasn't as fit as in the days when he was training Gorbals boys for football, or hill-climbing regularly. Even his attempt at a regular squash commitment went by the board as his time and energy went into problem-solving.

The development of community councils was at a crucial stage and Geoff was involved in a considerable number of community council meetings. He believed the councils, which had been established under the re-organisation legislation to represent the views of local communities to the authorities, could be key groups for the future. These grass roots organisations might even be able to put pressure on entrenched or unimaginative elected representatives and lobby for reform. When requests to speak came in he could not, or would not, say no.

One of Geoff's advisers on community councils was Andy Fyfe, a member of the Community Council Resource Team. It was an instance of the radiation of ideas from the Gorbals Group that the wee boy who, with his brothers, wouldn't go to sleep on Group meeting nights until Geoff had been in to clown around with them was now assisting the convener on one aspect of his work. Geoff treated young people as mature human beings. A lot is talked about racism and sexism. Geoff also avoided age-ism.

When invited to speak he did not avoid controversy. He opposed calls to bring back the birch for violent crime. Speaking in Glasgow on January 29, 1978, he said: "My colleagues in Strathclyde totally reject the extremist views of some politicians who know that the more grotesquely repressive the views they express, the more publicity they will get for them.

"We take a wider and deeper view of the problem of law and order, which is quite wrongly caricatured. It is thought of merely as softness or making of excuses. We genuinely believe that the early years of a child's family and social surroundings are important and can create problems which are at the root of crime. That is why we continue to support the Children's Panel system."

Convener Shaw claimed to be speaking on behalf of his

colleagues in Strathclyde, but more than a few within the party did not share his views and indeed regarded him as extreme. Geoff could never understand why working class councillors in a socialist party could support measures which he regarded as hard-line. He was also criticised for his repeated public support for the Special Unit at Barlinnie. He was a member of its committee and was a trustee for the charity established with the proceeds of Jimmy Boyle's biography, *A Sense of Freedom.*

In January the convener opened a new £1 million police headquarters at Maryhill. The following month he expressed fears that prison treatment was about to take two steps backward by the re-introduction of the special segregation unit at Porterfield Prison, Inverness. He wanted better training for police and more imaginative ways of dealing with offenders. He had earlier appealed to young people during a period of public alarm about rising crime figures: "To those young people who don't give a damn for the law or for other people, it is time that we were beginning to say 'Screw the nut yourselves'; for many of us are convinced that one of the signs of a truly civilised society is the extent to which control by force becomes less and less necessary."

He enjoyed this aspect of politics, the promotion of ideas which he felt would bring about a more humane and decent society. But was a second term at Strathclyde worth it? The question continued to nag at him as he went about his duties. He told Jimmy Semple he would stay in politics while he still felt he had something to contribute—"I think I've still got a bit of damage to do yet."

The *Glasgow Herald* for February 28, 1978 named Geoffrey Shaw as one of the front runners in its feature under the heading 'Who will rule Scotland?'

"The Strathclyde Regional Convener had a meteoric rise to power in local government. Within three years of being elected he was leader of its Labour group and the following year became top man in the Labour-controlled Region. At 50 he could go a long way in the Assembly, though he has not publicly committed himself yet. He has a fine record of social work to which he has devoted himself rather than accept a charge as an ordained Church of Scotland minister."

It was not just newspaper talk. Shrewd political judges in various parts of Scotland rated Shaw a very strong candidate for the highest office. He had a wide appeal. He was a man of proven integrity and ability. He would shine in a Scottish Assembly which, as a legislature, would offer more scope for ideas and debate than would local government, which was more decision-oriented. Yes, Shaw could well be the man to create a new and healthy political mood in Scotland.

The creation of a Scottish Assembly in the near future seemed to be on the cards. With the Government determined, the Nationalists on the rampage and the opinion polls showing apparently strong support for devolution, the Royal High School looked set for new occupancy. Labour's unity was paper-thin, however, as analysis of the indecisive referendum result was to show.

Thursday, March 9, 1978. The convener attacks fellow councillors, employers and health board officials for failing to turn up at a conference on employment for the disabled. "I have a great sense of personal disappointment at the size of the turnout," he says.

Friday, March 10. Social work seminar on addiction at Hamilton. Jimmy Semple notices the convener looks grey and urges him to see his doctor. In the evening, after a meeting, Bill Towill, tenants' association activist, talks with him. Geoff leans on his car, ashen faced, complaining of pains in his chest, saying he will go to see his doctor.

Saturday, March 11. Chairs a seminar on multiple deprivation in the morning. On to Garscadden for a walkabout in the Parliamentary by-election in support of the Labour candidate, Donald Dewar. Back to seminar at Dundasvale. On to Hampden for the Glasgow v. Manchester schoolboy international. Hosts a dinner for the teams and officials, making a witty speech, with good-natured jibes at the referee. Leaves at 7.30 with Councillor Harley. Talks for half an hour about the problems of the coming week.

Sunday, March 12. Geoff and Sarah at lunch and afternoon discussion with Len and Deirdre Turpie, Ian Lindsay-Smith (then editor of the *Glasgow Herald*) and Conor Cruise O'Brien. Evening: visitors. Geoff talks with a friend until 1.30 am.

Monday, March 13. Labour executive meeting. Secretary sees the convener sitting with his head in his hands. Jimmy Semple picks up Geoff, vice-convener Charles Gray and Councillor James Burns to go to a meeting with the press in Ayr. Geoff has a nap in the car. Jimmy Semple sees him suddenly grimace and clutch his leg. Geoff asks to be taken straight to hospital. The driver stops a policeman to get directions to the nearest hospital. The policeman jumps in and the car races to Kilmarnock Infirmary.

The news that Geoff Shaw had suffered a heart attack seemed to send shock waves through the West of Scotland. The news bulletins were followed by floods of letters and telephone calls expressing concern.

It seemed hardly believable that this fit, active and relatively young man had been struck down. Immediate arrangements were made for Sarah to stay at the hospital. It looked as if it might be touch and go.

Then Geoff began to get steadily better. The bulletins became more hopeful and he was pronounced as being 'off the danger list.' It was not long before he was sitting up. He asked to see Willie Quail and Jimmy Semple and they found their boss in good spirits—and could he have paper and pen?

There was one thing in particular Geoff wanted to do. He had been due to speak at the Conference of Scottish Local Authorities annual meeting in Oban and he wished to pay affectionate tribute to Sir George Sharp, the retiring president. Sitting up in bed in Kilmarnock he wrote the speech, which was delivered by Councillor Charles O'Halloran, in the convener's stead. Written in the same Old Testament style as the tribute to Dick Stewart it began with a brilliant account of the founding of COSLA and Sir George's election. The speech went on:

"And they shouted to him from all corners of the cities and the towns and the Regions and the Districts of Scotland—yea, even unto Penicuik. "Speak to us," they said, "words of wisdom that we may know the height and the depth and the width and the length of the future of

Scotland." And George stood before all the people and all the representatives of the people and he said, "It would be singularly unfortunate," and with that he departed to attend a concert of the Scottish National Orchestra.

"So COSLA appointed for itself wise men and scribes and chamberlains and magicians and those who could work wonders with numbers, and at their head was Graham Speirs—the greatest magician of all.

"So all the Convention said: 'We have appointed many stalwart staff and have put up fine offices, yea, we have also a president and a vice-president. Now indeed we are in business.'

"Yet did no one know what business they should be doing. So they enquired of Graham Speirs and he replied: 'First let us hunt for larger premises so that we can appoint more wise men. Second, give me but six short months, I and my staff, and we will think up some business for you.'

"But it was not to be. For the Lord sent to afflict them a new ruler of unparalleled brutality whose name was Bruce. And he called the representatives of the people together and he said unto them: 'Denis hath put the squeeze on my shekels. Therefore must I also grievously afflict you. Therefore hear this, all ye representatives. From this day on, seventy two and a half per cent becomes sixty eight and a half per cent.'

"And all the representatives of the people fell on their faces and smote their breasts and wailed loudly. And George Sharp said: 'All I can say is, this is singularly unfortunate.' And he led the representatives from the room.

"And throughout Scotland was there wailing and grinding of teeth. Peter of Lothian said, 'We don't actually use percentages in Lothian, but nevertheless, woe is I' (for, coming from Edinburgh he was very well educated.) 'Woe is me,' said Sandy of Grampian. 'Woe is me,' said Tom of Monklands. 'Woe is me,' said Highland Munro. 'Och-on, Och-on,' said Donald of the Isles. 'Woe is me,' said they of Cunninghame and Kirkcaldy, Fife and the Borders. Yea all of Scotland. Except for Ian Clark of Shetland, who said, 'Ah, Sullom Voe is me,' and took over the British National Oil Corporation.

"Thus did COSLA progress under the wise leadership of George Sharp, who in time became Sir George Sharp, 'Because,' said the Queen, 'I am proud of Scotland on a knight like this.'

"And the time came when Sir George announced that he would no longer seek to serve in local government, so all of COSLA gathered at Oban and offered to George their affection, their respect and their good wishes.

'Here endeth the First Lesson.'

The speech was received with tears of laughter and acclaim. Not only was it a brilliant effort, but the irrepressible humour was a sign of life.

On March 21 it was announced that Councillor Shaw would seek re-election at the Regional poll on May 2. He would not be able to take an active part in the campaign, but his election agent, Tom Murphy, and supporters, would work hard on his behalf.

All was not well, however. He suffered a relapse and was transferred to Glasgow Royal Infirmary. When Sarah went in she was told that Geoff's heart was beating too fast and that they were proposing to give him an electric shock to regulate the beat. The next ten minutes in the waiting room were agony for Sarah.

The treatment worked. The heart beat was back to normal.

Two weeks later Sarah had a call in the night. The same thing. Nightmare. Oxygen masks. Spotlights. Pain.

The next day Geoff told the staff that if it happened again, not to bring him round. He knew himself that he could not go on in that way.

But instead of becoming worse, Geoff got better and better. His strength seemed to come back. The heart specialist decided that an operation might be effective. Geoff was involved in the discussions and the date of the operation was fixed for May 13.

The time in hospital was a time to be treasured by both Geoff and Sarah. She came in each day to play Scrabble or to read to him. He particularly enjoyed *And the Cock Crew.* Sarah also brought in the many letters from well-wishers. He refused to be parted from one letter, from George MacLeod (now Very Rev. Lord MacLeod of Fuinary).

Part of the letter read: "This single word from me. Perhaps you are 'living in the mountains,' in which case it is not necessary. But should you occasionally feel you are 'on the beach,' this word—the greatest scientific discovery of this century was Einstein's, that there is no such thing as dead matter: the very atom is light energy. And Christ did not just say he is the Light of the Church: or the life of the converted soul. He is indeed both, because he is the Light of the **world.** In Him, every **thing** becomes every blessed thing.

"Christ is above you: yes, and 'underneath are the everlasting arms.' But science now validates that He is in you, vibrant in your corpuscles as well. 'We are no longer two, but one flesh: this is a great mystery I speak concerning Christ and the Church,' says St Paul. He is vibrant in what makes your brain: vibrant in your heart: vibrant in your corpuscles, really and truly. So leave it to Him, not to come down and lift you: but to take over his whole corpus that is you, **where he is already.**

"Prayer ceases to be pleading and becomes relaxed realisation (not resignation).

"Dance a jig in the mountains! God is blessing you. Amen means it is so. **He** is your future. Dance that jig.

"Yours ever, George."

When Geoff read the letter he wept and said, "I love that man."

For the first time in years Geoff had the opportunity to be be still and to think and to share it all with Sarah. It was a time for reflection and for tenderness, and sometimes for tears. The Royal Infirmary was hardly a monastery, but at least there was no crushing agenda. The man on whom so many people had depended for life-giving strength was now himself dependent and he was deeply moved by the experience.

Geoff had time to contemplate the possibilities before

him. If he died, he said, he supposed there would have to be a service 'in there'—rolling his head in the direction of the nearby Glasgow Cathedral. He was himself deeply aware of the ironies, but he knew that a service in the cathedral was appropriate to part of what he had become, a national figure.

He had no desire to live as a dependent person, a cripple who would have to be careful all the time and not be able to be fully involved. It would have to be all or nothing.

Geoff had wanted to be able to speak at the final meeting of Strathclyde Regional Council before the elections. He had been particularly keen to make a closing speech which would pick up the themes of his first speech as convener. He had to be content with a letter, written on April 24 and addressed to Vice-Convener Charles Gray. It stated:

"I am writing prior to the meeting of the Regional Council on Wednesday for a number of reasons. First and foremost, of course, must be to express my profound thanks for all the messages of good wishes I have received—from the council itself, from so many individual members and officials and representatives of the Press—and not least through Radio Clyde on my birthday!

"Try as I might, I could hardly have conceived a worse time to choose to be off with prolonged illness. The last few weeks of this four-year term of Strathclyde Regional Council were bound to be interesting and full. It has not been easy to see these weeks slip by without in any way being involved in them. But I wish to place on record my personal thanks to you for the way in which you have so willingly and acceptably fulfilled the duties of convener in addition to all your other commitments. I must add to that, of course, my particular appreciation of the convener's personal office and all those who have enabled a busy time to run smoothly.

"You will yourself, I am sure, during the course of the meeting, be referring to those who will not be back after May 1, the last day of this particular council.

"I am particularly sad that I cannot be present to say farewell and to shake the hand of those who, by choice, are leaving local government. It is a long list and all have, in their time, however short, contributed to the good of their community. It is hard for me to realise that at the next meeting there will be no Tom Fulton, a staunch colleague on so many occasions and a beloved adversary on so many others! Hugh Brannan, who has so ably chaired such a vital committee during these first years. Jean Craig, Anna Douglas, indeed to all I would ask you to convey my farewell and good wishes, along with those of the council.

"Again I would ask you to convey to the Chief Executive my public and personal thanks for his own work and through him to all departments my appreciation of the incredible achievements of the last few years.

"Finally I would want to refer to one particular job of the convener,—that of taking the chair at full meetings of the council. I want to express a special thanks to Mr Carlton and Mr Sharpe for their great assistance to me and to Mr Thomson for all his work in the background. But equally, I would want to thank the members. We have together forged some sort of satisfactory precedents of procedure and I am especially grateful that all the members have made the task of chairing the full council so easy.

"Like most of the members I intend to be re-elected on May 2. After a period of convalescence, I look forward to returning to take up, to the full, whatever duties may at that time fall to me. In the meantime may I again express my sincere thanks and good wishes to all."

Geoff wrote several letters at that time. Jimmy Boyle in Barlinnie was astonished to get a scrawled note of thanks for his good wishes. Len Turpie also. But what his friends wanted was to see him fully recovered. On Wednesday, April 26 Geoff wrote to a boy in Gorbals saying he was sorry he couldn't appear in court for him, but explaining that he had arranged for a substitute.

The next day he was visited by Dick Stewart and Charles Gray. He was glad to see them and they found him looking forward to the operation. When Dick swore at him good-humouredly Geoff was pleased, taking his arm and saying how he really felt at home again.

Nevertheless, there was a look about him which the two men did not like, and they left the Royal Infirmary in tears.

Friday, April 28, 1978. John Harvey sat typing a stencil for the Sunday service for St Mark's Church, Raploch, Stirling. The hymn was 'Lord of the Dance.' He was at the line 'I danced on Friday, when the sky turned black.' The telephone rang. His friend Geoff Shaw was dead. He had collapsed while walking down the ward, at 11.45 am.

His heart had finally given out. He had at last let go.

"Geoff Shaw is Dead" was the banner headline on the front page of the *Evening Times,* which went on to describe Geoffrey Shaw as 'one of the best-loved men in Scotland.'

The tributes poured in. Saying that Scotland had lost one of her foremost sons, the Prime Minister, James Callaghan, said he admired Geoff Shaw for his breadth of vision, his desire to serve his fellow men and his staunch principles.

Mr Bruce Millan, Secretary of State for Scotland, commented: "Geoff Shaw was a very good friend and one dedicated to ensuring a better way of life for the less fortunate. As convener of Strathclyde he displayed an unlimited amount of effort, zeal and efficiency which it will be difficult to replace. His untiring efforts in helping all, his guidance, kindness and advice will always be remembered and appreciated. Geoff Shaw was a man of conviction and compassion."

Lord Provost David Hodge of Glasgow said that Geoffrey Shaw could really be described as a man who laid down his life for his fellow men.

"The people who knew him as I did have lost a close and valued friend. The people of Scotland have lost a faithful servant."

A spokesman for the Scottish Council of the Labour Party said: "Geoff would be the very last man to say that he was irreplaceable, but those of us who knew him recognised him as a unique individual. He enriched the lives of all who came in contact with him and he clothed his compassion and sincerity in humour and warmth."

Church leaders of all denominations joined in the tributes. The Right Rev. John R. Gray, Moderator of the General Assembly of the Church of Scotland, said: "We in the Church are proud to have been able to give such a man of dedicated integrity to local government."

Archbishop Thomas Winning of Glasgow said that Geoff Shaw was a personal friend. He was a dedicated Christian devoted to the cause of social justice, and to the wellbeing of the people of the Region.

Strathclyde political colleagues and officials expressed their admiration. But it was not only those of Geoff's own party who were warm in their tributes. Councillor Gordon Murray, leader of the SNP group, described the late convener as 'dedicated, conscientious and sincere,' and Councillor Len Turpie, Conservative leader, said: "All the members of the group feel the same grief as one would for the death of a member of one's own family. Affection and admiration for Geoffrey Shaw ignored party and political difference."

The newspapers joined in the outpouring. The *Glasgow Herald* commented in its leading article: "The death of Geoff Shaw is a loss to Glasgow, to Strathclyde and to Scotland. During his political career he worked selflessly for the interest of all three and his untimely death is a result of the heavy burdens which he so willingly shouldered. His ability and his integrity took him to one of the highest positions in Scottish local government within a relatively short time. Few who achieve political prominence so quickly do so without losing the respect and friendship of at least some of their colleagues and opponents. Yet Geoff Shaw was admired and liked across the whole political spectrum."

One of the few to get behind the political significance of Geoff Shaw was Bill Hyndman of the *Daily Record*, one of the scourges of Strathclyde, who wrote: "Power did not really interest him. For he was far more concerned about the poor, the needy and the deprived of Glasgow and Strathclyde. He acted as host to visiting Royalty and civic dignitaries, as well as steering Strathclyde towards a new prosperity. But through it all he never forgot the folk he felt needed him most—the South siders, the minority groups, the suffering families in the many under-privileged areas."

The Observer referred to the loss of a man widely regarded as the probable leader of the Scottish Assembly and added: "In a part of the country where Labour politics had fallen into disrepute, his integrity and talents set him apart. From the outset Strathclyde faced a hostile public who regarded it as too big. Shaw proved that big did not necessarily mean ugly."

The *Catholic Observer* remarked: "A politician of the highest order who could have reached heights far beyond the convenership of Scotland's biggest Region, Geoff Shaw was so much more. He was a minister of the Church of Scotland, a man who saw his ministry in terms of service to everyone who needed his help—in whatever way. Though it was as a political figure that most Scots got to know his name, Geoff will be remembered by those who knew him personally as a man for whom people came first.

"To say he will be missed is an understatement. What is more accurate and more important is that Geoff Shaw, his ideals and his self-giving to the absolute limit will long be remembered in the West of Scotland."

The provincial papers carried tributes as well. The *Cumnock Chronicle* commented: "If the Region survives in its present form; if it finally comes to be accepted, then this will be due in no small measure to Geoff Shaw. Strathclyde—and Scotland—could ill afford to lose such a man."

None of these tributes was more important—nor more moving—than the letters, the cards, and the tears of ordinary Glasgow people who felt that as long as Geoff Shaw was around their interests were being looked after.

The funeral service had to be postponed until Wednesday, May 3, because of the Strathclyde Regional elections. A sweeping victory for Labour.

In the cathedral the solemn, silent processing of the representatives. Row upon row of sombre faces, straight out of a Who's Who of Scottish political and ecclesiastical life. The quietness broken by a housewife wheeling her baby through the church in a push chair.

"Christ is Made the Sure Foundation," sung with feeling. Lord, make me an instrument of Thy peace.

The service at Linn Crematorium was something of a Gorbals takeover. Geoff's friends, particularly his Gorbals friends, were much more at home there.

The staff of the crematorium had been bewildered when they heard about the arrangements. No hymns. No organ. The playing of a record! Was this really fitting for one of Scotland's leaders?

Yes, indeed. The service was a glimpse into Geoff Shaw of Gorbals and for some of the politicians and officials sitting there beside the former club boys and their wives and beside others who had obviously fortified themselves to face the occasion, it was their first real insight into what Geoff Shaw was all about.

John Harvey conducted the service and Walter Fyfe spoke about the significance of Geoff's life. Geoff's favourite Siegfried Sassoon poem was read. The record which was played was the *Tayvallich Singalong*—the camp songs sung by Gorbals youngsters which Geoff had had recorded.

It was moving to hear the raw voices of the Gorbals children sing out 'When I'm on my journey don't you weep after me', with its lines 'Every lonely river must go down to the sea/I don't want you to weep after me."

The lonely river went down to the sea at Peanmeanach, the place of the dream. The bare and silent hillsides seemed to echo with the happy laughter of Gorbals children as the ashes of Geoffrey Mackintosh Shaw were scattered—as he had wished—at this place of fond memories and high, high hopes.

> Everyone suddenly burst out singing;
> And I was fill'd with such delight
> As prison'd birds must find in freedom
> Winging wildly across the white
> Orchards and dark green fields; on; on;
> And out of sight.
>
> Everyone's voice was suddenly lifted,
> And beauty came like the setting sun.
> My heart was shaken with tears; and horror
> Drifted away...O but every one
> Was a bird; and the song was wordless; the
> Singing will never be done.